UEA PRO
NON-

UNIVERSITY OF EAST ANGLIA
CREATIVE WRITING MA
PROSE FICTION AND
NON-FICTION
ANTHOLOGY
2016

✳

NON-FICTION

✳

FOREWORD

*

GLENN PATTERSON

CHICKEN PAPRIKA, that's what I made, the night
in the early summer of 1986 that Tim and Kathryn came
round to my house on Thorpe Road. (You cubed a chicken
breast, cooked it off with onion and pepper before adding the paprika, and then – count to sixty – half a tub of
yoghurt… Ta-da!) My girlfriend, most likely, was working
– she had a job at the Berni Inn in Thorpe St Andrew: the
Berni Inreb as it pleased me, tireless (or –some) palin-
dromist that I was then, to call it. I don't know where the
other three were, the other three people I shared a house
with I mean, although I couldn't tell you either where the
other three people were who with Kathryn, Tim and me
made up that year's MA Creative Writing cohort.

Teaching had ended, so they may already have skedaddled, skedaddling at the earliest opportunity being part of
the UEA DNA. (I had been an undergraduate there too:
I had skedaddled myself more than once all the way back
to Belfast.) That said, since Christmas at least, Kathryn,
Tim and I had been circling our wagons a bit, a sort of
group within a group. This had nothing to do with the fact
that the teaching load was divided into Malcolm Bradbury
terms and Angela Carter terms – two to one, or (in our
case) one to two – with all the differences in tastes and
approaches that this entailed, although I had heard in
advance that some years split, as a result, into Malcolm
camps and Angela camps.

(Angela could have started a fight in an empty room –
well, a room empty of everyone but Malcolm – albeit with
a mischievous smile. She had an unnerving habit of describ-
ing rapid circles above her head with her right hand as she
searched for a word, any word it sometimes seemed, and
then just when you thought she would never find one – a
snap of the wrist and there it was, successfully lassoed: not
just a word, *the* word. Brilliant.)

However it fell out, then, it was, as I say, just the three
of us, Kathryn, Tim, me, that early summer night in the big

sitting room looking down the open-plan tip of a garden (no wall, or fence or hedge to interrupt the view) to Thorpe Road, the Post Office sorting office beyond, eating Chicken Paprika, discussing one another's work, draft chapters of our dissertations, circulated in advance, as the previous thirty weeks of the MA had taught us.

By post, I can only think. Or maybe bus.

There were reciprocal dinners, at Kathryn's and at Tim's, but it was a World Cup summer – a Northern-Ireland-in-the-World-Cup summer! – and my sense is that a football-shaped hole opened up in our meetings and never quite closed again. And yet when I think of my MA year those evenings come as readily to mind as the afternoon sessions (Wednesdays? 2 till 5?) with Malcolm and Angela and the rest of the group, and are more vivid in truth than most of them.

Perhaps because I had begun to realise that it was all coming to an end sooner than I had imagined back in the mists of October it possibly could, far sooner in other words than I was prepared for, and that I was going to have to come up with strategies for replacing the weekly workshops that I had come to rely on so much. For I was quite certain that without the MA I would never have got round to writing in any disciplined way at all. I was hoping that summer I could maintain the discipline for as much of the first post-MA year as it took to complete the novel I had started. Both Malcolm and Angela as it turned out were incredibly supportive and encouraging, long, long after-wards, but that seemed too much to hope or expect at the time. The advice and friendship of my fellow students was a godsend.

It is a mystery to me how that first year became thirty years, how the single raised digit (no, the other one) in answer to the double-barrelled question – 'A writer? *Written* anything?' – became a handful, two handfuls.

There are times though even now when I am sitting

with a draft of something new on my lap (old paper habits die hard) and I know exactly what Kathryn or Tim would say.

And sadly it isn't, 'You never gave me the recipe for that Chicken Paprika.'

Glenn Patterson

PROSE FICTION

INTRODUCTION

*

JEAN MCNEIL AND
HENRY SUTTON

SERIOUS FICTION KNOWS no boundaries, follows
no known course. It is powered by a relationship between
cause and effect. The impression it leaves may be quiet or
loud, but the pertinence and permanence of its hold on our
imagination and collective consciousness, the way it shapes
and expands our thinking and understanding, is why we engage with such literary endeavour. What strikes us as tutors
teaching on the MA in Prose Fiction each year is just how
dynamic, how flexible, the form and function of fiction is.
Each year we are privileged to be a part of this ever-evolving medium, in an ever-evolving world. The work collected
in this anthology is not just a reaction to that world, or the
workshop process, but the collision and distillation of a
moment, or rather a series of moments stretched over an in-
tense year (or two, for part-timers). It is both representative
of the past (in the way reading works), and the present, and
a point at which some letting go is required. This is the time
for a greater engagement with and acknowledgement of the
other key party in the process, the public reader.

One question we are often asked, as tutors and also
co-directors of the MA at UEA, is: do creative writing
programmes turn out writers who all sound the same,
or who end up writing about the same themes? Such a
homogenisation of fiction would be to deaden its appeal
and its artistic and political relevance, of course. But that
is not why our answer is always a vehement no. As you will
see here, there are no two writers in our cohort of some
thirty students who could be said to have adopted the same
approach, style, or subject matter.

The pieces collected here cover a huge stylistic range,
from carefully observed naturalism to raucous stream of
consciousness, from a comic approach to the social world
to the dank tragedy of the plague in seventeenth-century
Italy. To take a quick census of their settings is to enter a
time machine: New Zealand in 1791, the Ottoman Empire
in the sixteenth century, 1970s pre-Thatcher Britain during

the Grunwick Strike, Missouri in the interwar years, from a caravan park in coastal Kent to rural New York state in 1786, then back to a staggered London in the wake of the 2007 terrorist bombings. These kinds of whirlwind lists always trouble us; they are a shorthand to encapsulate something very difficult to describe: the diversity of our student cohort and their concerns. Each year we watch the abilities and interests of our students cohere, slowly and then with more clarity.

For all its remarkable energy and dynamism, divergence of opinion and solidarity, the workshop is a private space. It is part collective, part collaboration. From year to year the energies shift, the preoccupations differ, the resources change, yet the resolve doesn't – to shift boundaries, to do different, to capture a wider imagination and consciousness, by deepening that sense of what it means to be alive now, wherever you are from. We are all in this together.

Henry Sutton
Jean McNeil
Co-convenors, MA Prose Fiction

MICHAEL ALLEN

$*$

CARAVAN

STANDING ON THE MOUND, Ambrose can almost glimpse the sea through the clutter of rooftops and the vapours that rise and smudge the air with the whiff of chippy oil. The sky over Fairhills is lit pink with the festive neon of the Gala Club, and there is a faint melody of jackpots and spilt pennies and all things carnival gambolling on the breeze.

Ambrose cannot believe his luck. He trails his tongue along his teeth, lights a cigarette and settles down in a fold-up chair. Behind him sits a 2004 Ace Jubilee Globetrotter Touring Caravan. It is a fortress of plush salmon upholstery and walnut veneer that floats serene above the scramble of streets and frenzied traffic below. A washing line strung from the window is festooned with socks and underpants that dance like bunting in the breeze. Les had scouted the spot, and deemed it secure. The approach from the main road is lethal with gnarly waist-high nettles. Only a fortnight ago they'd parked her snug on the mound, let the air out of the tyres and laid her up on bricks, long stay. 'Ye shall tour no more,' Ambrose had intoned, consecrating the ground with a slop of foamy Tetleys.

It is early, but already the day is bright and unseasonably warm. Ambrose strokes his shiny bald head. He shuffles in his chair and flicks a small finger of ash from his sleeve, then spies a beer can down by his side, goose pimpled with condensation. He picks it up, gives it a light jiggle and a sniff. He balances it on his belly, then regards his belly sternly.

Ambrose has always been large. His father was large before him. The one time he'd tried wearing his belt up over his belly to hide his gut, he'd received gentle but genuine ridicule from Les. When he'd gone to the physio about his back, the lady had told him that his weight was the equivalent of carrying three full-term babies around, twenty-four seven. Ambrose had considered this, and had decided he quite liked the thought. There was something cosy about it.

He kicks off his boots and feels the breeze flow about his feet. He watches the leisurely procession of life in the park below: an elderly couple out for their morning walk, a thin figure in a dressing gown and welly boots staggering from the toilet block and tramping off in the direction of the Lodges – an orderly cluster of raised chalets with allocated picnic benches that go for a pretty penny.

There comes a cough and a wheezy sniffle, followed by another, phlegmier cough. Les approaches, walking up the mound with an armful of folded linen.

'You're not drinking that,' says Les.

'I bloody well am,' says Ambrose, taking a sip.

Les plonks the linen onto Ambrose's knees, takes the cigarette from his fingers and smokes it looking out over the caravan park. He is wearing blue jeans, jelly sandals and a black T–shirt with a design on the front that has become too faded to read. He has long greying hair and fuzzy arms. His tattoos look like old bruises.

'Piggott came over,' says Les.

'Piglet?'

'Piggott. Bloke with the teeth. When you were out.'

'Oh. What'd he want?'

'Didn't say. Asked if you were about.'

'OK.'

'Said I didn't know.'

'Right. Probably for the best.'

'That's what I thought.'

'Right.'

Les squishes the cigarette out on one of the flattened tyres of the caravan and pops it into a flowerpot filled with fag ends. He pushes his hair back behind his ear, takes the linen from Ambrose's knees and steps inside.

Ambrose feels triumphant. Fairhills glimmers at his feet. Eleven months on the road, from Plymouth to Swindon, Milton Keynes to Margate, and now they are

here, miraculously here. Each new morning is a strange and
complete kind of happiness. They listen to Eric Clapton
and Janis Joplin on the stereo and spend lazy days considering cleaning the barbecue. In the evenings they sit smoking
at the table beneath the glitz of the chandelier. As far as
Ambrose is aware, theirs is the only caravan in Fairhills
with a chandelier.

*

Autumn is asserting itself and the sweet reek of mulch fills
Ambrose's nostrils as he rakes a scattering of leaves into
a heap behind the caravan. The scent launches him into
a daydream. He imagines, with cheerful intensity, an abundant vegetable garden bursting with sweet tomatoes, spring
onions and bright green runner beans. He sees himself
tending to young shoots, idling among the radishes and
ripe aubergines. Or courgettes. He has an inkling that Les
prefers courgettes.

Ambrose lays the rake down and hoiks up his belt.
Right, he thinks. That's that. He reaches into his pocket and
pulls out a crumpled brown paper bag. He pours seed from
the bag into his palm and crouches next to a small area
that has been enclosed with wire mesh. Inside two plump
chickens squat in the mud, their feathers gently quivering.
He sprinkles the seed before them.

'Morning lads,' he says.

He stands and props a foot on a stack of wooden pallets
which Les has salvaged from someone's skip and instructed
Ambrose to repurpose as raised flowerbeds. A pleasant
ache enlivens his thighs as he bends to heft a long splint of
wood from a broken pallet and spikes a wet leaf with the
end of it. He twiddles the leaf before his feet.

Courgettes, he thinks.

He saunters over to the far side of the mound, towards
the main road. The ground there quickens into a scree of

black gravel and clumsy knuckles of rock before falling abruptly away into a ditch of nettles, cans and crisp packets. He kicks a stone off the bluff. It lands in the nettles and two birds, tiny ones, spring from somewhere, yanked up by their beaks. He watches their nifty plumage rise and evaporate into the heavens.

Returning to the area beside the caravan, Ambrose kneels with some difficulty and crumbles a pinch of soil between his fingers. The ground here is good. Good enough. He begins by measuring out the space, counting his paces and marking points in the soil with his stick. He feels the idea take root as he works, bending now to pluck a weed or collect a loose stone in his pocket. He stops twice to smoke a cigarette. When he is happy with the shapes he has plotted, he fetches a spool of twine from the caravan. He connects the plotted points with the twine, laboriously, then gets his spade. He readies the spade, lining its edge with the guiding twine. The ground feels supple beneath the blade. Good. He slices it neatly.

The washing line wiggles and a sock flops down onto the grass. Ambrose pulls out the spade and wipes his forehead with his sleeve. He notices a white substance on the tip of the blade, and kneels to inspect it. It's sugary. He lifts a crumb to his nose. It smells of garlic. He flicks it from his fingers, then looks up and watches in mild panic as Piggott trots uphill towards him.

'Good morning,' Piggott calls.

Ambrose straightens up. 'Morning.'

Piggott is wearing a zipped-up leather jacket with tracksuit bottoms. A plastic shopping bag sags at his side. It seems to contain a lone can of something. He stands next to Ambrose and looks out over the park.

'How's this for a glimpse?' he says.

'Yeah,' says Ambrose. 'It's something else.'

'Isn't it just? I should be charging extra!'

Ambrose smiles politely.

'Can you see the sea from here?' says Piggott.

'Almost.'

'But you can smell it, though.'

'You can.'

Piggott's hair is mostly grey but colours a little towards his ears – a dark, snotty blond. A few unshaven hairs jut idly from his chin. His ears and nose are aglow with broken capillaries. He is, thinks Ambrose, somewhere between forty-five and seventy. The years have been unforgiving or they have been downright brutal.

'Just came to see if all's fine and dandy,' Piggott says, unzipping his jacket and reaching into his inside pocket. He pulls out a pack of Rothmans.

'Yeah,' says Ambrose. 'Everything's fine.'

Piggott nods. 'Fine, fine.'

He lights a cigarette, pulls deeply, holds it out like a dart. He has a bloodshot, belligerent look. His eyes are yellowing somehow. Ambrose wonders if he has some kind of condition – jaundice, glaucoma, something.

'Now that,' says Piggott, pointing his cigarette at the chickens, 'is one pretty fucking ornate coop. Like, fuck me, it's a work of art.'

'You like it?'

'It's the fucking Xanadu of chicken coops.'

'Thanks. It's a work in progress.'

Les had always wanted to keep chickens, so on arrival Ambrose decided to surprise him with this, his gift – a chicken coop like no other – as a way of saying thank you, thank you for putting up with me so far. It has a geodesic dome frame with struts that splay out in a honeycomb pattern, which Ambrose plans to paint bright yellow. It's a little shaky in the wind, but Les had been very impressed. Inside it has three levels with ramps to give the boys as much room to run as possible. Ambrose would also like to whittle some elaborate filigree work as a finishing touch.

'Big chickens,' Piggott says. 'Do they have names?'

'Yep,' says Ambrose. 'Brian and Blessed.'

'Brian Blessed?'

'Brian and Blessed, yes.'

Piggott kneels and coos at them. 'Are they for eating?'

Ambrose leans on his spade. 'Not for eating, no.'

Piggott stands. He leans a foot on a wooden crate. On his feet are a pair of scuffed Reeboks with no socks.

'What are you plotting here?' he says.

'Ah, well. I'm thinking of growing some vegetables.'

'Yeah?'

'Yeah. Some runner beans, maybe.'

Piggott nods, then issues a hollow cough. 'Of course, there's no soil there,' he says. 'Dig an inch and you'll hit nothing but rubble.'

Ambrose raises his eyebrows. 'I see.'

'Only this here's very stony ground. It'd be hard work.'

Ambrose nods. He tries not to look too put out.

'Well,' Piggott says – he is now standing fully on the crate, licking his lips as if agitating from a soapbox – 'I'd say you're better off with an allotment of some sort. There are some available, I think, a few miles down the road.' He gestures vaguely behind him.

'Right, yeah. Thanks.'

Piggott smiles. His teeth are like a shooting range of broken bottles. He walks over the areas Ambrose has marked out with his twine, then looks at the spade.

'I'd beware of that,' he says.

'Of what?'

'That.' He points at the spade. 'I'd keep your chickens away from it.'

'The garlicky stuff?'

'That's not garlic. It's zinc phosphide.'

'Zinc –'

'Poison. For the moles. It doesn't seem to make a difference, they continue to eat the place up. Still, we put it down, wherever we see their little piles. The seagulls always come and binge on the stuff. Then they fly out to sea to die.'

'Oh.'

'And that's where we're all headed,' Piggott says with a sigh. 'Eventually, anyway. The coastline is eroding. Yep, there's no denying it. Soon enough we'll all be returning to the sea.'

Ambrose is silent.

Piggott grins. 'How's your breaststroke?' he says.

They look out towards the sea somewhere beyond the town, where the clouds curdle and the sky fades to the colour of a pale summer ale. Piggott looks on with watery eyes, his nose cocked into the wind. There is savagery in those eyes, thinks Ambrose. He wonders what Les would say if he stabbed Piggott in the belly right now with his stick.

'Well,' says Piggott. 'Best be off. You got that money for the next quarter?'

'Oh, yes,' says Ambrose. 'Yes – thanks for reminding me. I'll bring that over to you.'

'Ah, good. Fine.'

Ambrose watches him descend the mound in a kind of skittish tap dance. Les appears in the doorway of the caravan wearing a pinny.

'He's a funny bloke,' says Les.

'He is.'

SAMANTHA ALLEN

✳

CANAAN GULCH

In Canaan Gulch, California, the Gold Rush is coming to an end. When a feral woman is captured in the mountains that surround Canaan Gulch, her fate becomes intertwined with the fates of this failing boomtown and its strange residents.

CHAPTER ONE

There's a stack of meatless bones inside the cave: fish bones, bird bones, rabbit bones. Piled by the mouth of it. Scoop them up. Hold them to the light. Almost dark, but not yet. No meat left; sucked clean; cracked for marrow. Wind tickles her face. Too cold. Soon, no more heat, no more sun. Soon, berries rot and splat to the dirt. The meat dies or goes to sleep. Her cold and skinny season.

Eat, she has to eat. But there are men and fires – too close. Wait till dark. Gather up the leaves, get warm. There's a word for her cave, it starts with H. Hah hoh hit? She doesn't remember it. *Hit* makes a picture in her head: the man. His face. Pain in her belly. The bad taste of red. She whimpers. Grasps the corn husk doll. It makes a better picture. A woman and brown eyes. A smile. There's a word for her too. Mah meh mih mot – mota? No. She licks the doll. Rough, papery, good. Tastes like yellow. Not like red.

Yellow – like the bright round things swept here by the river. Wood things. Things that go on clothes? She has other things, too, collected from those banks. A box made of metal, rusted red; it wheezes music when she blows into its mouth. A big brown hat. A stick, good for black bears. Makes them run away. She takes the stick. Scoops the rest together, stacked like the bones. The doll sits on top to wait for her.

Then, dark. Smoke makes a cloud far away: the men. Be quiet. Flit down the slope. These rocks are hers. She knows them. Down below, the stream: black, cold, empty but for little fish that glint like stars. And the bushes. The place where rabbits run. Crouch, hide, be still. Like she was when the M woman got taken, dragged away. A bad picture. She sniffs. The dirt has water in it. Smells good. Wait, wait, wait. The moon rises high, starts to fall to the ground. So long to wait.

Leaves shudder. Not the wind. Crouch low, don't breathe.

A rabbit!

Uncoil muscles.

Launch from the bushes.

She'll have it. Meat.

No – too soon. Too far.

The meat disappears. Back underground. Too late. She plumbs the hole where the rabbit went. Chilled and damp but no fur. No meat. Too cold to wait again. Too cold to swim for fish. Back to the rock, the cave, the doll. To sleep.

Wait. A smell. Rich and sweet, like the wheezing box where it's rusted red. Blood. Not old. A cougar's kill? Not far away. She follows it, crouched low and ready. Holding the stick in her furred hand. No noise; she's a part of the trees, part of the dirt. Doesn't even stir a branch.

There it is. A deer. What's left. No skin now – all that red flesh, it waits. A trap? She growls. But her stomach does, too.

Get close. But careful.

Snap – a branch under her foot.

Freeze.

A breath? In the trees?

No. She's alone.

Try again.

Slow. Slow. Slow.

A crack.

Then ground that isn't ground.

Empty air –

falling!

A deep hole. Under the pine boughs and leaves.

She plunges into the earth, lands in soft black dirt.

Her mouth gets full of it. Cough, spit, cough. No scent of meat anymore. Just the sour taste of earth.

Up above there are voices now. The men. Whooping and hollering. Words she doesn't know anymore. She claws at the dirt, climbs. Falls. Too soft, too crumbly, it won't support her. She wails but the dirt eats her voice. A word comes back, she hasn't forgotten it – 'No no no no no!'

Above her head, the moon goes away. Blotted out. By a shadow. A man shadow. Grey fur on his head and black fur over his lip. She flattens herself against the wall. Crouched low. Stick in hand, point aimed up. A growl shudders her throat. Ready to claw, to fight.

The man's lips stretch and he shows her his white, white teeth.

CHAPTER TWO

Eliza wakes with a name in her mouth. 'Amos?' she whispers to the dark. But there's no one there, not even her husband's ghost. Of course not; there's no such things as ghosts. But there's a noise outside. It isn't coyotes, nor is it a bear. There are footsteps approaching her cabin. She throws back her quilt, grabs the rifle by her bed and hurries to the door. She peers through a chink in her cabin's wall. It's dark, with only scant threads of moonlight filtering through the aspens and pines. There's a sway-backed brown horse standing at the tree line.

Eliza nudges back the beam of pine wood that forms her flimsy door lock. The gun is already loaded – she keeps it that way – its lead ball nestled deep in the barrel. The sulphur smell of black powder burns her nostrils. She holds the rifle snug against her shoulder; there's only one shot so it had better be a good one.

A quiet voice squeaks, 'Don't shoot!'

It's a scrawny girl, no older than thirteen, white as moonlight with her colourless hair and skin like milk. She holds her shaking hands above her head.

Eliza lowers the rifle, holds it loosely at her side. 'You can put your hands down.'

The girl doesn't. 'You're Eliza Hawthorne.'

'Yes.'

'I came to ask for help.'

'What kind of help do you need?'

'There's a baby comin'. It's been comin' a long time. Pa thinks it's stuck.'

'Whose baby? One of the whores at Beaver Creek?'

The girl shakes her head, finally dropping her hands to her side.

Eliza squints at her. 'From what I've heard, there isn't another kind of woman here for miles around. Where did you come from, anyway?'

'Canaan Gulch.'

'There's still a town up there? I'd heard the gold was gone.'

'Please – Lil needs help real bad. Pa says she won't make it till morning.'

Eliza sighs. 'Wait here.'

She retreats back into the shack, her bare feet shuffling through the dust on the floorboards. She shucks off her nightgown, pulls on her heavy men's boots, and shakes out her blue wool dress, one of two she took with her from St Louis. It's cut to be worn with a hoop; the ends are bedraggled and brown with dirt, but stitching cloth is nothing like stitching skin, and she's never been good at sewing a neat hem. She slides her medicine bag out from under the bed. The black leather is cracking, but serves its purpose all the same, holding the needles and catgut and bandages of her trade: good quality instruments she brought when she fled to this godforsaken land. Inside, too, is a pair of forceps. She lifts them out of the bag, examines them in the gloom – no rust. Brushing the dust from her dress, she hefts the bag from the floor and carries it onto the porch, securing the door to the shack behind her.

Eliza unhitches Nut from his pen and tucks her skirts into her belt before swinging into the saddle.

'OK,' she says, patting her horse on the neck. 'Let's go.'

The girl nods frantically and clambers onto the back of her own skinny horse. They set off into the trees.

'How long has she been labouring?' Eliza asks.

'Three days.'

'And there's no crowning?'

'What's that?'

'Can you see the baby's head poking out?'

The girl looks at her with wide eyes.

'Ain't nobody looked.'

The girl nudges her horse and it jogs ahead, leading Eliza deeper into the forest, following some imperceptible path.

'What's your name?' Eliza asks.

'Bess.'

'And – what's her name – Lil? She's your sister?'

She shakes her head, long pale hair swinging around her face.

'I been takin' care of her day and night since we found her nigh on a year ago.'

'What do you mean, found?'

'In the woods. Pa found her and brought her back and she's been livin' with us ever since.'

'An Indian captive?'

'Don't think so. She don't talk.'

'Not at all?'

'Don't think she can.' The girl lowers her voice. Eliza can barely hear her over the clip-clop of the horses. 'She ain't like a normal woman. Pa says she ain't even human.'

Eliza's heard a story like this before. The miners at Beaver Creek have told it, and so have the Indians she trades with. A story about the Hairy Man who roams these parts. The Indians believe him to be gentle – but the miners claim he has a terrible appetite for flesh. A ridiculous story; goose bumps rise on her arms anyway.

'Not human,' Eliza says. 'Then what is she?'

Bess glances back over her shoulder at Eliza and shrugs.

'Well – you'll see when we get there.'

They trot along for a while in silence, riding up a steep ridge and then down its rocky slope. Bess leads them down into a gully where they meet a river swollen with snowmelt. This is the river that draws all the men with its scant promise of gold. It winds deeper into the valley still until they come upon a kind of canyon, walled in on either side by the mountain's granite cliffs. The canyon narrows; their horses splash through the shallows of the river, and the sloshing of their hooves echoes through the canyon in a way that sounds like whispers.

The canyon is dark, in shadow from the low angle of the moon. It's bereft of the moonlight that lit the open valley and conjures the feeling of a tomb. Eliza thinks of Amos and guilt settles thickly in her lungs – a familiar feeling, one that's as constant as her breath. In her mind's eye she sees him enclosed in a pinewood coffin, his eyes flashing suddenly open, accusing.

The canyon mercifully widens again, emptying into a narrow valley choked with evergreens. They've ridden for more than an hour – the moon is drifting now towards the horizon. In the distance, Eliza can see whorls of smoke rising from some unseen hearth, whisked away by a cutting wind that blows down from the mountain. Above the valley looms a towering, snow-capped peak that gleams an otherworldly white against the unbroken black.

The valley is beautiful, but the camp is not; it's little more than a gathering of tents and rude cabins leaning like drunks below the mountain. Mud sucks at their horses' hooves as they ride into the camp. The place smells of old grease fires and livestock, the stink of piss and unwashed men. Their voices echo through the valley; she hears a man's shout, a braying laugh, a crude song yelled tunelessly around a campfire that belches foul smoke. As they move towards the centre, Eliza sees the skeleton of a cabin, and then another – torn down when the occupants left, timber stolen and put to some other use. The structures still intact are rough and incomplete, with logs so poorly stacked they leave gaps in the walls like missing teeth. They pass a canvas tent with holes that flap open in the wind. Eliza catches a glimpse of the men inside: filthy and bearded, huddled around flickering lanterns, playing cards. A man staggers out of the tent when the horses clop near. He wears nothing but greying longjohns and a hat with a broken hawk feather in its band.

'Wanna suck my pecker?' the man shouts at them. 'Give ya dime fer it.'

Another pokes his head out of the tent to join in.

'Mayor's girl been wantin' it.'

Four more men emerge. One yells, 'Come 'ere girl, show ya real biggun.'

Bess ducks her head, hides her face between pale curtains of hair. Eliza won't look away; she spits into the dirt at their feet.

*An extract from
a short story*

ADAM ANDRUSIER

✳

SPIDER

AFTER AN EXHAUSTING night of shallow dreaming,
Sharon Salmon opened her eyes to clock – with horror – an
enormous spider staring down at her from the ceiling.

She'd been having her usual recurring nightmare about
falling from a tall building: essentially, a set piece based on
her eight-and-a-half hours of continuous television viewing
on 9/11, but also with its roots in a dream of falling she'd
had as a young child.

What disturbed Sharon about the dream was not the
falling itself; rather, her dream character's automaton-like
arm and leg movements in descent. There seemed to be a
complete resignation to fate – no shouting or screaming of
any kind. It concerned Sharon, who was a successful crim-
inal lawyer, that she should need to project such a feeble
self-image onto her dream, when she was such a capable
person in her daily life. She was someone who always stood
up to authority, in its various guises. She wouldn't hesitate
about questioning a suspect item on a restaurant bill; she
fought unfair parking tickets; she'd several times complained about uneven walking surfaces in public buildings.
She also advocated for others, during a weekly volunteer
shift at a drop-in centre for asylum seekers, where she
answered queries from worn-out and poorly-informed
desperate people. Sharon followed up ruthlessly, on the
asylum seekers' behalf, with phone calls and emails to
other professionals.

Despite its terrifying realism, the recurring nightmare
about falling had become something that Sharon had
learned to live with. This was thanks to the assistance of
a hypnotherapist in Crouch End, who'd helped her to put
a 'cinema screen' around the dream; the idea being that
each time it started up Sharon could identify herself as
a *spectator* rather than a participant. The hypnotherapist
had insisted that, as time went on, Sharon would be able
to pause the dream – or 'mind-film' as he preferred to call
it – rewind and forward wind it, and eventually stop it

altogether with the aid of a hypnotically-suggested remote control zapper that she could hold up to the 'screen' and press buttons on, although this virtual gadget had failed ever to materialise. Still, she was relatively content with the cinema screen technique, which she felt more or less justified the £700 she'd spent on ten successive hypno-treatments.

During a recent and confronting silent weekend retreat in Kent, Sharon was floored by a realisation that her fear of spiders went back far further than any dreams she'd ever had about falling. When she'd first had the nightmare – aged about six – it had, in fact, just been her body's way of trying to distract her from what was, already at that age, a paralysing case of arachnophobia. Once the dreams about falling began, Sharon thought a good deal less about arachnids, or at least the first part of the day tended to be clear. And she stopped insisting her mother search her bedroom at night for spiders, spiders' webs and traces of venom.

Another more recent interpretation of Sharon's, occurring during an 'Aha!' moment in a craniosacral therapy session in Hyderabad, was that the dream's original function, as concocted by her six-year-old self's brain, had been less about distracting her from her morbid fear of spiders, than about giving her worn-out parents a merited break from their exhausting morning and evening ritual searches of the house, which had been causing arguments and general unease. Since Hyderabad, Sharon had been feeling extremely angry with her now ageing parents, for not only had they completely failed to recognise their daughter's extraordinary self-sacrifice – in subsituting a fear of spiders for a debilitating fear of falling, essentially for their benefit – but they had also repeatedly expressed great relief that the spider obsession, as they called it, had finally run its course. They even *congratulated* themselves for having helped their daughter to recover.

Sharon had felt it right and proper to confront her

parents with the new theory. So, she arranged to meet them, on neutral territory – the lobby of the Marriott Hotel, Swiss Cottage – and spent several weeks building up to the meeting, discussing in detail with her psychotherapist how she imagined the conversation might go. Nothing could have prepared her for how traumatic that meeting would be. Her parents' inability to hear, let alone *understand* their daughter's point of view, seemed so pathological that it reminded Sharon – in fact, brought back in technicolour – how they had always washed their hands of her, emotionally. Perhaps, Sharon screamed at the old couple across the lobby, if they'd taken more time to tune into her trauma when she was still a *child*, she wouldn't have had to spend her entire twenties, and the first half of her thirties, crying into the arms of therapists. She might, instead, have been dating men, doing bungee jumps and uploading photographs of herself to Facebook, and whatever else it was that normal women did.

The conversation proved entirely fruitless, and Sharon felt she had no choice but to break off contact with her parents. For the following three months, she communicated with them solely through brief handwritten messages passed back and forth by her brother, Steven, who seemed to know better than to get involved in any other way. (Steven had tried in the past to explain everyone's positions to each other, but he hadn't really understood the positions, and couldn't seem to understand why anyone needed to be angry with anyone; nor did he seem to have any idea what his sister even meant by a 'difficult relationship'.)

Sharon's psychotherapist of nine years couldn't help noticing that, despite her client's new and seemingly important discovery about the recurring nightmare's true function, the dream itself had not gone away – and nor had the discovery made any difference whatsoever to Sharon's crippling *daytime* fear of heights, flying and getting into lifts. One explanation put forward by Sharon was that she'd

been having the falling dream for so long that it had caused
a sort of *habitual* fear of heights (and anything that might
fall from one). But she had to admit it was mystifying that
the fear of heights she experienced in her waking life was so
much more spine-chilling than in her nightmares, when she
was more preoccupied with her dream-character's inability
to call out for help and her generally useless demeanour,
and not bothered so much – more sort of mildly irritated –
by the falling itself.

Another thought had also crossed Sharon's mind,
which was that the reason the dream might still be recurring was because it still had some kind of *live function* for
her as an adult; that it was trying to pass on some kind of
message to her. This was a particularly perplexing worry for
Sharon, and the only theory she could entertain was that
the dream's continued function was to wake herself up to
the fact that she was still – even now, aged 36 – trying to
protect her parents from the true extent of her anger, past
and present. That by being a constant reminder that all was
not well, the dream prompted an awareness that an important score had yet to be settled.

It seemed to Sharon bizarre, even funny, to consider
that a dream whose original function had been to *protect*
her parents (both from their daughter's true morbid fears,
and from the exhausting parental chores that the fears
had set in motion) now turned out to be about *exposing*
them for their failures. But this new understanding did
seem much closer to the truth than any of the suggestions
put forward to her over the years by phobia experts and
therapists of various kinds, some of whom had even made
ridiculous insinuations about Sharon's name – both first
and last being the same six letters long as the word 'spider',
and also beginning with the letter 's'. Others were quite
certain she must have had an early traumatic experience
of a spider falling on her face or suchlike, although try as
she might, she could locate no such memory. In any case,

since the meeting at the Marriott, the falling dream had become more frequent, which made it all the more difficult for Sharon to focus her attention on what her early fear of spiders might have been about in the first place.

The awkward fact – Sharon had to admit it – was that she couldn't truthfully *remember* the nature of her early fear of spiders, largely because when the falling dream first started, when she was six, it had taken over so convincingly. Thenceforth, she'd become so completely preoccupied with high-up things, lifts, staircases and falling objects, that spiders became a very distant memory indeed, and took a back seat in Sharon's psyche – unless, of course, she happened to see one. One psychoanalyst, whom she'd only ever met for a single consultation, had made a link between arachnophobia and mothers and pubic hair. But that was ridiculous and Sharon wasn't even going to begin to go there; she had even managed to argue her money back after that session and had held a deep distrust of psychoanalysts and psychoanalytic psychotherapists ever since. Her preference now was for Jungian and/or existential therapists, or therapists who at least had an integrative approach, and weren't interested in 'labelling' her or 'putting her in a box'.

Sharon was frozen on her bed, her arms outstretched on either side, clutching onto the bedsheets. She stared up at the spider, who in turn seemed to stare down at her, with his three or four sets of eyes (she imagined – she practically convulsed at the thought). It was difficult to think of any way forward in what was essentially a stand-off, or even a hostage situation.

It was then that a primitive survival instinct twitched inside Sharon. She knew she was experiencing a panic attack, and she also knew that she'd get out of it alive. It was during this moment of clarity that Sharon remembered there was a phone on her bedside table, and it was really just a question of getting to that phone and dialling her neighbour Jill, who was usually in, and had a spare key, and had successfully removed spiders from Sharon's flat in the past. The only trouble was that she couldn't, for the life of her, figure out how to get to that phone without looking away from the spider. And she feared that to lose eye contact with it, for even one second, would risk the spider making a sudden lunge down onto her, or else give it time to scuttle to a different position and make itself essentially *still in the room but non-locateable* – a thought subtly more petrifying than it staying in its current position, with its various pairs of emotionally-dead eyes locked onto her.

But the theoretical possibility alone of a phone call, combined with Sharon's deeply-held belief that if she could only get to the phone then a kind person would help her, sustained her in her predicament. And this was when, serendipitously, Sharon remembered a panic attack routine she'd once learnt at an evening seminar in Fulham. She couldn't quite remember how you were supposed to do the 'let the panic attack know who's boss' stage, so instead she went straight into deep-breathing and counting to twenty, and then to a section she'd tagged on herself, which involved putting a 'cinema screen' around the whole situation and trying to imagine she was watching the scenario unfold from the outside.

A short story

JAMES BARNES

*

499 DAYS WITHOUT
A RESURRECTION

MY DAILY ROUTINE: Wake up, bran, my cousin
Roach picks me up from lay-by next to nearest petrol
station, drive to work, update whiteboard in staffroom,
gear up, head out into area of forest in which we operate,
track down Our Lord Jesus Christ, (ideally) tranquillise
Our Lord Jesus Christ, humanely euthanise Our Lord
Jesus Christ, go home, macaroni, bed.

Yesterday, the whiteboard in the staffroom read '498
days without a resurrection'. Today it reads '499 days
without a resurrection'.

*

I say part of my daily routine is that we '(ideally) tranquillise' Our Lord Jesus Christ, but strictly speaking that isn't
true. To be honest these days we don't bother. Christ never
ever shows *any* signs – facial, verbal or otherwise – that He
is experiencing any form of human pain. When we chase
Him, when we catch Him, when we put Him down, His
body goes through the motions of a life-and-death struggle
but His face looks glazed, daydreamy, sometimes like He's
forgotten we are even there. So these days we don't bother
tranquillising. These days we do whatever.

One time my cousin Roach dispatched Christ with
a cricket bat, for example.

Clunked His neck into an eerie right angle with the
wedged side of a cricket bat.

One time, when we found Christ tangled up in ivy
vines, struggling, Cousin Roach pushed a sharpened stake
through His chest with the tongue-biting care of a man sliding a control rod into a nuclear reactor core, and Christ just
yawned contentedly and watched a squirrel. The squirrel
rotated an acorn in its tiny hands and watched Christ back
while I pretended to clean out a thumbnail.

Roach is a maniac but he got me the job. And he is
family, I guess.

Me, I usually dispatch Christ with a scoped, bolt-action rifle, from a distance, through the head. I will lie in the stringy, wet, yellow-rooted grass of the forest and wait, prone and slow-breathing, until I spy pennies of Christ's bright white shawl blipping through gaps in the rowan leaves. Failing this, ideally I will fall upon Christ from a low branch and slip a knife into the soft oval dent of flesh at the base of His skull.

What I'm saying, basically, is that Cousin Roach is prepared to commit extra time and energy to *elaborating* the euthanasia of Christ, whereas I'm prepared to commit extra time and energy to *simplifying* the euthanasia of Christ, and I think that says something about each of us.

That said, if it's getting late in the day and Christ is still unaccounted for, and I'm tired, and Roach is tired, and the walkie-talkie starts sneezing to life with complaints from our supervisor wanting to know when we'll be wrapping things up, I'm not beneath tackling Christ to the ground when I spot Him and half-heartedly thumbing around in the mud for His eye sockets.

Or spraying the foliage at hip-height with a fully-automatic weapon in response to the sound of snapping twigs.

Or shucking cans of nerve-paralysing gas into any badger dens that I suspect Christ may have taken shelter in.

*

The situation:

• The Second Coming of Our Lord Jesus Christ occurred one spongy Easter morning in the Mendip Woodlands.

• Why the Mendip Woodlands? None of us has any idea. I have been assured by multiple regional history enthusiasts that the Mendip Woodlands are of zero scriptural significance.

- There are a lot of caves in the Mendip Woodlands, though.

The problem with the situation:

- Christ's return was, at first, manageable.
- Christ emerged from the forest. He appeared to a butcher. He appeared to a lollipop lady. He appeared to a Mindfulness of Breathing seminar. He was not believed.
- Christ was provided with an old sleeping bag and a paraffin lamp (which were later discovered neatly abandoned by an Oxfam bin), made known to the authorities whose business is the wellbeing of the homeless, then, come evening, was not seen again, He having shuffled, unfazed, back into the rustling lungs of the Mendip Woodlands.
- So, fine.
- The next day, however, Two Christs emerged from the forest.
- The day after that, Four.
- Then Sixteen.
- When, come Thursday, no fewer than 256 Christs were counted milling around the extremes of the Mendip Woodlands – talking amongst Themselves, absentmindedly levitating, and (with the same enthusiasm you normally see in someone kicking a can along the pavement) performing minor miracles, such as the transformation of all the leaves on a single tree into Ulysses butterflies, which promptly detonated upwards in spectacular, warping-blue gobs – the council blocked off road access to the area and anxiously yanked up a sheet metal perimeter.
- Friday's 65,536 Christs were well-mannered, didn't appear to need feeding, etc., but there were now credible fears that if serious action was not pretty immediately taken then, that weekend, the limited resources of the Mendip District Council could have up to 4,294,967,296 Messiahs on its hands. Bear in mind that the resources of the Mendip District Council, only a couple of months previously, had

been stretched to breaking point by road gritting.

• Mercifully, come Saturday, the Numbers had not increased.

• Still. In such overpopulated conditions the Christs grew restless and discontented. They snuck out by night in groups of Four or Five to drive Satan out of local cattle. They would recklessly multiply bread crusts snatched from nearby duck ponds, and trout lifted from brooks. They piled the bread and fish into huge heaps that attract- ed clouds of hungry birds, so many that soon it started disrupting global migratory patterns, tampering with ecosystems thousands of miles away from the Christs. When at Their most sedate, the Christs would pace around in circles, One every ten feet, padding out the whole forest with low murmuring. When at Their most frustrated, They would lash out at One Another, bitterly, with One Jesus, for example, converting the cranial and circulatory fluids of Another Jesus to wine, which resulted in increasing sight- ings of floppy-limbed Christs with deeply-creased brows and eyes that pointed in opposite directions.

• All the while loomed the fear of another exponential jump in the Christs. I had vivid daydreams in which, to the sound of distant rumbling, over Four Billion Christs swelled up out of the wooded landscape like the froth on a fizzy drink, smothering the horizon. Local government concluded this was not a risk that could be lived with.

• Ultimately the Christs had to be pulped.

• Then the forest was back to One Christ per day, which was when Roach and I were brought in. Up till then we'd been mowing roundabout grass for minimum wage. 'Is this a promotion?' Roach asked. Our supervisor hummed encouragingly as though that was a good word for it. That night I dreamt of freshly printed nametags and a world without hay fever or circling traffic.

Some of the rules of the situation:

• Christ rises from the dead once every twenty-four

hours in one of seven known caves.

- (The wording of the whiteboard in the staffroom is, strictly speaking, not accurate – but we only see resurrections in which Christ successfully evades us for a period exceeding twenty-four hours as 'counting'.)
- If Christ successfully evades us for a period exceeding twenty-four hours, an Additional Christ will appear. Forty-eight hours, Four Christs, and so on.
- If we attempt to booby trap a cave, Christ resurrects in a different cave. If we attempt to booby trap *all* the caves, or simultaneously observe all the caves with disguised cameras, or fill in all the caves with cement or entrapping foam, another cave will appear – which is why we have to hunt Him down ourselves.
- Christ has a demeanour of apathy but does actively hide from us and does actively flee from us when discovered.
- Every time Christ regenerates, He does so wearing one bright white shawl and one pair of primitive sandals.
- Every time Christ regenerates, He bears the wounds He received at the crucifixion, but none of the ones He received from us the day before. I am grateful for this because sometimes I have nightmares in which Christ appears to me with almost 500 consecutive euthanisations' worth of wounds about His person.

Some interesting characteristics of Christ:

- Other than the characteristics you would expect from Christ – a wide selection of forgiveness-conveying eyebrow arrangements, for example, plus general calm, an aura of detached politeness, a gait suggestive of a weight-less conscience and a piss-irritating habit of brushing ferns with the tips of His fingers as He passes through them – Christ also has a surprising capacity for improvised camouflage, and the ability to take advantage of the alarm calls of certain birds.

The staff:
- There is me, there is Roach, we hunt Christ.
- There is a secretary.
- There is a caretaker.
- There is our supervisor.
- There is a team of three who deal with the disposal of the body of Christ post-euthanasia, a process Roach and I have nothing to do with.
- There is an additional team of all of the above who carry out the same tasks at the weekends.

*

Today Roach is armed with – I suspect without irony – a nail gun. His nostrils punch cigarette smoke into the air and he corrugates his brow against the sunset, which is bright red and marbled with clouds, like a slab of uncooked steak. Still no sign of Christ.

Roach growls. He spits. His knuckle hairs distance themselves from one another as his fingers tense around the nail gun. If Christ doesn't show we're looking at an all-nighter.

If Christ makes it to midnight, an Additional Christ will be generated and we will have to deal with Him also. If Christ makes it to midnight I'll have to wipe the whiteboard in the staffroom. I'll have to wipe it and correct it so it reads '0 days without a resurrection'. Then put the kettle on. Then go into the toilet and pat my face with water so I wake up a bit. Then stare at my own reflection in the mirror above the sink, the mirror above which our supervisor has affixed a sign that reads – I suspect without irony – 'Don't forget to wash your hands'.

I say part of my daily routine is, 'go home, macaroni, bed', but strictly speaking that isn't true. Lately I've begun to pray. Monday evening I prayed for three minutes. Tuesday evening I prayed for nine. Today is Wednesday and tonight I'll pray for twenty-seven. I guess I'll pray on foot.

I try to pray but I keep on making false starts.

'Father God, forgive me for I have…'

'Father God, forgive me for I knowingly continue to…'

'Lord, is there any way I can convince You that I am not a man of ingratitude?'

'Lord, please forgive me. Please forgive me and please continue to forgive me indefinitely, or at least until Legoland or the paintballing arena get back to me.'

Roach has stomped off, heading west. I'm heading east, stepping carefully through the undergrowth like a heron.

'Lord Father God, You have made the accommodation of Your Son on this Earth a logistical nightmare, so I do this so others don't have to, I do this sin, I take it and absorb it, the sins of the other people of a potential future, so is there something Christ-like in what I do and why I do it, or is even thinking that just another huge, massive sin in Your wise eyes?'

'Lord Father God, witness my applications to Legoland, witness my applications to the paintballing arena. They are not the applications of a man who is proud, who covets. They are sincere –'

I freeze by a stream as I spot a light shape in the distance, distorted by the white noise of the midges that are suddenly all around me. Could be a shopping bag, could be Christ. The forest is fairly still and the bright red sunset is starting to clot. The stream is muttering to itself. I raise my rifle and lower my voice.

'As I was saying, they are sincere. Help me be better. Send me a sign.'

A short story

ROSS BENAR

*

HYENA

I WALKED OUT to the dumpster behind my store with
another box of unsold bananas. Stark shadows thrown
by the security light, something felt wrong even before
I saw her.

Out of her dark little patch with a gun in her hand.
I saw the cute little two-step out the corner of my eye when
I dumped the fruit. Turned around and stared her dead,
my stone not slipping and her face in shadow so I couldn't
even see.

Don't like guns. Make little people feel big, like they
can take me down just cause they got a couple hundred
bucks and a clean record.

Too far, too far, no chance I'd make the spring. Just
get cut down. If she was closer this story'd have a different
ending.

I stopped calculating the distance and I looked at her
– for real this time, not for scaring off – and I realized she
wasn't a pro. The gun shook a little, and she had it pointing
between my eyes. That's not a safe shot for a shaker. She
should have kept it trained on my chest. Center-mass, they
called it in the army. Less chance of missing.

I took a step towards her and she took a step back, half-
in the shadow-patch. Then she shot me and it fucking hurt,
and now one of us was going to die.

The bullet clipped my shoulder and I know I must've
hollered but no one called it in. My store isn't in the
best area.

Plus there's a drag bar across the corner and even back
by the dumpster I could hear the horns and cries from
something the girls were blasting. Maybe no good citizens
even heard the shot.

Then I laughed, because why was I thinking about the
drag bar? She didn't seem like a queen – short with thick,
dangerous legs. A black hoodie, no fishy dress.

Still nothing from the girl and now I was bleeding and
my dumpster had a bullet-hole. Just to get it over with I said,

'You want my wallet? Eh? You gonna let me pull it without playing cowboy?'

She repositioned her fingers on the gun and nodded.

I pulled the wallet and I was gonna throw it on the ground but I didn't. No reason for her to know who I was, if this was just a mugging. Sometimes even the greatest get clipped. Instead I held it open upside down and let the two dollar bills fall out and drift a little in the summer heat before they hit the ground. I watched her eyes but they didn't follow the bills, they kept on me. Fear can make you smart, keep you alive. Kept her alive, then.

But maybe she did know who was I was, because she didn't just leave when the carcass turned out more gristle than meat. She kept the gun on me and pointed at the back door to my store. Didn't say a word.

I liked that wordlessness. Opposite of Molly.

I moved slow. The door would have been a problem for her, except I had left it open. Who dares to flit in, rob my store, *my* store, behind my back?

As we passed the dirty, shabby little aisles in the half-bright fluorescent, I realized I was embarrassed. I'd always thought it was my castle and keep, but I suddenly saw how others must see it. I saw it through her. Trashy little corner shop, cigarettes and beer and chips and candy, with grime and muck and the smell of old farts and dirty little children. A few drops of blood, from the gash on my shoulder.

That arm still isn't moving too well.

I knew what she wanted, and I just went behind the counter. Shutters on the storefront were down, only the emergency lights on, and even if anyone could've seen us through the dark and the grate it would just have been one of the poor queers across the street. God knows they don't need any more trouble.

I don't like guns. Most shopkeepers you see in TV and movies have guns behind the counter. I don't hang out with those guys in real life though, so who knows if it's true or

not. But I don't like guns and I don't have one behind
my counter.

She kept her distance still and now I had a fucked arm
and the register between us. I liked her even more. Out
there hustling – not proper hustling but getting what she
had to get. I felt myself stirring and wished I could go with
her, back to being young and lean and hungry, look into my
madness and despair all ye who breathe here.

But I had Molly, and her hoarse, *hubby* whispers when
she liked me, decided to want me that night. Fights with
cheap slut and *lousy faggot* in the air.

No Sale-Enter on the register and the cash drawer
sprang out, medium-thick with light bills. Ten years of too
slow and too fat to be in the thick of it, ten years of manning
the shop, and not much more than what was in that register.
One thousand, eight hundred thirty-two dollars. As I gathered them up out of the little slots, I had a brief vision of the
girl naked, sitting on the counter while I fucked her, a hand
on my ass, pulling me into her, the other holding the gun up
to my temple while she moaned.

She looked at me and I could almost feel her disgust,
as if she knew what I'd been thinking. I saw her eyes. They
were hazel, like mine and like Molly's, and I wanted to ask if
she was Irish but I didn't.

When she reached out to take the money off the counter, that's when she made the mistake. She didn't make me
stand back, she didn't make me head into a corner.

I grabbed her wrist, the one outstretched, without
the gun. Hauled back hard, wrenched it so I could feel the
bones splinter under my fingers, and she was slammed
against the counter then dragged across it towards me. Her
finger wasn't on the trigger because she got greedy, focused
on the cash instead of her own ass. I took the opportunity
to clamp my hand on top of hers, stripped the gun out of
her fingers. Probably they were slack from the pain in other
parts of her body. Her sudden shriek thrilled me; finally I'd

heard her voice.

Shattered hand, no gun, half-stunned. I couldn't hold back the old blood-smile as I brought her face close up to mine, and I roared for ten years of humiliation and pain and hatred before hurling the cub off my counter, onto the floor where she looked up at me pale and mewling, before scrabbling up and out, rushing through the open back door which she slammed behind her.

I laughed, despite the pain in my arm and in my brain. It had been a nice try, a very good opening move from an early professional still stumbling.

Then I gathered up the bills to put them back in their slots, pinned by the flimsy plastic arms. Just because I had had it beaten into me so it's an automatic reaction, I took a count, double-counted. Both times I was missing a hundred-dollar bill.

I didn't bother searching the store for the little scrap of fat.

ANNETTA BERRY

✳

THE BINDING FRAME

PALERMO, 1624. *A time of plague.*

The shutters were closed against the heat of the day. Sofonisba leant into a thread of light and looked up with rheumy eyes. Her irises were half-concealed beneath heavy lids, which were red-rimmed and bald, as though the lashes had been plucked. Antoon found them strangely compelling, the way the light glazed the pupils. Lead white highlights: that would be how to paint them. A very fine sable brush. He rested his silk elbows on the grimy arms of the chair.

'I have never been to Venice,' Sofonisba said slowly. 'But I remember seeing the Titians in Madrid.' The effort of memory seemed to use all her strength. 'There on the walls, everything in motion. The vivid colour of dreams. Naked skin in buttery strokes. Unstable, shallow spaces; feverish, opulent skies. Europa, faceless, snatched from the shore on a bull. Everywhere violence; flickering brushwork; patches and slashes of paint. The surface of his canvases alive.' Sofonisba's breathing had quickened and each intake of air began with a dry sniff of her nostrils. 'My heart is beating so fast,' she whispered, pressing her chest.

'Should I call for someone? A servant?' Antoon asked.

Sofonisba shook her head. Gradually her indisposition subsided and she regained her composure. 'Your portrait of our viceroy, young man. They say it is exceptional. The textures: starched lace, crimped silk, the gilding on the metal. That, in places, you hardly blend your brushstrokes. But, from a distance, it looks incredibly real.' She straightened her bones in the chair. 'I wish I could see it.'

Antoon looked away. The sunlight through the join of the shutters was like a seam of gold. 'You are kind.' He spread his palms on his thighs. How pale and unmarked the backs of his hands appeared against the black silk – like the hands of a gentleman. 'Your own name and work are still highly acclaimed.'

'Oh,' she said, lowering her eyes, 'I am entirely

forgotten, Señor van Dyck. Although, I had some success. In my day.'

What must she be? Almost a hundred. Antoon had never before met anyone so old. The structure of her face was drawn and fragile, a series of sloping planes, with a long straight nose and finely flaring nostrils. He thought that once she might have been attractive, although probably not a beauty. Now her skin was papery, taut over her brow bones but folding and sagging in bags on her cheeks and jowls, creasing in deep lines which ran from her nostrils past the edges of her thin lips to her jaw. Several tufts of thick grey hair sprouted unpleasantly from either side of her chin. Looking at Sofonisba was like peering into a tomb. Antoon shuddered and hoped he would not have to stay too long. As the motes swirled in the light he thought of all the flecks of shed skin and hair as she returned to dust. He tried not to breathe too deeply and his fingers twitched to brush down his black satin doublet.

'You painted for Philip of Spain?' he asked.

'I was in the queen's household. Elisabeth of Valois. I taught her to draw.'

'And you portrayed them? The king, the queen, the king's son, Don Carlos?' Antoon vaguely recollected some scandal.

'They paid me a small pension for their portraits.'

'You are too modest, Signora.' The thread of sunlight now touched the parakeet's cage. 'It puzzles me though, how a girl, a noblewoman, could have been trained?'

Sofonisba paused. Was it pride or pain that flickered across her face?

'I began in Cremona, at home. Drawing my sisters and brother, God rest their souls. Six daughters without dowries.' Her lips wavered, but failed to turn into a smile. 'My father nurtured our talents. At fourteen, with my sister Elena, Bernardino Campi taught us to paint. Not in his workshop with his male apprentices. In his kitchen, among the pots and pans.' Her speech came in wheezing, short snatches. 'We copied his paintings, in churches. Drew each other. Our servants. But mostly we painted ourselves. I still don't know why my father did it. Such pride and belief in the skill of a daughter. He set me apart from other women. Placed me on a path of my own.'

'Remarkable. A remarkable man.' Antoon thought of his own father. He brushed his palm along the knee of his breeches. Antoon no longer gave his father the credit for arranging his apprenticeship with Van Balen, and it had been a good position for a boy of ten, a reputable master high up in the Guild of Saint Luke. All he remembered now was the disgrace – his unmarried sisters with no suitors – and Isabella.

'So, you were Rubens's assistant.' Sofonisba raised her shoulders and shifted her spine in the chair.

'Yes. Now he is more like a prince than a painter. One of Antwerp's richest citizens. I was seventeen and had already set up on my own when he sought me out. He honoured me by trusting me with his most important works, introducing me to his best patrons, considering ways to make my name known.' But, Rubens had always carefully managed Antoon's success, and his own competition. Antoon had not realised how frustrating painting in the manner of his master would eventually become. For too long he had sublimated himself to Rubens's style, his own hand constrained and always invisible. He thought of the sea and cities separating them now, the wealth and freedom of all he had seen and experienced in Italy. He cursed Palermo's locked gates. How would he ever get out alive?

The clock ticked. The dust settled. The pungent odour of the leather wall hangings infested Antoon's clothes, seeped into his pores, tainted his hair. The heat was making him drowsy. The air was heavy with the smoke of musk and amber burning in the *profumatòio* in the grate.

'You must wish to return to Antwerp.'

'Yes.' What Antoon wanted was Genoa and hourly sittings with jewelled bankers' wives. 'But the port is still closed, Signora. Due to the pestilence. No ships may sail.' He bent over to reach for his sketchbook, his gold chains weighing against his knees.

'Must you go so soon?' She sat forward, blinking; her shoulders dropped. Antoon felt her disappointment like a stone in his chest. Then, he realised that the old woman's loneliness was of a quality only he could satisfy – the loneliness of a painter.

'My sketchbook,' he said, holding it out towards her. 'Might I ask the honour of drawing your portrait? To remember you.'

Her eyes brightened and she spread her elbows, her veil enclosing her in a broad triangle of white against the dark wall. 'Of course.'

Antoon selected a blank sheet, unstoppered his ink and dipped his nib. He wondered whether he should ask to let in more light, but decided he could manage without.

Sofonisba hunched forward in her chair, squinting and spreading her fingers across the pommels of the armrests. Her bent shoulders, bead-bright eyes and long straight nose gave her the appearance of a fledgling crow.

'I know of a ship. A Genoese galley at Syracuse,' she said, her eyes narrowing. 'The shadows cast by my wrinkles are not too dark if I sit like this?' The considerations of a portraitist had never left her, and she appeared conscious of every move she made.

'No. That's perfect,' Antoon said. A galley! How could she know of a galley? Shut up here in the dark with half of Palermo dead. Antoon peered at her. Was she just saying what he wanted to hear?

He began with the kink of her mouth and the flare of her nostril. These first few strokes were heavy with ink, then the line of her nose and her cheekbone, fading up into her brow. A new nib of ink and the left eye, the socket, the

eyelid; the jowls of her age-squared jaw. Her appearance
captured with a dozen marks. Then twenty or so sweeping
strokes for her veil and the suggestion of the gown and the
chair. No hesitation, no changes of mind, absolute certainty
of purpose between his eye and his hand. He blew on the
page to dry the last beads of ink.

'Would you like to see?' he asked.

'What? Is it done?' She held out her hand.

Antoon sensed she had been anticipating something
more, the work of several hours, the strong modelling and
high finish of a presentation drawing by Michelangelo;
something, he imagined, more akin to her own antiquated
style. He stood up and carried the open book to her. She
took it from his hand, her brow furrowed as if sceptical
about what she would find.

'Could you…?' she raised her right palm towards the
window.

Antoon drew back the bolt and slipped his hand
through the ring on the left. He pulled the shutter a crack
wider. The heat hit him like opening an oven. Orange
blossom, sea spray, the stench of rotting meat. He could
hear a man ranting in the street; the cathedral Angelus bell;
a woman weeping; the screech of swifts. The noon sun cut
a beam across Sofonisba's cheek and shoulder, bleaching
her velvet gown to a dust-flecked grey. She shaded her eyes
with her hand, the open sketchbook on her lap reflecting
the brightness up into her face. He could see the bones of
her fingers through her skin. She looked too frail for the
sunlight, like a night-dwelling creature caught in the flare
of a torch or emerging from the earth. She flinched and
turned her face away.

'Señor…'

Antoon closed the shutter and opened the other, an-
gling it so the light now fell in a bar across the floor, diffus-
ing more gently off the polished bricks. He'd not previously
noticed the crest painted in the centre of the ceiling – her

family emblem, he assumed – or the tarnished brass pricket candlesticks without candles lined up along the mantelshelf.

Sofonisba lifted the sketchbook up to her face so her nose was almost pressed to the paper. He imagined her damp breath on the ink, feathering his outlines; minuscule droplets of her caught on his page. She squinted and moved the drawing slowly beneath her gaze. Then she tried bringing it closer to and away from her eyes. At first Antoon wondered what she was doing, then with the knot in his chest rising into his throat, he realised she was almost blind.

'I am better with colours than lines,' she said, laying his sketchbook down and closing her eyes. Antoon stared at the marks of his rapid drawing, upside down on the old woman's lap. He had made her admit to a greater loss than either of them could bear.

'May I… It would be my honour…to paint your portrait in oils.'

Sofonisba laid her hand on the open page. She ran her fingers slowly to the edge of the paper and then folded the volume closed. Raising her head and looking up, the clouds in her pupils caught the light.

'Señor van Dyck. Throughout my life I have painted my self. Self portraits.' Her breathing was laboured, as though exhaustion were overtaking her. 'As a girl, and as a woman… I have watched and recorded my self take shape.' She paused to catch her breath. 'My hands are steady. Look.' She held them out towards him. They did not tremble. 'If it were not for my eyes, I would be painting still.'

'Yes.' He believed she would. Antoon thought he had offended her again, and inwardly cursed himself.

'My greatest regret: I can no longer paint.' Sofonisba knotted her hands in her lap and leant back in her chair. 'I must make my self for the final time. Before it is too late. You will paint my last. My final *self portrait*. Only *you*. You will come back the day after tomorrow,' she said.

NICK BRADLEY

*

AUTUMN LEAVES

'I WANT YOU TO slap me in the face and force me to suck your cock,' whispered Mari in English. 'Really jam it in.'

George was not sure what to say. He made a low groan.

'OK?' She looked up from her coffee and stared him straight in the eyes. 'Will you do that for me? When we next have sex.'

'But why?' He shifted in his seat uncomfortably.

'Because I asked you to. That's why.'

'But I love you. Why would I treat you like that?'

'If you love me, do what I ask.'

'But why?'

'Because it would make me happy.'

The two of them sat in the Mister Donuts in Kōenji, drinking black coffee from red cups. George in his forties, Mari in her thirties, they were on the top floor of the doughnut shop and could see the station through the windows. The sun was shining in, and the café was becoming quite hot for an autumn morning. Outside the sky was blue, and the air conditioner was humming into life, stuttering after a long summer keeping thousands of customers cool. There were only a few other people nearby: an old man with a cane sitting by himself, three high school students sitting together giggling, and a group of young mothers, all looking at their smartphones, idly rocking their babies and shhhh-ing them if they called out or cried.

Mari was picking at a doughnut she'd ordered. George took out a cigarette and lit it. She took up her dog-eared copy of *The Catcher in the Rye* and carried on reading, bringing a choked end to the conversation. George picked up his biro and continued scribbling away on his yellow notepad, his cigarette hanging loosely on his lips.

They'd first met in fall
At the largest park in town
The trees flamed red gold

He had been so drunk
While she was stone-cold sober
On that autumn day

He had been drinking
All night and had not stopped
Until the sun was high

Each year without fail
She took a fallen red leaf
Pressed it in her book

Pages and pages
A catalogue of colour
leaves of history

He'd spoken to her –
She'd been alarmed at that –
His voice faltering waves

'What are you doing?'
'Nothing. Collecting red leaves.'
'How about this one?'

'It's fine, I suppose.'
[must finish this stanza]

'Fancy a coffee?'
'What? With you? Right now?' she asked.
'Yes. Why not?' he said.

George paused. It took a lot of effort to write everything in
the haiku format. The strict 5–7–5-syllable structure hurt
his head. He was a purist. He didn't like it when Westerners
translated haiku into English and lost the syllabic structure
of the poem. He'd been reading a lot of Matsuo Bashō in

translation, and it annoyed him when he noticed an
extra syllable in a line or, equally, when one or two were
missing. Why couldn't people respect the form? Why call
it a haiku if it lacked the structure? He longed to read the
poems in the original. A step at a time, like the haiku by
Kobayashi Issa:

蝸牛
そろそろ登れ
富士の山
O snail
Climb Mount Fuji,
But slowly, slowly!

Mari was reading *The Catcher in the Rye* for the tenth time
in English. It was her favourite novel. She loved everything
about it. She'd first read it in Japanese at high school. She
remembered that initial thrill of reading about another soul
like her – a boy her age, isolated and different – lost in a
massive mega city, an alien New York. She could relate to
him. As a teenager she'd imagined meeting Holden, he'd
be much taller than her – blond hair and blue eyes – wearing that famous red cap. She'd take him to Tokyo and look
after him. They'd be happy together. They wouldn't be lost
anymore because their lives would have meaning.

She snuck a look at George as he was writing. He
looked so cool concentrating. She loved his leathery face,
blond hair and blue eyes. The ash on his cigarette was
building up, but he didn't let it drop. She wished she could
photograph him like that. Her very own Holden. Her
hopeless, lost *gaijin*. True, he wasn't from New York, nor
even America. It had taken her a while to adjust her ears
to his stuffy British accent with its terribly repressed, hard
syllables. It was nothing like the accents of the string of
American guys she'd dated before meeting George. At
first she'd found it a little bit of a barrier. She missed the

looseness and openness of the Americans.

This British man was just like a Japanese man. Exactly what she didn't want in a partner. But the way he looked, she could imagine him as an American. What could he be writing? Perhaps a novel like the one she was reading. She allowed herself to fantasise a little about her life as the wife of a foreign writer. She'd write about it too, in Japanese. Perhaps they'd live in New York, but she would travel back to Japan to appear on chat shows, to promote her latest novel. She went back to her book.

George needed to take a break from writing. He looked at Mari reading silently on the other side of the table, her sharp cheekbones hovering over the open book. Her black hair was cut short, like a man's. Sometimes she looked so fierce, but now she seemed softer, more approachable. He wanted to talk to her when she was like this. He coughed and slid his notepad towards her. She didn't immediately look up from her novel, so he waved the notepad under her nose. She furrowed her brow.

'*Mari-chan, Mi-te,*' he said, the foreign syllables stumbling off his tongue in an effort to impress, to become closer to her. His tongue, when he tried to pronounce her name in Japanese, froze midway and fell neither here nor there. He never struck upon the correct sound for the consonant.

She ignored his Japanese.

'Mari. Look,' he said in English.

'What?'

'I'm writing a story about us. About how we met.'

She put her book down and sighed. He passed her the yellow notepad, and she rolled her eyes as she took it. She read through the poem quickly.

'Great.' She handed him back the pad.

'You don't like it?'

'Well… it just seems a bit…'

'A bit?'

'Insubstantial.'

'Oh…' George flicked his cigarette into the ashtray. The mountain of ash fell, and he took a sorry-looking drag on his cigarette. It would be finished soon.

'Why don't you write it as a story, instead of a poem? And maybe set it somewhere interesting, like New York?'

'But, well, I wanted to make it a haiku.'

'Oh, really? But it's not a haiku…'

'Yes it is.'

'No it's not.'

'Well, each stanza is a haiku.'

Mari didn't know what the word 'stanza' meant, but she didn't want to admit it. The fact that George had used an English word she didn't know made her a little angry. 'Haiku are supposed to be written in Japanese.'

'I don't think so.'

'*Yappari gaijin wakaranai ne,*' she said quickly under her breath.

'What?' George couldn't catch her fast Japanese.

'Anyway, it doesn't have *kigo*, George.'

'*Kigo?*'

'Yeah. You know, like, a seasonal word. Every haiku is supposed to have a seasonal word that relates to one of the four seasons.'

'I see.' George put down his pen and bit his lip.

*

Mari would check his browser history whenever she got hold of his laptop and he wasn't around. George looked at a lot of porn. Such a wide variety too. It didn't make her jealous. It fascinated her. What was he into? His search terms were things like *Asian cumshots. Classy girl gets fucked. Cream pies. Girls dressed up in high school uniforms. Cuckold porn.* Every now and again in the history there would be something super-kinky, like *ladyboys* or *bisexual* stuff. She liked to watch the porn he'd been watching and slip a finger inside herself while she imagined him masturbating.

It wasn't George that she fantasised about. It turned her on to imagine being in the porno he'd been watching. She thought about how great it would be if he clicked on a video to watch and suddenly saw Mari in the scene, being gangbanged by seven or eight muscular men with massive cocks. She'd just look directly into the camera – straight into his shocked eyes – taking the loads of all the men shooting sperm all over her face. She would climax thinking about things like that. Then she would be gripped by a feeling of melancholy, and would tidy away his laptop in exactly the same place she'd found it.

Then she would go wash her hands.

George imagined a lot of things when he was on his own. One of the strange ideas he'd had was a daydream about sticking his cock in Mari's arse. In his imagination she would pop just like a balloon. Her skin would turn to rubber, and bits of it would fly all over the room, just like a burst balloon at a child's party. He would scurry around trying to get her all back into one piece. Thinking that if he did, if he held all the bits of her in his screwed-up palm, she might come back to life again.

When he'd really fucked her in the arse one night, it had been an entirely different experience. She'd taken it well, and had seemed to enjoy it. After he came, he'd pulled his cock out of her arse, and a bit of shit had popped out onto the bed. She'd obviously sensed something, because she scrambled underneath his weight, wanting to know what had happened.

'What was that? Blood?'

'Don't worry about it.' George grabbed a Kleenex from the bedside table before she could turn round. He scooped up the bit of turd and hid it from her.

*

'I had the weirdest dream last night,' said George.

'Urgh.' Mari screwed up her face in disgust.

'What?'

'It's just. No, well, I hate hearing people's dreams.'

'What do you mean?'

'Well, they're just always so boring.'

'But this one was so vivid.'

'I'm sure it was. Vividly boring.'

'Just hear me out, OK?'

'Go on then.'

'So, I don't know why, but we'd been cryogenically frozen – you know, like when they do it in science fiction movies. When people travel to far off planets, it takes light years for them to get there, so they get into these tanks and freeze themselves. Their bodies won't age. Kind of like rich people who want to live forever and have their bodies frozen. Anyway, we'd both been frozen, for some reason or other. But we got chopped in half – right down the middle. So we had just one arm, one leg, one eye, half a nose, that kind of thing. We were lying on the bed as just two halves. And the machine had broken, so we were thawing out naturally, and we both knew that we were going to die. We could see the insides of each other, and everything was just slowly melting, our organs were dripping everywhere, and we were just becoming all squishy, like an ice cream. We couldn't speak properly either, because we were still partially frozen. But we both knew what we had to do. We crawled together, and we matched up the sides of our bodies that had been cut away. We became this hideous one whole body, composed of the two halves of a man and a woman. And we lay together there like that until we died.'

'Hmmm,' said Mari.

'What?'

'I dunno. That's just one of the dumbest things I've ever heard.'

The beginning of a novel

ROSALIND BROWN

*

POSITION OF TRUST

I STILL THINK it's the best word in the whole language
even after everything

Ashcrofts

two pure open vowels   a cushion of consonants

the white capital Λ on the dark red sign a paragon of
symmetry and elegance   and the rest of the word in unem-
barrassed serifs

the apostrophe   missing in action somewhere   once
it had been Sir James Ashcroft's School for Girls est. 1893

and now agitated English teachers every few years
wanting it corrected

but I think it turned out for the best

Ashcroft   no too naked

Ashcroft's   no no   too fastidious

Ashcrofts

Ashcrofts

yes   settled and steely   and safe

*

so ten-year-old me   back in what 1997   on a tour with
my mother getting a sense of the place

a good sense we got too   endless rooms all well-lit full
of patient industry   we stood in doorways watching heads
bent over maths problems   small smiles busy pencils
girl-chemists wearing actual protective goggles tending to
actual Bunsen burners   looks of alarm at obscure words
in a French *dictée*

no energy misdirected   nothing untoward

all very   *toward*

a geography lesson with a grey-haired geography
teacher   about coastal erosion I think

she interrupted her teaching with whiteboard pen
sketching out a diagram and came over to the door   spoke
a few words to my mother   looked at me   asked my
name

I said nothing
    after a long pause   the girls in the lesson craning their
necks   my mother said she's Charlotte she's a bit shy
    not true   I had never been shy
    but that teacher was giving me such a look   an exami-
nation almost   like she was testing for the thing in me
a lump of quartz or   a burning ember perhaps   whatever
it was that marked a girl out for Ashcrofts   like I was a
piece of rough iron they would extract from me on day one
and spend seven years firing and tempering and hammering
into place until I was an Ashcrofts girl through and through
    and being looked at like that I found it hard to reply
    I was burning already with a blue flame

*

when we got home I went up to my room and sat there on
my own
    like the ignition button on a gas stove held down
    spitting sparks
    waiting

*

on the day of the entrance exam we were taken round again
in a group this time
    through endless corridors across a lawn round corners
up stairs   finally into a room where they arranged us in
alphabetical order at desks for the exam
    another grey-haired teacher   Mrs Miles if I remember
rightly   said there's no need to be nervous
    she threw a general smile around like a handful of
flowers
    I was pretty studious by nature   but now it swelled
raised itself to several powers   demanded perfection   so
I took my pencil sharpener and began to sharpen my pencil

slowly　　one turn　　at a time　　shaved　　inspected the
point　　back in the sharpener　　just one more turn　　and
one more

the teacher said　　now girls firstly let's write our
names at the top of the page　　full names please first name
surname

my pencil was so sharp that when I pressed it on the
paper tiny flecks of graphite broke off and spattered across
the page

and when I started the first sum the pencil lead dis-
lodged itself entirely　　rolled across the desk and off onto
the floor

I had to start again sharpening then　　the time ticking
on

(honestly this ten-year-old aesthetic crisis which had
appeared out of nowhere)

finally the teacher appeared next to my desk　　like
a horse putting its head over the fence　　do you need a new
pencil she whispered

I thought of my mother saying something that began
with but if you don't get in　　and my father saying hah and
draining the last of his wine and asking why on earth
I wouldn't get in

cue the end of the miniature neurosis　　I nodded at the
teacher　　sorry it keeps breaking

she gave me two maroon pencils with silver lettering
Ashcrofts School for Girls
and I nicked them both

*

friends romans and countrymen　　I said to my three pri-
mary school friends　　(all local boys I had managed to get
the upper hand over)　　I will not be accompanying you to
the community college to my great distress and devastation

I had slobbed about there in leggings and sweatshirts

running about with the boys like a mad thing   trailing
at least one shoelace and getting ten out of ten in every
spelling test

my father summed it up with the phrase big fish in
a small pond   and now I knew I was going elsewhere this
was more obviously accurate

for example two of those boys couldn't remember
things like history dates or the words of school hymns or
the correct punctuation for contractions and I could do all
that almost without effort

Peter (the third one) was a bit sharper   but he still
struggled with long division and I had to help him quietly
when the teacher was at the other side of the room

and now these boys all about to disappear from my
life   or rather me about to disappear from theirs

*

the Ashcrofts school uniform shop was open two afternoons a week and grudgingly on Saturday mornings for
those mothers who might actually have jobs   at least that
is how my mother characterised it to me as we parked the
car and went in

I doubt I was interested   I was probably in a rebellion
about having to wear a uniform at all   certainly it was
under protest that I went into the changing room with the
armful of hangers

undressed   stepped into the maroon pleated skirt
and slid up the zip   too big for me and had to hang on my
hipbones   with its sharp pleats like thumbnail folds

then the maroon shirt and the maroon v-neck jumper

I looked at myself and felt very   very Charlotte
Elizabeth Davies   it was like I suddenly knew the exact
weight and heft of my own intellect   I wanted to rush
home to a clean white exercise book and write an essay
I barely knew what an essay even was

a hundred and forty-two pounds it all cost I remember that
precisely   my mother covered her enormous yawn with
her right hand and signed the slip with her left

the woman wrote down the transaction in a large ledger
and said   now make sure you look after these young lady
they have to last

Mum said a hasty thank you and ushered me out of the
shop before I could say anything cheeky

but a sudden thought put my irritation on hold   wow
that was so expensive I said

yes my mother said   it is

*

we drove home and she went upstairs to lie down and
well   and she didn't get out of bed for four days   I think
that was the start of it

but at the time I didn't notice anything was wrong
I took the huge plastic bag bulging in my arms like a fat
white seal and went through to my father in his study to
show him   he let me change and parade in front of him
in the new uniform   I even tore the maroon tights out of
their wrappings and wrestled them on and suddenly had
dark thin serious legs

very nice he said   not smiling

I told him about my urge to write an essay

christ I wish my undergrads felt the same way he said
so what are you going to write about

don't know I said   I don't have a topic

ok he said here's one   school uniform is a lazy way for
educational institutions to pretend they inculcate a sense of
community   discuss

I made him write it down for me on a sheet of lined
paper   he wouldn't tell me what the word inculcate meant
so I had to go and look it up

spent a while starting sentences and crossing them out

got ink on the cuff of my new shirt   before going back
into my father's study and admitting I was stuck
    he gave me twenty socratic minutes on school uni-
form and its sociological implications but nothing at all
about Ashcrofts itself or what was going to happen come
September when I entered this world of Clever Girls

*

luckily however I entered it with great aplomb   and
worked and worked and worked   and proved myself
a Clever Girl over and over again

*

those maroon pencils are still in a pot on my desk in my
old bedroom
    (amongst other fragments broken off my life)
    both still with the silver lettering and one perhaps half
a centimetre longer than the other
    neither is sharp now

The beginning of a novel

DESMOND BYRNE

✳

MONTH'S MIND

A LOSS AGAIN, of course. This month, like the months before, descends to naught, continues below; and the private chest near exhausted, perfect naught ahoy. Fintan rolled his neck and to gristle-crackle his circling gaze took in: Bridget at her desk; long-dead bluebottle, black through clouded bowl of ceiling shade; scratched remains of gilt letters on pebble glass in office door; his own petrol-blue mohair thighs and crotch – concertina-creased look, destroyed this whole bloody get-up; Bridget again; Bridget's glasses, late morning sunlight glint in lilac tortoiseshell. Pausing his circuit here, he called to her:

'All our righteous deeds no more than filthy rags.'

Bridget, at stubborn rest, ignored him, turned a page of the fat paperback before her.

In one of her snots is she? Or fatigued just, after the customary Friday morning convocation? The burly bouncing-boys paid and dismissed to new missions – to the doors men! Who else but ye bould musclemen could guard such doors – shower of thugs. And grievance and plaint aired and heard; no lack of spleen and ill humour this morning at the lack of work. Not one of them any match for Bridget Una Buckley though, for all their oul' bluster and bull – grace *and* grit Bee by Jesus you're worth your weight.

No slouch with the figures either, worse luck – page after pitiless page of noughts and crosses-to-bear with nothing for sport but hangman in their margins. He considered again her ledger, borne earlier, with no little gravity, from her desk to rest on his own, the concluding rite to the Friday reckoning and this final Friday of the month; her even hand, frank, assured, the inky knots and flourishes of his own revisions on roughs and scraps scattered about the desktop. A loss again, of course, not a new penny made, a handful of wretched notes left, gone warm from being counted and every one of them spoken for and more besides. He'd have to make it up himself, again.

'Doesn't make an ounce of sense Bee,' he said.

'Speak for yourself.' She glanced at him and at the floor and returned to her book.

'These Olympian men.' Fintan picked up the thin sheaf of fives and ones that lay on his desk, thumbed them again absently. 'You'd think the phone would be leppin' off the hook with the bookings.'

'Any brawny fool can stand at a door and say yea or nay,' said Bridget. 'And isn't the town full of bowsies only dying to, and fit for it. No shortage of swaggering bulls who'd have the hand off you for the pound note alone, never mind the *say-so* for the night. *These* brutes able to pick and choose, sure 'tis like crown and feckin' sceptre to them altogether.'

Fintan's gaze had rested on the skirt of her skirt-suit and he noticed it now. A dear cloth as usual, a hound's tooth, and high waisted, taut around her thighs and hips, sat as she was, straight-backed in her swivel-chair. Her elbow was on her desk and her pale hand hung lengthily from its wrist, a More Menthol 120 smoked between its fingertips. An awful shame about the dial on her. The spit of her oul'fle. Raw deal altogether for a woman that: a ride from the neck down and a whoer-to-go in the saddle but the head off her ugly oul'fle God love her. That moon face and big beak and the big huge thick glasses, straw hair you can see through nearly – half an hour's teasing and tousling every morning to make it look like a head of hair even – and the teeth, of course.

'That's all I'm saying,' Bridget was saying. Fintan, at a loss, said:

'That's it, yeah, absolutely.'

Bridget regarded him warily. Her lips formed a sideways O to expel smoke. The rapid little stretch and purse then – her oul'fle does exactly that as well, the family tick to try and hide the tombstones.

Back to the grindstone. Fintan turned again to his figures. The numbers rewritten from Bridget's ledger, rewritten again, modified, amended, each new column getting straighter and tidier but the numbers at the bottom the same each time, the noughts lining up and at the sight of them the airy bloom in his gut and the blood running to his cock, the pulse of it there after each curt little minus before each new expense. Down to nothing and growing stiff at the sight of it and further down below that as well, the difference to be made up again with his own money. And the day soon that the last of *that* would go into the last envelope and the last bouncing-boy would bounce off out the door with it – the fine line of noughts that will be, a fine figure indeed, the royal horn altogether at the sight of it.

His cock fattened again at the thought. He'd had the horn on and off him since he had woken up, a ferocious head from the night before and the horn to go with it – nothing like the horn on you when you've the terrible head. Let it cook for another while and then over to Young's for the cure. A good oul' pull in the jacks before but. Maybe ask Bridget even. Then again maybe not, if she's the snot on her. The weight of the world on her poor oul' Bee Bee sometimes. Her oul'fle in another scrape is it? Sorrows of the woman's calendar perhaps?

A memory then, dimly: Bridget's face close to his own in Young's the night before, her voice urgent and earnest above the racket. Is it me she's browned off with? He leant in closer over the figures, shaded his brow with his hand and peered at her through his fingers. She had remained in firm repose, unmoving, save for the terse circling of a chest-nut-mid-heel-loafered foot. More Menthol smoke hung in the air around her and she just then wrangled another *O* and blew through it.

'So anyways Bee,' said Fintan. 'Not ideal, what?'

Bridget made an *mmh* sound and continued reading.

Humped off definitely. Fintan cast about inwardly, strained for recollection, yielded nothing but the proximity of Bridget's nose and teeth, the evening murk and mumble of Young's behind her.

Abruptly then, the thought of Hato. Where was the little amadáin? Away off somewhere and a reason for it. Fintan took a breath, said:

'So where's the bould Hato, Bridge? Do we know? At all?' His forced cheer withered as he spoke.

'It's like you're the new man everyday, d'you know that Fintan?' Bridget spoke to the air in front of her, turned then and met Fintan's gaze.

'What?'

'Every day new born the day before forgotten.'

'How d'you mean like?' said Fintan. Prelude to a proper row this, was it?

'Nothing,' she said. She ground out her More. 'Hato's out off away beyond to see that eejit Egan, he'll be in soon.'

'Grand. Right so.' Fintan drummed the desktop. 'Egan's a few bob owing hasn't he?'

'The last of it,' said Bridget, a steadiness to her gaze now, wounded and questioning.

'The last of it, OK so,' said Fintan.

Bridget raised an eyebrow. Fintan, conceding, said:

'How d'you mean?'

'He's finished with us. I told you *all* this last night. Gone with another crew, some shower of northern gun-slingers. Hato's gone out beyond to collect what's owing and that's *it* like. I told you. Another loss like that and we're sunk.'

'Right so,' said Fintan. Fuck off Bridget, browned-off bloody gob on her. Amn't I the boss? Isn't it my loss sure? Sunk. I have to laugh. Weren't we sunk the day we started?

'And Reed?' she said. 'You'll have forgotten all about Reed then as well will you?'

Fintan made to speak, paused, he cast his gaze about; noonish now and the low cold spring sun lit the office, filtered through the grey grain of the window's three re-maining panes. The fourth had been replaced by a sheet of

ply, cut to approximate size and glossed cream, in its centre
was mounted a cream coloured sootily burnished broken
fan. *Expelair*, he read again.

'Indeed'n I have love,' he said. He lit a cigarette and
stretched out in his chair. 'Tell me again, why don't you.'

Bridget closed her eyes, tilted her head. Air whistled
backwards through her nostrils; and her eyes, open again
then and intent, shallow little nods of her head as she spoke.

'So Reed right,' she said. She took another More and
lit it, swivelled her chair in Fintan's direction. 'Where
to begin.'

A flush of excitement now, less of the fed-up look to
her. Fintan, emboldened, hand wringing and winking, said:

'Isn't this grand now, an oul' scéal from me oul' pal Bee.
And isn't it well she knows how much I love a good yarn.'

'Grand, so just be quiet and listen.'

'Sorry Bee. Away you go. Tell us.' Fintan's lips and
brow wriggled against laughter, an effort now to hold
Bridget's gaze.

'So,' said Bridget.

'Fádo fádo in Érin,' said Fintan, lilting.

'Will you fuck off Fintan out of that for fuck sake.
You're like a feckin' child so you are.' She planted her feet
firmly apart, a palm on each thigh. Fintan glanced into the
darkness between her parted knees, met her gaze again.
'A loss again boy. Not a feckin' brass farthing of a float to
see us through to the busy season and here's me with the
solid work that'll be the makings of us and you acting the
feckin' maggot.'

'Jaze Bee I'm only codding you,' said Fintan. 'You're
in quare humour altogether today d'you know that.'
The thought immediately: shouldn't have mentioned the
humour, wigs on the green now wait'n you see.

'D'you know what.' Bridget turned from him, her
upheld palm trembling before her. 'Why don't you go on
ahead and get some other eejit to organise this shower of

gobshites for you. Honest to God what am I like sure?'
She busied herself with her desk, aligning and realigning
objects on its surface. 'Tribe of feckin' loolahs. Trying to
get them to remember a rota you'd swear it was feckin'
Aristotle or some fucking thing. And then me like an eejit,
on to my Da to get them out of scrapes, them after *starting*
the trouble they were meant to stop. And isn't it me who
has to arse-lick half-wits for the work for them in the first
place? Butter up town dunces who think they're *it* because
they run a nightclub or a pub or a pool-hall and half of them
not able to write their own name sure. What am I feckin'
like at all, 'tis my head I need examined.'

'Ah Bee. Bee, Bee, Bee, fuck sake love.' Fintan leant
forward, reached out a hand. The crackle of the hangover
sharper suddenly, the beginning of a headache, the horn
receding now leaving a cold patch of seepage in his underpants. 'You know I'm well aware.' He passed the flat of his
hand over the desktop. 'Well well aware, without you, all
this, I'm not even sure if I'd… Sure y'know yourself sure.
Bee? Bee love.' Bridget gave in to a sideways glance and met
his eye. He added a grave little nod. 'So tell us love. Please.
Tell us about this Reed.'

ROSANNE DAVIES

*

BEYOND, THE FIRE

NEW ZEALAND, 1791

Aroha stares at the hulking mass of flesh in front of her. Her younger brother, Hemi, stands to her side, his chest moving in, out, in, out. She can see him in the eye of her mind, but her open eye is looking at the thing in front of them. Is it dead? No signs of breathing. The sweep of it is like the horizon, the size of it so big and the sky behind it so bright they are standing in its shadow.

They came to the bay for clams. Their baskets were dropped at the top of the dunes when they saw what was on the beach and their footprints followed them like shadows, first through sand hot and soft, then through sand thick and wet, until they stopped, hearts thrumming, beside it. Waves pool around the thing and Aroha, taking a few steps back, peers over its flank out to sea. The water is grey-green today, and gentle, but the tide is coming in.

She takes Hemi's little finger. It is rigid.

'What is it?' he whispers. Aroha doesn't know. Not yet.

Wind blows and she sniffs. The smell of the air and the sea, but closer, from the blue-black flesh. A higher note. Not yet rotten. Her belly rumbles.

'Should we tell Father?' Hemi asks, louder. His little finger has gone limp in her hand. Aroha shakes her head.

'What do you want!' the boy shouts at the thing. Bravery makes his mouth tremble. He is scared and angry. Aroha isn't. Yesterday it was not here, and now it is.

The thing doesn't answer. Hemi tries to kick at the sand, to make it feel his flinted impatience, but his foot catches in the heavy gloop and he stumbles. Aroha pulls on his little finger to say, *stop that.* She wants to work this out for herself.

She thinks she knows what this creature is but the shock of seeing it has stopped her from rushing. Then something swims past the eye of her mind, its shuddered boom and spray above the sparkling surface of the water, its earth-deep moan as it dives. But is this one? It is in the wrong place.

Her mother's words hover by her ear, waiting to be listened to. *You must do things with slowness, my girl. And show Hemi slowness, too. He will learn it as he hardens into a man. Help him. Teach him. A dot on the horizon is all he must see. A man will protect you from such a dot one day, Aroha.* One day. It is in the future because her blood has not come to her yet.

She looks at the new horizon in front of her, at the way its blue-blackness falls in a long, long line to the sand, a large leaf at its tip. Red streak in the water that swirls around it then, but she will have time to think about that later.

'Hemi,' she says. 'I know what it is.'

'What?' he whispers.

'A whale.'

Silence from her brother. Aroha lets go of his hand and walks the whale's length. Nice and slow. It takes her fourteen steps. She wants to touch it but is fearful about what her touch will do. If it is dead then it is sacred. If it is alive? No. It cannot be alive, out of its home, although its home is so near, reaching with salty arms up the beach. She looks out at the sea, at the green waves rolling. They don't look strong enough to take the whale back. Her father's voice this time. *Don't let small waves fool you, my girl. The ocean has a heartbeat we cannot see.* Maybe it doesn't want the whale back. Tangaroa, God of the Sea, has gifted this whale to the land. To us. She smiles.

She looks at the tail on the sand, and tentatively sticks out her foot. Hemi whimpers.

'What?'

'Don't touch it,' he says.

But her patience has crystallised into curiosity. Maybe after she sees whole whale she can touch it, and then she can tell the whole tribe and they can eat. She walks round to the ocean side and sucks in her breath as shock runs through her body. The whale's belly is white, but something has been plunged in its side and it has opened, like the mouth of a small red cave. Long things have spilled out of it, black-red and purple, their ends swaying like seaweed in the water. Another gust of wind and Aroha covers her nose and mouth. She feels sick.

'Hemi, don't come round here,' she says quietly, but of course when she says *don't* he *does* and this time it is a different silence from him. This whale is not a gift, she thinks. Something has already taken it and attacked. But what?

And then Hemi does something she never thought he'd do. He splashes past her and pats a part of the whale's belly that is still white, pats it and pats it before Aroha can stop him.

'Go back!' he shouts.

'Hemi!'

'Go back, go away!'

'Hemi, it can't. It's dead. Don't touch it, Hemi. Please don't touch it.'

'Aroha!'

Sister and brother look up at the shout. Someone has called her name. Father? No. The voice, carried on the wind from the dunes, isn't as deep, but it is a man's. Are they hidden by the body of the whale? The eye of her mind rushes to their baskets, left in the grass. Empty.

'Aroha!' the voice calls again.

She peeks around the tail and sees her older cousin, Amiri, marching down the beach. As he walks his staff points out in front of him, and his feet sink in the sand just like theirs did. When he looks up and sees her, he moves faster. No one else is behind him. How is that possible? Has no one else seen?

'Aroha,' he says for a third time, but she can tell he is distracted by the sight, and Aroha is grateful to the whale. It has taken the telling-off out of Amiri's eyes.

'What's this?' he says, coming right up to her, his eyes widening, and she knows what he is thinking. Treasure.

'It's not a gift, Amiri,' she says.

'What?' he says, confused, and then, 'where's Hemi?'

'Hiding.'

'From the whale?'

'No, behind it.'

'I'm not hiding!' Hemi stomps round as best he can, the sand sucking at his heels. One of his hands is red. The dark green lines on Amiri's face come together as he frowns at the sight of the boy. Hemi has not yet learnt to be frightened of his cousin's strength and pats Amiri's belly.

'Look what we found!' Hemi says, his face upturned, and Amiri's face cracks and smiles.

'You found it?' he says, laughing. 'You didn't find it, little man.' He splashes to the whale's head and calls back, 'it found you!' But this is all wrong, Amiri sounding excited, not knowing about the blood. He might run to the chief and tell him that the tribe is a lucky one. This is the opposite of luck.

'Amiri!' she calls, walking back to the ocean side and the guts. 'Look!'

His head appears over the part where the tail curves down. 'I'm looking, Aroha.' The smile in his dark eyes.

'No, Amiri,' she says. 'Look here.'

He joins her on the other side. Like wind passing over water, the smile leaves his face. He doesn't say anything. Pronging his staff in the sand he crouches, perhaps from shock, perhaps to get a better look. Aroha doesn't want to see this side of the creature again but she has to be strong. Soon the birds will shriek and cry overhead.

'Hmm,' is all Amiri says. Then he straightens, and without looking at her commands, 'Take Hemi and go back to the village.'

'But what about the whale?'

'What about it?'

'It's dead!'

'I can see that, Aroha.'

'But it shouldn't be dead like that. Not already bleeding.'

He frowns. 'Why not? There are sharks out there, and other creatures with teeth.' He pats the whale's flank. 'We have found some treasure.'

'I found it.'

'Aroha.' His voice has dropped in the way that it does when he wants to be mean and nice. 'Take Hemi back.'

Hemi appears at her side, a scrape of blood across his cheek.

'What do you think, little man?' Amiri says, bending down and grabbing the boy playfully by the shoulders. 'Your first whale!'

'Amiri!' Aroha says. Her voice is breaking and she doesn't want to cry, but he doesn't understand. Why is he ignoring her? Why can't he see it?

'What?'

'What if something's done that to the whale's body? Something bad?'

Amiri glances out to sea then back to her and chuckles.

'What are you worried about?' he says. But she doesn't know how to explain. It's like a monster curling inside her belly, stretching and flexing its claws.

'I don't know,' she says, defeated.

'Come,' Amiri says. 'I'll take you back. You've come much further than Manawa asked you. She will need an explanation.' He picks up his spear and strides up the beach, Hemi tottering behind. Aroha wants to drag him back and make him stand in the waves. She wants to say, *You didn't look hard enough. You didn't look long enough. You didn't look for dots.* But she has to follow.

When they reach the top of the dunes they come across their baskets, cradled in the long grass, and she knows any protest will be useless. Amiri stoops to pick one up and stares at her over Hemi's head. His look dries her out from the inside.

    'Manawa will be angry,' he says, his voice soft and deathly.

    'Let me get some shellfish now. It's still light.'

    'No. You'll come back tomorrow and get twice as many.' He slings the basket over his shoulder and strides down the path, into the trees. Aroha doesn't want to think about tomorrow. She picks up her own basket, slowly, and uses the time to glance back at the bay. Her home. The bruised sky and the yellow streak of the horizon; the headland, curling like a sleeping arm far out to sea. The waves, surging further and further up the beach. But there is something new now, something bleeding. And something coming.

A novel extract

NICHOLAS DEPHTEREOS

✳

BLACK RIVER COUNTRY

1786

One morning, some weeks before my sister's wedding, I came down to find my mother hovering over the kitchen girls as they cleared the furniture from the front sitting room.

'Mind you that side table,' she said, jabbing a finger at two pink-faced girls hefting a table between them. 'It was a gift to my late husband. From the Earl of Dunmore. Governor, before the war. Or was it from Monckton?' The girls set down the table in silence and stood away from it as though it might spring to life at any minute. My mother swept across the room, her shears and keys rattling in the folds of her gown, and ran a finger along the table top for dust. Finding none, she narrowed her eyes, thin and dark as iron turnings, and flapped a hand at the girls. 'Go, go,' she said, and they scrambled to stack chairs and benches against the wall. I wondered at their task, but did not wish to cross my mother in asking.

Coming off the steps, I made for the kitchen, hoping to avoid my mother's gaze. Like a fool, I opened my mouth in a wide yawn before catching myself.

'And here you are, Judith,' my mother said, 'mooning about, bed-wrinkles still across your face.'

I fumbled to pull stray hairs beneath my cap. 'Good morrow,' I said.

'Hm. And what do the Proverbs tell us of the slothful?'

'That the soul of the –'

Before I could finish she cut in, loud enough for both the kitchen girls and me to hear her every word: '"the hand of the diligent shall rule, while the slothful shall be put to forced labor." Proverbs. Twelve. Twenty-four.'

I glared at the floor, listening to the girls straighten the chairs, and felt myself twice the fool in front of them.

'No breakfasting today,' my mother said. 'Go and tell Sibby to put your beans and porridge away. And fetch you a broom and tidy this floor while you're looking at it.'

I nodded.

'Of all the days to laze about, Judith. Really.'

From the corner of my eye I saw the kitchen girls, shoulder to shoulder, hands folded against their aprons. My mother was too busy with me to dismiss them.

'Anna's wedding looms before us and you think only to rise when it pleases you? He comes today.'

'He?' I asked, letting the word slip out of my mouth. 'Reuben?'

'Are you dim-witted, Judith?'

I held my lips together concentrating on the floor.

'He comes today. Monsieur Dubois. From Albany.' She clicked her teeth with a sound like metal chips and grabbed my chin. I looked up into her eyes and I smelled the sharp spice of her ambergris perfume. 'Monsieur Dubois,' she said again.

'Who –'

'To fit your sister for a gown.'

I realized now her rush to rearrange the furniture: she was staging a fitting room.

She dropped my chin, spun around and faced the kitchen girls. 'Go up to my rooms,' she said to them. 'Bring down my screen. The one with the Chinamen. Not the other one. Set it up here – no, here – in front of the fireplace.'

I began to slink away to the kitchen.

'Are you dismissed, Judith?' she called, still facing the girls.

I stood still where I was.

'No breakfast,' she said. 'And the broom. I want this place looking decent for Monsieur Dubois.' As an afterthought, perhaps only for herself, she added, 'Not the hole that it really is.'

When Monsieur Dubois's carriage pulled up to the house my mother called us all to the foyer. She thrust Anna out in front of her, as if an offering, and gripped her by the shoulders. Anna's face was limp, and though she was scrubbed and dressed and brushed just so, she couldn't have looked more bored at the prospect of a fitting. My mother, on the other hand, fidgeted and sighed and yanked stray hairs from Anna's scalp. I stood beside them and strained to see out the frost-laced window for a glimpse of the great Dubois.

His carriage was small, an ordinary chaise, but an astonishing emerald green. I had never seen anything of its like in the county. A coachman wrapped in three or four coats stepped down from the seat and swung open the door. From inside the shadowy cab a man emerged, rotund and swathed in fur. A Scotch cap, the same brilliant green as his carriage, was perched like a soufflé on top of his head. For all his weight, he leapt gingerly from the step and made his way with a curious skip to the front door. He knocked – *rat-ta-tap-tap* – on the door and Sibby opened it, giving the slightest curtsey as she did. His size, his fur, his cape and his great jaunty cap took up the entire frame, and a wild, Oriental smell of bergamot and mandarin filled the room as he stepped inside. For a moment we did nothing but stare, open-eyed, at my sister's dressmaker.

'I,' he said, loosing his furs and throwing them onto Sibby, 'am Dubois.'

For a moment more, even my mother said nothing.

'My man will bring in my things,' he said. 'Where to set up?' he looked around the foyer. 'Not here. No, no, no, not here.' To my surprise, he had no accent at all. I had been expecting a Frenchman.

At last my mother cleared her throat. 'Monsieur Dubois,' she said, 'we've prepared the sitting room for you especially.'

'*Magnifique!*' he said, pronouncing the word in plain English.

'Right this way,' she said, leading him to the sitting room.

'*Etienne*!' he called to his coachman. 'Bring my things within. *Tout de suite*, as they say.'

In the sitting room he made for the fire and rubbed first his hands, then his backside, by the flames. 'Yes, yes, yes,' he said. 'This'll do. This'll do nicely.'

My mother looked over at Sibby who was still struggling to hold up Dubois's pile of furs. Her face could scarce be seen beneath the heap. 'Sibby,' my mother said, 'fetch Monsieur something to drink. An apple toddy, perhaps.'

'Yes, ma'am,' mumbled Sibby beneath the mound.

'No!' said Dubois, still rubbing himself by the fire. 'Nothing strong. Chocolate, perhaps. Yes, a pot of chocolate.'

Chocolate, as a rule, was never served in our house. It was, my mother said, an indulgence, and kept locked away. In a rush, my mother unclipped a key from her chain and handed it to Sibby. 'In the chest beside the tea caddy,' she whispered. 'As much as he likes.' I nearly gasped: my mother was serving chocolate by the pot.

'And who is the bride-to-be?' asked Dubois. 'Which of them is my muse of the hour?' He looked at Anna, then me, casting his eyes – wide as a bullfrog's – over us from top to bottom.

'My eldest,' my mother said, hurrying back to Anna's side. 'Anna.' She gave Anna a push, nudging her forward so that she stood a few inches from Dubois's nose.

'Ah,' he said, 'the blonde,' and sighed. 'Very well.'

Just then, Dubois's coachman came in carrying a lacquer box under his arms. It was long as a man, flat and thin, and held shut with a golden clasp. Except for Anna, we looked on in wonder.

'Over there,' Dubois said, 'set it over there.' The coachman set it down in front of the Chinese screen and Dubois came forward, taking a better look at Anna. He placed a hand on either of her shoulders and spun her round and round again. 'Hm,' he said at last. 'And where is Mademoiselle to stand?' He looked around at my mother, then Sibby, then me. 'Surely you do not mean for Dubois to measure a hemline on his hands and knees? A stool. Someone fetch me a stool!'

My mother hissed at Sibby and shooed her out the room before hurrying out herself in search of something for Anna to stand on.

When someone had at last found a footstool, Anna mounted it and Dubois circled her several times, sighing and puckering his lips.

'*Etienne*!' he called again to his coachman. 'The dress form. Bring it in. And the samples – the taffetas and satins. Bring me the blue-greys, the ivories, the silvers. Her skin is very cold, very blue. Anything else would wash her out.'

Etienne nodded and hurried back out to the carriage.

Dubois took another turn around Anna and she stared down at her bare arms, looking, perhaps, for blueness.

I heard Sibby in the kitchen, busy with Dubois's chocolate, and from the dining room I could hear my mother rattling though her china cupboard pulling out her best pot and cups. There were only three of us in the sitting room then: Dubois, Anna and myself.

'You,' Dubois said, looking down at me.

'Yes?'

'What is your name?'

'Judith, sir.'

'Judith, you are to help me with something very important. Do you see that box over there?' He pointed to the lacquer box beside the Chinese screen.

'Yes.'

'I need you to hold open the lid as I remove its contents. It is quite, quite fragile.'

I nodded, but felt myself suddenly very nervous.

We approached the box and Dubois lowered himself over it with great strain.

'Open it Mademoiselle Judith,' he said. 'And take

care to hold it very steady.'

I unhinged the golden clasp and lifted the heavy lid.
A smell of tea and jasmine burst forth into the air, the smell,
I thought, of a Turk's harem. Dubois peeled back a crisp
sheet of tissue paper, and revealed inside a long, spectacular
mirror, its corners traced in swirling scrolls of gilt. As I held
open the lid, he prised the mirror up and set it on its legs.
Then, as though it were a juggler's trick, he unfolded the
mirror until there were two, then three, then four mirrors
side by side like an open bellows.

'*Et voila*!' he said. 'You may let go of the lid now,
Mademoiselle Judith. And I thank you. See, now, there
are four Judiths staring back at you.'

Indeed there were. Reflected in each of the long and
flawless mirrors I saw myself. I turned, laughing, trying
to glimpse myself from every angle. Dubois positioned the
snaking mirrors so that they circled Anna, and her white
and listless face blinked tiredly four times in the glass.
How she could be lukewarm in the sight of something
so marvelous I cannot say.

Etienne came back in carrying an ivory-handled case
and opened it before Dubois. Inside, little squares of satin,
uncreased and perfect, shimmered in the light. Blues the
color of sea foam and robin's eggs shone like jewels beside
patches of pure silver and pale sapphire.

'Exactly so,' said Dubois, snapping shut the lid. 'But
I must have Mademoiselle Anna's measurements first.
For that I need sustenance, Etienne. Run and see about
my chocolate. And tell the girl I want three sugars. No,
no. Four.'

A novel extract

JEHANGIR JILANI

✳

TRANSPORT

LONDON, JULY 2007

The attacks on the city, a brutal rupture of metal and flesh across three tubes and one bus, had that rare quality of touching every category of Londoner. There weren't many events in the age of the modern city that could lodge directly in the minds of the wealthy and over-educated as well as the poor and illiterate. It might have been something my cleaning lady thought about as she ironed the shirts I would wear to the office; perhaps she would reject the bus and walk to the other side of Brixton in the afternoon, guaranteeing she would arrive home safely before her daughter finished school. It would only cost thirty minutes of her time. Was that a fair bargain? Similar space-time calculations were deliberated by tube travellers across London and many of my colleagues altered small details of their commute to favour more time on the edgeless surface. The prospect of injury didn't concern me but I still ended up changing my routine: being of South Asian origin I thought it prudent not to carry a backpack or holdall of any sort. No need to stoke the general anxiety. But it was here, in the aftermath of the explosions, during the time when I had never seen the city so paranoid, it was at this moment that two strangers presented their gift.

The general concern was most acute after the second round of bombings – the ones where the devices didn't result in any deaths (unless you count the Brazilian man mistakenly shot by the police at Stockwell tube station). The latest suspects didn't achieve their objectives but two attacks in two weeks had a bruising impact on the spirit. Underground, there was an urge to move on swiftly. The subterranean air hung thicker; you could taste it on the lips, swelling your thirst as you walked among the crowds. When you stepped outside the atmosphere had an uncommon sweetness.

Several times the focus of attention seemed to bend towards me. I had an appearance similar to those who had killed and another attack couldn't be discounted. I was statistically more likely to be a threat than a white man. It was simple mathematics. That's what I thought, at least in the beginning. I was a few years into my corporate career, in a position earned on merit. I dealt in practicalities; it was about getting the job done efficiently. There was nothing to be gained by examining motivations. But as the days wore on some of the journeys stayed with me, stretched out and illuminated by little bursts of sentiment and I found it hard not to be affected. I could sense the uneasiness of a stranger near me. The attention had an exclusionary element, like they were turning their back on me. This was the cold isolation of judgement I remembered as a child and I couldn't stop myself from trying to unpack it once more. My body was being used against me, yet it was pitiful evidence for a decision, there was so much more I could show. If only they would speak to me! I could explain that I was a lawyer for multinational corporations and finance houses. Look at this suit, see how the lapels roll smoothly across the contours of my chest. It fits more like a sweater than a jacket. I wanted to stand up and recite highlights from my life. I wanted to ask what they were thinking. Were they afraid I would kill or did my genetic association impose some responsibility for the deaths? I wondered if this were the lot of a beautiful woman sitting quietly on the tube, to be relentlessly scrutinised, susceptible to countless unknown and creative sequences.

The commute to the business district was different though. The corporate crowd were less interested in me or at least that's how it appeared. They stared hard at nothing, brows rutted in concentration; too much to focus on that morning, too many egos to snake through and tiny details to assess to waste time considering the remote possibility of disaster. Making an error was the great fear, not dying in an explosion.

It was on the journey to work that I encountered two

smartly presented women, perhaps lawyers or actuaries, on two consecutive mornings. The business-as-usual attitude on these trips allowed me to ease into the day. I had a seat and silently ran through the main points of a talk I was to give to the new trainees. Someone leaned forward towards me, a young woman with thick plastic glasses tanned brown at the top fading clear below. I lifted my head to accept the query as if she were a trainee. Her lips were slightly apart and glossed a delicate pink and I waited for some movement as she put her question to me. The seconds ticked and all was still and I was transfixed by her mouth which had become an indistinct mosaic of rose and white, yet no question arrived. Oh Jesus, I thought. She thinks I'm a killer. But there was something confusing in her manner. I couldn't map fear or anger onto her expression; there was no tension in her eyes, just a deliberate and calm regard, taking in the whole of me as if I had been cut in one piece from the dirty green cloth of our seats. A man in a brown tweed jacket walked between us and broke the connection. The doors were open. Moorgate station. I left.

That evening I was drawn back to the encounter with the woman. There was a nagging sense that I had missed something, like I had read a document that I knew had some relevance to a case, either in favour or weakening our position, but didn't quite fit into current lines of argument. Something a superior would spot instantly and explain in a subtly condescending tone.

The following morning I considered how I could run into the same woman again. It was basically impossible. I figured the only chance, and this was stretching the definition, would be to sit in the same carriage of a train passing through the City at the same time as before. Could I manipulate the transport system as I would a regulatory structure? Was it possible deliberately to position oneself close to someone on the tube? I wasn't sure of the precise moment I had crossed the interchange at Stockwell station

the previous day, but I'd definitely walked down into
Brixton at eight-fifteen as I always look up to the digital
clock when swept along in the flow to the ticket barriers.
So I left the flat a little early and reached the station at
eight-ten. I paused at the broad entrance and saw a man
selling incense on a fold-up table. Six sticks were smoulder-
ing on individual wooden cradles and he stood stock rigid
behind them, not even moving when errant stubbles of ash
floated back to his cotton kameez. Presumably each joss
stick had its own scent and I wondered if I could distinguish
them at close quarters. I scanned my watch to see if I had
time to walk up, then realised how ridiculous the whole
endeavour was and went inside.

The train was somewhere under the river when a
woman sat down opposite. Her black suit jacket was edged
with a yellow trim which kept catching the fluorescent light.
I thought she'd noticed me admiring her out fit a fraction
too long but again I was met with an unexpected look.
There was no recrimination in her features but a kind of
urging; her slate-blue eyes were wide open in encourage-
ment. I replied with a resigned look: I don't have any answers for you. Surely this woman could accept the choices
I had made to be here, sitting in her shadow with some
overlap of professional obligation?

My silent plea had no effect and she remained a study
of patience. She was on the cusp of smiling, the corners of
her mouth just tingling her freckled cheeks. Her lips were
broad and I could make out folds of plump bare flesh. In
fact her whole appearance appeared utterly without make-
up and suggested an unconditional openness. Then all
locked in place, what she and the other woman required:
a measure of truth. Enough truth to put them at ease.

I obliged. My eyes softened and face relaxed to a deep
smile. Of course you may look at me; I will show you what
you need to see. Absence. Of that thing which swelled up
inside those young men at the end. Of what ultimately

moved them to detonate their vests and murder the working men and women around them. We both know I could never hide that from you. The woman dropped into the smile she'd been threatening and sat back. The working day regained its momentum.

That communication took on a significance as I turned it over in my mind. I thought it a beautiful dialect, one that could only have been instigated by someone with a particular sensitivity. It was clear that I had lost some of this since arriving in the city. How many other attributes had I shed in pursuit of this career?

I was so far behind these women when they offered to connect; and they'd waited so patiently from a higher place. I think it was the first time anyone in a suit had stirred an emotion in me.

The beginning of a novel

ADAM BENNETT KEOGH

✳

EVERY OTHER PLACE

DAY 1 – EARLY EVENING

I found her in the woods, curled up in a ball, covered in moss and heather and bits of fur. She had a fever. She still has a fever. She was sweating, roasting hot. Wouldn't wake up even when I poked her in the arm with a stick. This little body on the ground, under an overhang to shelter from the weather. It was surreal, like looking at a diorama in a waxworks. That midday half-light you only get in dense pine forests, the bare branches clawing at your face, the needles under your feet soft and copper and dead. She's real enough though.

What is she, seven, eight? When it started raining I took my jacket off and lay it over her. Luminous yellow with breathable waterproof membranes. She almost looked normal. I shouted. I walked a perimeter. There was no one else around. It started lashing then. Nothing to be done.

DAY 2 – AFTERNOON

She's sleeping again, snoring as I write. Been unconscious almost the whole time. The state of her when I got her in: hair matted; fingernails an inch long, sharp, black; deep ridges of scars across her neck and shoulders; bite marks all up her arms; some ratty old nightshirt down to her knees, torn to bits, streaked with dark brown, green and amber, a faded purple unicorn on the front. I heated up a basin of water, undressed her, wiped the crust of mud off her arms and legs and face. The smell of her made me gag. She mustn't've had a bath in years. Her breath like a dog's, teeth pointed and yellow and black. I put her in one of my old T-shirts, some freebie from a team-building workshop years ago. Paintball, girls vs. boys, *Femme Fatale* emblazoned across the chest in pink. She's swimming in it.

She woke earlier and I fed her some soup but she sicked it up. Vomit everywhere. Days' worth. There were bits of undigested bone rolling around on the bedsheets. She

couldn't speak. She just nodded her head and fell
back asleep.

The glass is rattling in the frames. When I got here
I remember thinking how lovely the windows looked, little
squares set deep into the mortar, wavy and translucent, like
they'd been melted down from discarded wine bottles. The
walls are three feet thick. Made me feel like I was living in
a bunker.

Now, though, the windows make the whole place sound
weak and whiny. You can hear the gusts whistling through
the gaps. At any one time I've three jumpers and a fire going
against the draughts. I'm just waiting for a crash and a tin-
kle, and one of the little squares will be on the ground letting the air blow through and sending these papers flying.

Doesn't seem to bother her though. She just sleeps
through it, little moans escaping whenever she wets
the bed.

DAY 3 – AFTERNOON
Two nights and a day now and no let up. It's dark in here
even at high noon. I tried going out in the morning, but
even the walk to the woodshed nearly blew the skin off my
bones. The valley was in bits, uprooted trees floating on the
black surface of the lake, the heather pulsing in waves on
the far hill. I was out all of twenty seconds and I looked like
I'd gone swimming. We can only wait, I suppose.

I've been running on adrenaline, not a wink of sleep,
pacing back and forth in front of the fire, feeling her forehead, piling her with blanket after blanket until she groans
under the weight, still unconscious. My mother would've
had something to say, just the right balance of scorn and
concern. She'd have told me right enough. Phones never
worked up here at the best of times.

She looks so peaceful when she sleeps, curled into an
apostrophe facing the wall. Reminds me of myself, still
sucking a thumb at seven and a half. Here I am struggling

to keep warm with a fireplace and a monthly food delivery.
And she's been out there. And her so small.

Get out, I thought. Get away. Cut yourself off. Escape
and give yourself time to think. And then this happens.
It's all just so fucking typical.

– EVENING

She was awake. Half-awake maybe. I'd drifted off in the
armchair but when I woke up her eyes were just open,
looking drugged and dopey. I got up, slowly, carefully, sat
on the edge of the bed. She kept looking at me, her head
still propped against the pillow. I tried to smile but I think
I was too worked up, just flashed my teeth maybe, opened
my eyes a bit wider than normal. I reached out to feel her
forehead – still too hot. When my hand touched her skin
she shook all over and seemed to want to get away, but she
settled after a moment or two. One of her little hands came
out from under the covers and wrapped its fingers around
my wrist. She squeezed it. Hard. She kept squeezing and
prodding her fingers into the flesh around my hand, little
mewls and grunts coming out of her, her face screwed up.
She pushed my hand away then. Rolled on her side and
started snoring.

DAY 4 – MORNING

She called me '*Lucy*.' I think she called me. I was over by
the fire heating water and honey and lemon, and she said
it in her sleep. '*Lucy*,' she said. Her voice was raspy. '*Lucy*.'
She was almost crying it.

I didn't want to make a fuss. I didn't want to shock
her again. So I just kept facing the fire. 'No,' I said calmly.
'Grace. I'm Grace.'

'*Lucyyyyyy*,' she said again, upset, like she was trying
to contradict me.

'Ok,' I said. 'Lucy it is then.' She drifted back under.
When the water came to the boil I took it from the fire and

poured it into a mug. I blew on the surface and watched
her breathing.

That was the first conversation I've had in about
three weeks.

DAY 5 – LATE EVENING

She's still sleeping a lot. She only wakes up a few minutes
at a time, her eyes still only half open. I'll look up from the
little table by the fire and see her watching me and get
a fright. 'Jesus, Lucy,' I'll say.

'*Juhzuz, Lucy*,' she'll say right back, like she's gagging
on the words. I laugh, then she coughs. I sang her *Lucy
in the Sky with Diamonds* and she just cocked her head,
confused. Reminded me of Digby. Stupid dog. I still miss
him, though.

The weather's getting better, still no good for going
anywhere though. I can see the far peaks through the sheets
of rain at least. The roads will be a state. Give it some time
and wait till she's ready. Francis will be up in a day or two
with the food. I'll tell him to send for a doctor, if he can
find one. The Gardaí? Social services, maybe? Who
trusts them anymore?

She's slept for nearly five whole days. She must be
starving. She looks it. Honey and water's the only thing
she'll keep down, poor yoke. Rest is what she needs.
A break. A breather.

DAY 6 – EVENING

She's improving, I think. She's eating. She was sitting
up and looking around like in a dream. I took her some
flatbread, an apple, a hunk of cheese, cut off a raggedy slice
of ham with the penknife. She sniffed at the plate, picked
up the ham, licked it, wrinkled her nose and threw it on the
flagstones. 'Hey,' I said. She just hissed at me.

She took the bread though, tore at it with her teeth,
chewed with sticky, open mouth. It was gone in an instant.

She licked the palms of her hands for crumbs, brought the
bedsheets up to her face and sucked at the fabric to catch
any strays. When she finished she looked at me again,
all eyes.

'More?' I said.

She cocked her head.

'Do you want more?' I pointed at the plate, the gap
where the bread had been. 'Moooore?'

'*Mo-wer*,' she said. She sounded ninety years old, twen-
ty-a-day. '*Mo-wer, mo-wer, mo-wer*,' hitting the plate with
her hand. I gave her what was left and she hoovered it up.
Lay back against the pillow then, satisfied.

She dozed. I carried on with my work.

In a moment of low tide I looked up and saw her watching, trying desperately to keep her eyes open against the
weight of the lids. I started singing a song my mother used
to sing whenever I was sick, whenever she was still lucid
enough to care. I hummed it at first, the words tumbling out
after a few bars: 'dum dee dum dee dum dee dum/ you're in
for a big surprise/ if you go down to the woods today/ you'd
better go in disguise...' After the second verse the smell
of shit was so strong I nearly gagged. And her just lying
there, big smile.

DAY 7 – LATE AFTERNOON

Francis'll be here tomorrow. Even with all the madness
I'm trembling. Here's me, the jumped up survivalist trading
food for favours, getting all shaky at the thought of him.
Him and his van. Him and his dog. Him and his wet wool
jumper the colour of turf, the smell of it too. Him and his
big hands. His back. His weight. Christ.

Poor bastard doesn't know what's happening to him.
He thinks he's beholden to me. There's some good people
left, I suppose, only I'm still not sure he's one of them. All
the same, get a hold of yourself, Grace; he's a culchie fuck-
tard the size of a transit.

She's coming round. She sits up and watches me for hours at a time now. I try to talk to her but all she does is echo.

'Hello,' I say.

'*Eh-oh.*'

'Grace,' I say, finger on my breastbone.

'*Geyssss*' – hers in her belly.

'You?' I say, pointing at her.

'*Yew?*' – pointing at me. We stay like that for a moment, a stand-off. Pistols at dawn.

'Lucy?' I say.

And then she's off like a rocket, bouncing up and down on the bed on her haunches: '*Lucylucylucylucylucylucylucy,*' calming down only slowly, losing energy bit by bit, her strength still not back yet, all quiet again after a minute or two. She's had the last word. Nothing more to say.

The beginning of a longer story

DM LYNCH

✳

CANICULE

SANDY-EYED, A LITTLE CREAKY with dream salt,
but feeling good, whole – morning-sex residue swinging
gummily in his pyjama pants – Michael comes down to the
kitchen to see:

    – clear young sunlight on the red tiles of the floor
    – clear young sunlight in the combed grain of the table
    – a tissue crumpled like a tea rose on the windowsill
    – his garden framed by the proscenium of the window
    – the heart-snagging beauty of the waking garden
    – the neighbours' dog hanging from a chain over
    the wall
    – three blue tits dancing through the clear young –
    …

Michael looks back at the dog, at the stiff limbs and the
tongue coming out of the mouth, and feels the texture
of his Sunday change around him. The air thins and the
light grows hair and sour juices move in his gut. He blinks
rapidly then brings his knuckles up to his eyes, receiving
a sudden sense of himself – a man in a dressing-gown rubbing his eyes with his knuckles, a cartoonish, desperate per-
formance. He grinds his vision to pulp. Dispel this illusion.
When it's over and the world coheres again the Noonans'
dog is still there, in sharper focus now. A shitsoo. Shidzu?
Small, white, fine-boned, anyway, a toy breed, a forgery.
It hangs about three feet off the ground, just over the hya-
cinths. The fur on its head is tied with a blue bow. Michael
can't remember its name, only the pitch of its voice, shrill
down the nights, and how he dreamt it dead.

    It can't weigh much, but the chain coming over the
garden wall is taut with the load.

    Michael sits down carefully at the table. His head drops
and he brings his palms up to catch it. The fragility of all
Sundays is a kind of treachery. He draws his hands down
over his cheeks, past his nose, smelling Amanda on his
fingers. There's something melancholy in the smell, like the
trace on a breeze of a snuffed-out fire. Champagne blush

behind the bedroom curtains, linen cool against his skin,
night scents pocketed in Amanda's folds – all gone now, lost
to history. The dog is made all of the morning, the way the
world collects abruptly around the corpse in the road, the
lump in the skin. There is nothing now that is not the dog.
The kitchen smells of dog. Michael's own body feels stiff-
limbed and furred, a phantom collar closing on his throat.

He glances up at the clock on the wall. Twenty to nine
– Amanda will be out of bed soon. Lily should be awake
now too. God, if Lily sees, before he can pre-empt her. But
he can't imagine what form an evasive manoeuvre might
take – un-noose the dog, stash it in the freezer, torch it in an
oil drum, give it a gangland burial on some remote hillside,
dip it in cement and throw it in a canal. He imagines the
Noonans moistly emergent next door, Yvonne shuddering
with Peter in the pupal sheets, their own small child – what
is it, Jack or James, Lily's age – four, four and a bit – coming
methodically to consciousness as his daughter must be upstairs. It's as if there are, between both houses, two different Sundays happening like adjacent microclimates, a dog
in one and a dog-shaped hole in the other. For all Michael
knows the Noonans are at this moment looking out on the
blank, total doglessness of the garden beyond *their* kitchen
window, studying the tension in the chain, calculating,
silently reconstructing. There's a queasy intimacy to this.
He's still looking up at the clock, he realises. Squinting.

He squints harder. There's something wrong with the
clock: the 6 is coming unstuck from the face, peeling melt-
edly away by the neck, the guillotine of the second-hand
bearing down. Michael's never noticed this before, the 6
coming unstuck. It might have happened in the moment
before he looked at the clock or over the course of unknow-
able time, for as long as they've owned the clock, for as
long as they've lived in this house, a wilting as agonised as
the puddling of glass. How many mornings and evenings
– weeks or years – has he sat with his family at the kitchen

table while, just above their heads, this imperceptible de-
cline was in progress? What else in the house might be failing, fraying? He begins, thinking about the clock, about the
6, about the Noonans, to think about the deep soft reaches
parcelled in his skin and bone – which makes him think
about the dog again, feeling the pressure around his throat,
the stony curdle of rigor mortis, and his heart stammers
and his lungs grab for air. His left arm tingles, or his brain
in its eagerness to get ahead of the symptoms coerces it
into tingling. He'd like to know how many cardiac episodes
are accidentally self-willed, the body running through the
catalogue of indicators until the heart itself does its bit. His
chest feels tight: what does that mean? The patient will experience a tightness in the chest. What's a tightness? But at
least a heart attack now would be formulaic, predictable, a
foothold in the chaos eating at the borders of his morning,
symptoms organising themselves in line with the words,
unlike this dog dangling beyond language.

He hears the Mass bells ring from outside then:
a tape-recording playing in the church down the road,
tannoys in the belfry. They've passed through him almost
without his noticing every week for years, but now the false,
chintzy carillon (tocsin, klaxon) recalls the Sunday of his
childhood, putting the taste of the wafer back in his mouth
– the papery, disappointing taste of Jesus – and, in his nose,
the smell of the incense, headier suddenly than the fading
smell of Amanda, the chimeric smell of dog. The patient
will receive unusual sensory inputs. In the beginning were
the words.

'Michael.'

He jumps.

'Michael,' she says, 'is that –' while from his other side
comes his daughter's gluey breathing.

'Yes.'

'Jesus, it is. God. How –'

'Waaaaaah,' Lily says, just like that, *Waaaaaah*, as

though pronouncing a word, counting off the *a*s. Then something opens or shuts inside her and the true cry comes.

'Shush, pet,' Michael says. He stands up and steps to block her line of vision. Her face has gone pulpy and red, like a crushed tomato. 'Don't look now, it's all right. Don't look.'

'B-b-but G-G-G-Gizmo!'

Fucking Gizmo. 'It's all right, Lil, Gizmo's just…' Resting? *Hanging out?*

'Gizmo's just had a wash and they've hung him up to dry,' Amanda says quickly, running a hand through Lily's curls, which appear to be full of snot, somehow.

'A – wash? But I – I thought – I – you said Jack – and his – mum – and – *a-huh* – dad – were gone away –'

'No – yeah,' Amanda says, turning to Michael, 'yeah of course, Yvonne told me they were going to her mother's for the weekend, she wanted me to keep an eye on – oh, God.'

'They're not home?' Coring out his relief, he feels the sudden emptiness of the house next door as another betrayal.

'Due back sometime today, I think.'

'Mummy you said – we could go in and – feed Gizmo – this morning.'

'We will, I promise, just as soon as he's dried out.'

'But if Jack – and his mum – and dad – aren't there' – Lily clenches her fists and takes a huge breath – '*thenwhoputGizmointhewash!*'

'Fairies,' Michael says. 'Come on, Lil, will we go in and see what's on the telly?'

He glances the question at Amanda too, who nods, but complexly.

'Won't be long,' he tells her. 'We'll sort this.' Then, 'Hup!' he barks to Lily in his robust-patriarch voice, bending to collect her, meaning to hoist her smartly on the beat of the syllable, get her a little airborne, make her laugh, stumbling back a pace instead with the weight of her. She whimpers into his chest. It astonishes him every time, the sheer, paradoxical density of matter gathered in her tiny frame. Usually it makes him smile. Now he can only think of the dog again, this body in his arms not much bigger than the one at the end of the chain. She feels almost dangerously vital to the touch, coiled and animal, the skittish tissues under his hands transmitting their sickly heat. He has to fight the urge to reject her, surrender her to her mother. 'Ssh-ssh,' he breathes into her hair. He carries her through to the living room and sets her down on the floor and gets some shapes and colours happening on the TV.

He waits until the sobs falter and her eyes glaze to miniatures of the screen. He searches the pockets of his dressing-gown for something to wipe her face with, but there's nothing. The living room is at the front of the house, the window here a portal to an alternate morning, dogless and unspoilt. The front lawn spreads like pressed linen, threaded with the deeper green of cuttings left by the mower, down to the road and the houses in their prim crescent beyond it. Shadows of trees and lamp posts condense as he watches, recoiling from the hard blue sky. Neighbours are emerging, many perms kindling in the sunlight, many pairs of spectacles flashing. He glances to his left: the Noonans' driveway is empty. He breathes. Space opens. The church bells have run to the end of the tape and he imagines the summoned bodies – couldn't be more than a handful, a bare clutch arthritic with prayer – and the incense mingling with the smell of their breath, each tongue itself a little fuming censer. He hasn't been to Mass in years. The dog might be a punitive measure for his absenteeism, cranked down from on high, or the prelude to a more expansive round of vengeance: The Plague of the Hanged Pets, about to descend.

He's wasting time now, standing as though he could yearn a channel into this morning that might have been. But he stays where he is. He feels like a visitor to a museum,

examining a diorama through the glass partition. Break
through to it, he thinks, and he'd encounter only waxwork
and papier mâché, houses carved from plywood, the sun
a lamp being slowly winched across a painted vault.

Mary Foley appears then in her driveway across the
road and spots Michael before he can shrink from the window. She salutes and Michael raises his arm in reply, then
she throws her head back to the sky and puffs out her lips:
We're haunted with the weather today thank God. Michael
nods frantically back with a smile that feels maniacal on his
face. As Michael's about to turn away the ancient, nearly
hipless Tommy O'Brien comes oaring along the footpath
on his Herculean morning stroll and Mary stops him,
pointing out, first Michael, who has to wave again, then
the sky, as though Tommy might need help in being made
aware of it, and the two of them stand there, looking up and
shaking their heads, like feudal peasants at some inscruta-
ble celestial event. They're right, though: this will be a day
to be marvelled at in kerbside discussions for weeks, the sky
as empty of cloud as though disembowelled, the great raw
sun harrowing all beneath it to a brilliant, painful clarity. It
will be very hot by noon. Michael wonders how long they
have before Gizmo starts to spoil.

Extract from a novel set in
Australia and Poland

LUCY MALOUF

✳

WHERE THE LIGHT
GETS THROUGH

WHEN MUM TURNED UP on our doorstep that Wednesday, it was a bright spring afternoon with magpies warbling, sunshine flashing between wispy cotton-candy clouds and the first magnolia buds bursting into life along our street. I'd just got home from walking the dog, keys on the hall table, leash on the floor, when the bell rang. Nerves still tingling with the pleasure of it all, I strode to the door and there she was.

'Mum! This is a nice surprise.' I leant in to greet her, but at that exact moment I saw something like panic flit across her features and she turned to look back over her shoulder, leaving me off balance, my kiss lost in the space between us.

'Hallo Paul,' she said, turning back to face me, her expression unreadable again. 'I come for a visit. OK?'

I had a vague memory that one of her Senior Citizen Clubs was somewhere out our way, but this sort of unannounced visit was unheard of. It was even more extraordinary that she'd managed to find our new house as she'd only been here once, for the big family dinner we'd had shortly after moving in.

'Have you been to one of your Club afternoons?' I ventured.

'No love, I bin to the Council offices,' she said, which puzzled me even more.

'Well come in and have a cuppa and you can tell me all about it.'

She followed me through to the kitchen and sat at the table, both hands clutching her handbag tightly, while I muddled around with the kettle and teapot. She seemed disinclined to chat and I had the uneasy feeling that something was happening right there in front of me; something I could just about glimpse, but not see clearly.

'I don't understand which Council offices you've been to,' I said eventually. 'Aren't the Kew ones back closer to your apartment?' I set mugs and milk jug down on the table and returned to spooning tea leaves into the warmed pot.

'I did have to get away from my apartment because of the police.'

'Police?' I turned slowly to look at her.

'They bin' watchin me,' she said, cool as you like, pouring milk into her mug, and it felt like she was avoiding my gaze. 'This morning they did come to my place to find me, so I must go away.'

'What are you talking about Mum? What police?'

But she shook her head and frowned, her bottom lip all scrunched up – which reminded me of how she used to look when Dad grilled her about the housekeeping money.

Now I was certain there was something going on, and I didn't have the foggiest how to get to the bottom of it. Call me a wuss for not trying harder, but when Mum had her stubborn face on you might as well save your breath.

And when Rosie and Bas arrived home a short time later, this was how they found us: sitting in a slightly strained silence at the kitchen table, late afternoon sun spilling onto the formica, sipping tea, dipping butternut snaps, Mum still holding onto her handbag for dear life.

*

I can't, now, get it all in the right order. The memories fizz and jump like cells firing, like synapses sparking. I shuffle the events around in my mind trying to decide what came next. Was it the arguments Mum began having with her next-door neighbour about him playing loud Polish music in the middle of the night? Maybe it was the day Rosie and I arrived to take her out for lunch, and found her wedged into the corner of her tiny kitchenette weeping. Taken in isolation either of these things might be explained away as the stuff of daily life. Then she started hearing the same Polish folk tunes at the tram stop – and we even managed to convince ourselves that there must be a simple explanation for that oddity, too.

There's none so blind as those who will not see, as my ex-wife is always saying, and in the end it took several weeks to recognise Mum's mental deterioration for what it was. But what I do remember quite distinctly, is that *that* afternoon with the flashing sunlight and the butternut snaps and the early-blooming magnolia came first. That was when it all began. When things started to go wrong.

*

'There's nothing wrong with your mother,' Dr Kalan said, when I took her in for a check-up two days after the unexpected visit. It was a tedious session, with lots of loud talking and repeated questions, but he ploughed patiently through the competency test, working down a list of questions about prime ministers and seasons and days of the week, and Mum aced them all. She managed to count back from twenty perfectly, in Polish *and* English, and only began getting cross when he asked her to mark ten past five on a printed clock face; but she did it, all the same, with reasonably good grace.

'To be honest, she's as strong as an ox,' Dr Kalan concluded. 'The tests aren't showing any signs of dementia and I don't think there's anything seriously the matter with her – other than being eighty-seven, of course. We all slow down and get forgetful when we're older, so it might just be a question of everyone being a bit more patient. I'll give you another prescription for her arthritis pain meds and you do need to make sure she's always got batteries in her hearing aid.'

Later on, my sister and I had to exercise an awful lot of self-control not to remind Dr Kalan of that blithe assessment: *There's nothing wrong with your mother*… But the thing was, when you discounted the police stuff, Mum did seem to be managing as well as ever. Mondays, Wednesdays and Fridays saw her trundling around Melbourne on the tram to her three different Polish Clubs. She was still getting to the supermarket and even making it across town to her favourite continental bakery for rose petal jam *pączki*. Competent. Coping. Fiercely independent. Same old, same old.

We weren't looking for the right things, of course.

Probably we were in denial a little bit, too, each for our own reasons and in our own way. But things weren't happening quickly, or in any obvious way. So we drifted along for a few weeks, Kate and I avoiding any serious discussion, moving away from the awkwardness of it all, afraid to reach out and grab hold of whatever 'it' might be.

*

In the end, it was Mimi who brought matters to a head. Kate rang us in the middle of *Masterchef* and said that she'd died.

'Mum's beside herself,' she said. 'I thought things were getting bad when I dropped in last weekend. Mimi was out on the balcony screeching and yowling. It was bloody awful.'

'Mum told me she'd taken her to the vet, but I didn't realise there was anything seriously wrong.' I was juggling my glass of wine with the phone handset, gesturing at Rosie to turn down the volume.

'Her kidneys were packing up. It's quite common with elderly moggies, apparently.'

'When did it happen?'

'This morning, I think. Although she just rang me about it now. It would have been much better to have her put down, but you know what Mum's like about death and dying. She'd have done anything to keep Mimi alive.'

'Jesus! That poor cat.'

'Anyway. I can't get over to see her for a few days, so

d'you reckon you can go to Mum's and… you know…'

'What? Get rid of the body? Thanks a bunch.'

'Thanks, bro! I owe you one.'

Rosie and I drove over to Mum's apartment the following morning, nice and early, before the worst of the traffic started up around the Junction. Predictably, she didn't hear us banging, so I opened the door with my own key. The place was in darkness; silent, stuffy and hot.

'Christ it stinks in here! Where are you, Mum?'

We moved through to the living room where I raised the blind and opened the door onto the small balcony to let in some air. I was mainly worried I'd trip over the dead cat, but as the early morning light washed through the room I got a different shock altogether. There was Mum, sitting in her usual telly-watching chair and staring, empty-eyed, into the gloom. She seemed not to notice us.

'Mum! Why are you sitting in the dark? It's like a cave in here.'

'Pavel. What you doin' here?' Her voice was distant, not her own.

'Have you got your hearing aid in Mum?'

Nothing.

'MUM!' Louder now, leaning in closer. 'YOU OK, MUM? WHERE'S YOUR HEARING AID?'

'What you say Pavel?'

'Fuck's sake. Let's get some proper light in here. I can't see a bloody thing.'

We moved swiftly through the few small, cramped rooms, opening curtains and windows, letting the day stream in, letting light shine on the chaos. It was clear that things were not OK. Not OK at all.

The bedroom was bad enough, bedclothes sliding off the mattress, a mess of dresses spilling out of the wardrobe, a trail of scrunched up tissues on the bedside table, a thick drift of talc on the carpet. And why was her suitcase out of the closet?

But the kitchen was the worst of it. Looked as if a storm had whirled through. The sink was full – nearly overflowing – with greasy brown sludge. The work surfaces were crowded with a mishmash of crockery, saucepans and frying pans, tinned food, packet food, jars of jam and *Polski ogorki*. Fridge and freezer doors were wide open and their contents appeared to be piled up on the floor underneath the kitchen table, along with mounds of newspapers and a wodge of recyclable shopping bags. There was a dried-out pan of soup on the stovetop, which was itself thick with grease and other unidentifiable food spatters. I counted three open tins of cat food on the window ledge and the reek from the litter tray made me want to gag.

'Bloody hell, Paul,' Rosie muttered. 'What's been going on here?'

I walked back through to the living room and began rifling through the clutter on the sideboard, looking for Mum's hearing aid.

'Ha. Found it.' I picked it up with the very tips of my fingers and handed it to her.

'MUM! PUT IN YOUR HEARING AID. WE NEED TO TALK TO YOU.'

Rosie shunted a half-finished tapestry and a tangle of embroidery threads off the sofa and sat down close to Mum while I crouched on the floor.

'What's up Mum? Things don't look so good.'

'No Pavel. Things not so good. And last night I did sleep not so good. Next door, always he play the music so loud.'

'Again with the damn music. And yet she's as deaf as a post whenever you want to have a conversation with her.'

'Helena, are you feeling OK?' Has something happened?'

She swivelled round to look at Rosie, eyes watery and pale, and I noticed the strange grey cast to her face, how her hair was stringy and flat against her scalp, how hollow her cheeks were. A smell of dust and something sour, like vinegar, pricked my nostrils.

'The police, they bin watchin' me again. And they say they will come and get me. They say I must go back home.' The words were choked and scratchy, like feathers in her throat.

'What are you talking about Mum? You *are* home.'

'No, Pavel. They tell me I must go back to Poland. I must go back to prison.'

JACINTA MULDERS

✳

MONTAGNA

ANNALISA DROVE THE CAR up the side of the dark
ridge. The valley below spread out cold and full of sharp
lights. By the roadside, Pia glimpsed vineyards, their vines
spindly and dead; the stiff outlines of beeches and pines.
The snow, hedging in the squat houses, lent a softness to
the surrounding night. Gino sat hunched-shouldered in
front of her. She could hear him breathe. They wove around
the hairpin bends, Pia bracing her bag to her stomach to try
and quell the nausea. She tried to follow what Annalisa was
saying: 'Dino and I will be married in autumn it will be difficult to find a house, unemployment is so bad, we may take
the apartment upstairs from Dino's mother then we don't
have to find anything, they have two dogs I adore dogs their
names are Pepi and Milo – ' The car swung into a driveway and bumped to a halt, its headlights splaying across
the stone façade of Gino's house. 'Here we are!' Annalisa
said. Pia clambered out and swallowed cold air. Her breath
condensed when she breathed out. The view of the sky
was bounded by the tops of houses.

'*Ciao*!' came a yell from above. In an open door in the
side of the house, Pia's great aunt Maria was leaning over
a railing and waving her hand. Pia pulled her bag over the
cobblestones. Even before she got there Maria had her
hands out, grasping at the air in front of her, seeking out
Pia's body. She pulled Pia against her collarbones, wrapped
her arms around her and pressed her into the side of her
neck. She wore a grey kerchief around her head and what
looked like a blue factory worker's coat over her clothes.
She led Pia through a hall full of prune-coloured light. On
the walls, they passed black and white photos, a wooden
crucifix, and a collage of a mountain cottage pressed with
bark and pebbles. The kitchen was very hot, and Pia was
immediately swamped by the smell of mushroom risotto.
Already light-headed, she felt her stomach writhe. Maria
gibbered over her shoulder in dialect. She would be sick.

'Zia, is there a toilet?' She untangled her arm from

Maria's and pushed the bathroom door open, locking it
behind her and turning on the tap while she bent over and
retched. Only bile. She pressed her forehead against the
tile. What were you supposed to eat when you were preg-
nant? What about the wine she'd been drinking in Sydney
with Tom? She lowered her mouth to the tap, rinsed, and
swallowed a careful mouthful. She splashed her face, patted
it with the hand towel, took a breath of damp air and went
back into the kitchen.

'– no, but seriously, they wanted two hundred for the
flowers, I said I'd get Dino's sister to do it,' Annalisa was
saying. The table was laid with four plates of steaming
risotto. Annalisa turned to Pia and lifted her tumbler.
'Giuseppina you have to try this, Enzo's uncle made it, you
can taste the grape.'

'The fridge is the only place for red wine,' Maria said,
nodding and rubbing the back of her spoon backwards and
forwards on the table.

They started eating. 'How was your trip?' Annalisa
said.

'Long,' said Pia, picking up her fork and lightly touching the rice on the side of her bowl. Maria watched.

'Aren't you hungry?'

'Sorry, I'll be back in a moment,' Pia said, leaving the
room again.

When she returned her forehead felt hot.

'You can't *say* it like that, Zio.' Annalisa circled her
wine glass gently. 'The Africans need homes too. They're
always having wars…'

Gino squinted. 'The north has been holding this country up since unification. Southerners don't know how to
work, and now Italy is full of Moroccans.'

'They want the jobs,' said Maria.

'There are no jobs.' Gino turned to Pia. 'Annalisa's
fiancée has to work at a bresaola factory the valley over.'
He flung a hooked finger into the air, as if to indicate which

valley it was.

Pia's risotto looked like it had solidified as it had
cooled. She shrugged. 'Europe has a difficult past.'

Maria dropped the serving spoon with a clatter.

'People should stay where they come from,' Gino
said, without removing his eyes from her.

Maria put her in a dark room with heavy furniture. Sitting
on the bed, she could see her blanched face suspended in
the mirror across the room. It hovered over a statuette of
the *Pietà* strung with aqua rosary beads. She turned off
the light.

When she woke, her abdomen hurt. She twisted up, almost
yelping in pain, then lay back down and touched the area
lightly with her fingertips until it lessened. Raising her
phone, she saw that Tom had sent her some messages and
a photo of a bowl of broth. No emails from Mum. She
dropped her phone to the floor and hugged her stomach
harder.

In the kitchen, Maria, who was wearing the same
worker's coat from the night before, turned from the
stove when Pia entered. 'Did you sleep well?'

'Yes.' She sat down. 'Zia, is there somewhere I can
use the internet?'

Maria looked back blankly.

'I want to call Mum but my data won't – '

'Call your mum? You can do it here!' Maria strode over
to a beige landline sitting on a small side table next to the
television. 'Wait a minute,' she said, picking up a notebook
and beginning to flick through, 'Where's the code for
Australia, oh God I'm so forgetful…'

'Don't worry about it, I've just realised she might not
be at home.'

Maria looked up, the notebook limp in her hand.
'What? But it's night, where else would she be?'

Pia pressed her teeth together and looked out beyond the meagre lace curtains to the mountain tops across the valley.

'No Zia, actually, I need it to send an email for work.'

'Oh… for work,' she said, nodding. 'Enzo has a computer. Or Annalisa's house, they have it there.'

'When's Annalisa arriving?'

'Soon,' she said, pointing to the clock above the stove and tapping her wrist. She wasn't wearing a watch.

When Annalisa arrived, she accepted a coffee from Gino and Maria and sat down. Chatting, the three of them slipped gradually into dialect, until Pia lost all understanding of what was going on. Occasionally, Annalisa would stop and look at Pia in a bewildered way, then, as if suddenly remembering, let out a breathy laugh and apologise, before speaking in an Italian that was loud and plodding. She looked at Pia encouragingly as she spoke.

*

'So many people want to look at you,' Annalisa said as they picked their way up the track to Santa Chiara. Pia had had to refuse tea and coffee in every house they'd visited among the houses below.

'What? Only water?!' all her relatives had cried, rolling their eyes and wringing their hands. They had all tried to make her eat cake, if not cake then biscuits, if not biscuits then fruit. She knew her refusals would be taken as rudeness. The smell of coffee in *grappa* had threatened to send her out of many rooms. Following Annalisa, Pia found herself losing breath. She tried to focus on Annalisa's blonde ponytail bobbing above her, but the light coming off its slippery strands made her feel ill. As Pia bent over to get her breath, a cramp shot through her. She whimpered softly and waited till it went away.

'Giuseppina! I'm up here!' Annalisa's voice called from

somewhere in the mist. Pia walked up the the path, turned a corner and came abruptly against a high stone wall. She followed it until she came to the front of the building, which she could see now was a church. It was not ornately designed. The walls were very straight and plain and made of large square blocks. At the front there was an arch, with a boarded up wooden door inside. A small bunch of faded plastic flowers was wedged into a holder on the side of the portico. Annalisa stood leaning against the door, rubbing it with her hand. 'The inside is very beautiful,' she said. She pointed in the other direction. 'Out there, if it's clear, you can see over the valley. But you can't see anything today. It's too misty.' Pia walked over to where Annalisa had indicated, but she couldn't see anything at all. Turning, she couldn't even see how high or large the church was – every time she stepped backwards the ground became rubbly underfoot. The tops of the walls were smothered in white.

At the front of the church, Annalisa had picked up a wet piece of paper from the ground and was looking at it carefully. 'Look, Gianni died,' she said, pointing to a box that said '*Deceduti*.' 'We'll have nicer paper for our wedding program,' she said.

Pia's mouth felt wadded as she looked down. The black, cursive letters on pink paper pulsed. 'Can I talk to you about something,' she said.

Annalisa looked up. '*Certo!*'

'You can't say anything.'

'I won't,' said Annalisa, leaning forward and looking at Pia with wide blue eyes.

'It's delicate.'

She nodded.

'I need to talk to Mum.'

'Yes.'

'Because… because I think I'm having a baby.'

Annalisa inhaled.

'I only just found out but I couldn't – '

'But no one in Australia said anything about – '

'I wasn't, I mean, it's not, I haven't told this to many – please, Annalisa, don't tell anyone.'

'Who's the father?'

'His name is Tom.'

'Are you together?'

Pia paused. 'I don't know, it's early – '

'You mean… you're not a couple?'

'I don't know, I – '

'Oh, Giuseppina.'

'No, it's not that, it's just, I've been having these strange pains – '

' – pregnancy is painful, I've been reading about it.'

'You have? No, I mean, *different* pains, like not right.'

'Listen.' Annalisa put her hand on Pia's arm. Pia gently stepped back till it slipped off. 'Giuseppina, I'll talk to my mum about it. She can help you. There were complications in Enzo's niece three years ago. They took her somewhere near Livigno, I think, apparently it's very good – '

'I don't want that!' said Pia, feeling her cheeks become hot. 'I just want to speak to Mum.'

'But at the clinic they would – '

'I don't want to go to a clinic! I need to call home.'

Annalisa looked at Pia as though she couldn't understand her anymore.

'Please don't tell anyone,' Pia whispered. The pale sky watched, indifferent.

Extract from a novel

FELICITY NOTLEY

*

THE ANIMATOR

IN MR LAWRENCE'S CHAMBER is a four-poster
bed, the canopy of which is pale blue like the sky. So it is the
sky that looks down upon us as he turns away and divests
himself of his garments. When he turns back to me again,
naked, I stare. He has been called handsome and indeed he
is. He has a fine frame and his limbs are in proportion, his
features fair. In short, all is as it should be, but his mascu-
line parts are strange to me: raw-red, like meat in the butcher's shop, nested among a great quantity of black hair.

'Do not delay, my little one,' he says.

I am accustomed to the help of a female companion
when undressing, be it a maid or, as of late, Flora Chorlton,
and now my fingers tremble and I want to bid him help
me, but how can I make such a request, naked as he is?
Notwithstanding, after a short delay, he walks around the
edge of the bed and unfastens the back of my dress, where
I require assistance. I shiver and he strips me.

We stand together beside the bed. The flat of his hand
rests on the rosebud of one breast. His other hand touches
my belly with a light sweep. And now he forces two of his
fingers inside me, as if I were a bird for stuffing.

'Are you a virgin?'

'The Lord knows that I am.'

'You are so open here. I would not have expected it.
And you are wet.'

I am conscious of movement within me: Mr Lawrence's
two fingers paddle like fingers made to walk to amuse a
child. I experience nausea. It is as if he is rifling through my
childhood lonelinesses, selecting one, discounting another. I
want him to desist; yet I move with him, hearkening to the
rhythm. When he withdraws his hand, I feel the loss of it.

He lifts me onto the bed.

For a reason best known to himself, Mr Lawrence made
over his son's bedchamber to me as a study, and it is
here that I sit on many a sunny afternoon, recording my

observations, sketching, painting, preparing a manuscript, which I hope to see published one day under the title 'The Natural History of the Insects in the West of England'.

To think on the former occupant of this room is a distraction which affords me both pain and pleasure. Indeed, when I requested a room for use as a study, I was dismayed to find that this was Mr Lawrence's choice. I thought perhaps he was not so much the sponsor of my industry as he had hitherto declared himself to be. Was it his intention that I should never open the door to this chamber? Did he hope I would never measure, never catalogue, never uncover new wonders? Sometimes I think it must be so.

On the first day that I came to this room anew, calling it by a new name, my study, I understood at once my folly in thinking that by the avoidance of a particular chamber I had avoided all thought of the boy. In truth, I think on him every day and, though to sit beside his trundle bed – Mr Lawrence would not suffer it to be removed – causes me fresh grief, it also offers me solace and has been the cause of something approaching communion with the boy.

In the bedchamber, Mr Lawrence lies on the far side of the bed. Since the first night of our marriage, he has not shown me his nakedness, nor touched my flesh.

It grieves me and I know it causes him disquiet, for once he tried to tell me the reason for his coldness. 'I would do it,' he said, 'but you do not have the smell on you of my first wife. I would do it, but I cannot.' I enquired of him if my scent displeased him and he told me that, just as a phantom is said to bear no shadow, he would find it hard to identify the smell of me. According to him, I have no scent at all.

It is morning. The bed sheet is pushed back, for the day is very warm, and I see that my husband is aroused, his body animated by a spirit of new life. There is no danger that we shall be disturbed. If I ring the bell, Emma will bring tea in a silver teapot, but if I do not touch the bell, we will be quite alone.

I move towards him and he kisses me in the parting of my hair. I lie close alongside him. I push back the heavy cotton sheets a little further. He is on the point of suspecting me, so I must act now if I am ever to do so. I guess at what is properly called for. I lie upon him like a common woman of the street. He rolls me over. The weight of his rapture probes, nudges, knocks against me. At last he finds the place which will give way to him. We move together in wretched anticipation: I, brazen, full of lascivious desire, he – I later surmise – in a state of some consternation, as the swell of him, the physical manifestation of the will of man crumples away beneath him.

My thoughts flee to Jamie very often. I can barely mix a colour without the notion of him here, behind my shoulder. How I regret every day spent with him, that I did not relish it tenfold, that I did not cherish him more fully. I did not know then that a lifetime's love should have been imparted in a mere six months.

This afternoon I sit with a smile on my lips to see a bumblebee which has fallen in mid-flight, by the look of it, upon the very page I had intended for the study of a moth. In my fancy I sense Jamie watching me with approbation. I turn quietly, but he is not here.

The bumblebee, hind legs in the air, one wing yet outstretched, has fallen as a fielder might fall heavily on his shoulder in a game of cricket. My delight with this intruder is exceedingly great. The markings on this one could best be described as mustard yellow, a kidney-shaped saddle on its abdomen and another similar marking on its thorax just behind the head. Its fur is soft. It invites stroking and, just as the yellow is not pure yellow, the black is not pure black, but nuanced, brown in fact. On the tip of its right hind leg is the claw. Have I ever before had occasion to see it so clearly? The tail of the bumblebee is white. The sting, protruded in death, as must be expected, bears a drop of moisture on the tip, the size of the point of a pin.

I take up my quill and begin to write, breaking off after every few lines to sketch a likeness of what is before me and then commencing once more. The wings – why have I never noticed before that bumblebees have wings as delicate as the wings of fairies, creatures only of the human fancy, too wondrous to live and breathe in this world?

Such is my delight and, it may be believed, my dis-tractedness, that I do not at first take notice of Meg, Mr Lawrence's white mare. If I do catch sight of her at all, it must be with only the half of my being, for when I at last raise my head, I am astonished to see her walking un-hindered through the young trees which lead into more significant woodland, adjoining Mr Lawrence's garden. I stand and watch her go; she appears to me a white unicorn from a story book.

But I am not yet such a ninny that I would let Mr Lawrence's most beloved mare plot her own departure. With neither bonnet nor mantle, I am soon lifting the latch on the garden gate, granting myself permission to depart, and hastening into the woods in her pursuit.

July is the month of highest beauty in the woodland garden and I believe myself to be quite blessed, for the white and yellow flowers peep on the forest floor and the singing of birds quiets my anxiety. Perhaps I will go so far as to say, my soul joins the birds in their song and the wings of my heart fly with them. I congratulate myself on this good accident, which renders free as a girl once more, and furnished with the most compelling of arguments, for do I not undertake this task, take each and every step, not like Red Riding Hood, straying from the path, but in my husband's service?

WILL NOTT

∗

HUNTING

EVERY EVENING AT SUPPER the boy ate a plain
baked potato and sat alone. The rest of us laughed and
called his name. He ate his potato and looked up and smiled
but didn't say anything. He only spoke after he had been out
with the beagles. He would sit in the warmth of the dining
hall and say 'today we caught a rabbit.' Sometimes he came
back with a pile of skin and fur.

I only saw him with the dogs once. I was out on the
rugby field and it was raining very hard. I heard the dogs
howling and moaning far away. The sound got louder and
louder but I still couldn't see anything apart from the torn
mud of the playing fields and the rain. Then the pack
appeared, quite close and moving fast along a line of oak
trees. The dogs' tails were all wagging together.

Behind the dogs were a master and a group of boys.
The boy from my house was at the back, running in a torn
pair of tracksuit bottoms and covered up with a Barbour
jacket. He stumbled every few steps and his hair was stuck
to his face. He looked so weak that I expected the dogs to
turn around, smell him out and tear him to pieces.

'We caught a rabbit today,' the boy said when he came
back soaking and shivering, into the dining hall. The
portraits of old white-haired men watched him as he took
his long socks off and sat at the table. The rest of us ignored
him. He ate his potato and then got chilblains in his toes
and had to go to the Dame. He sat up in her study and let
her feel his toes one by one as he told her about the hunt.

He was in an English class with me and when we read
Gawain and the Green Knight he made a small o with his
mouth and stared at the master who was reading. When
the lord of the hidden castle went hunting the boy looked
around the room and tried to meet our eyes. The poet told
of the gutting and gralloching of the animals killed in the
hunt. The boy listened and nodded as the narrator told how
the skins and furs were peeled back and the joints were
popped and the entrails pulled out. The boy touched my

arm as we all got up and left the classroom. 'It's just like
that you know,' he said. 'I can skin anything.'

That night a few of us waited for him after supper.
He ate his potato slowly and we stood around in the hallway outside the dining room. He was one of the last boys
out. He didn't seem to notice us all standing in a line. We
followed him up the stairs and he still didn't seem to notice,
his eyes were open but closed and perhaps the hunt and the
lord of the castle was all he could see as he tripped up
the stairs.

When he got to his bedroom door we grabbed him and
took him inside. He asked us what we were doing but then
he kept silent. We passed him around under the posters of
British flora and fauna and shelves on beagling and hunting.
I found the boy's suitcase in a cupboard. It was black and
large when I zipped it open. When we tried to tip the boy
in he fought but within a few seconds we had bent his arms
and legs and squeezed him inside. The others held the lid
down and I zipped the bag shut.

We wheeled the suitcase down the corridor to the
shower room. The showers were all in a row and the
showerheads looked like faces on long necks. We dragged
the suitcase into one of the showers and then turned on the
water. It fell directly onto the suitcase and soaked through
the material. We stood back and said goodbye and then
opened and closed the door to make the boy think that we
had left the room. Then we watched in silence.

A few minutes passed and nothing happened. I ran into
the shower and unzipped the suitcase to check on him. The
boy was soaked and he had curled up into a ball. His hair
was stuck to his head just like the time I saw him in the field
with the beagles. He didn't move his eyes towards the light
and he was frowning with his lips tightly pushed together.
I stood up and backed away to give him some space. He
jumped out of the suitcase and ran past us and back to
his room.

My father drove up and took me for tea when the school called and told him what we had done. He told me that the men in our family never attack the weak. It was our duty to help them. He prepared a scone very gently, putting on the jam and then a spoonful of clotted cream.

He was quiet and he looked uncertain of himself. He looked like he wanted to go and finish his cream tea in a corner of the room where nobody would talk to him. I said it was a joke and that sort of thing happened to all of us at one time or another. He nodded when I said this and looked at his scone.

My father was always reluctant to come out on my grandfather's annual pheasant shoot in Devon. After a family breakfast he always tried to hide in his cottage. The dogs barked and scratched at his door and ran around the courtyard. My grandfather shouted his name until he appeared.

From a young age I had run through the woods with the dogs and pushed up the birds. Later my uncles taught me how to shoot a gun and I stood in the line of men and fired at the pheasants. If one was still alive when it fell to the ground I didn't need to be told what to do, I went up to the bird and broke its neck. My father was different. When he shot a bird he ignored it afterwards and never touched the glossy brown feathers or its lizard eye. My uncles would joke when he finally came out of the cottage. Once I tried to join in and he said my name and stormed off down a mud track to the field alone.

Everybody was given a position by my grandfather. His eyebrows were huge and wiry like the tail of a fox and he wore glasses that made his eyes look large and open. He had a horn that he raised to his lips and swapped for his voice. I imagined my father trying to speak up and explain that he didn't want to shoot and my grandfather blowing the horn at him and covering up his words.

My favourite drive in Devon was a small wood that was

half sunk by a deep bog. The water was black and covered with a silvery sheen. Tree trunks covered in moss grew out of the bog and wood pigeons roosted in their branches. Pheasants liked to hide amongst the cold brambles and fallen leaves.

On the morning of the shoot my grandfather positioned my uncles, my father and myself around the wood and then the dogs were walked through the middle by local men. At first there was quiet, the faint sound of the wind nudging the trees and the low calls of birds. Then my grandfather's horn rang out across the valley. The beaters called to each other as the dogs started to crash through the undergrowth and scare the birds out of their hiding places. Then I heard the first few shots. They came one after the other and I heard the men in my family calling to each other across the wood: 'Forward – pheasant', 'back – woodcock.' I listened out for my father's voice but he never joined in the woodland chorus.

The birds came fast over the treeline like cricket balls. I shot a bird and it fell through the trees and landed a few feet away from me. Its wings were broken but its legs could kick and before the head knew what was happening the bird had run across the field and dived through an ancient hedgerow. I put down my gun and ran after it.

The hedge was thick with hawthorn, elderflower bushes and brambles and I cut my hand when I tried to push through. I watched the bird on the other side as it ran across the open view of the next field. Then I saw my father. He was standing at the edge of the field. The tall woods hung over him. He was very still and silent and he had his gun pointed at the ground. The air rang with shots and then from across the trees the wind carried my grandfather's voice. 'James! A pheasant is coming your way!'

My father watched the bird as it came out over the trees. He lifted his gun to his shoulder, aimed it at the ground in front of him and fired. A burst of earth erupted

and the pheasant flew overhead unharmed. My father
reloaded the gun's smoking barrel and then stood back into
position, still as a rock. I watched him. More birds came
towards him and my uncles and my grandfather called out:
'James! Another one coming you way!' My father shot into
the ground every time and said nothing. The birds flew
on unharmed.

At lunch we crowded into the old dark Jacobean
dining room in my grandparents' house. A piece of meat
on a silver platter was brought out and put before us. My
grandfather carved it up and my uncles took large slabs and
filled their plates with juice. Then my grandfather asked
my father how many birds he had shot that morning. My
father cut his meat into thin strips. 'None,' he said quietly.
My uncles joked and shook their heads and my grandfather
smirked.

The boy from my house left Eton that term but none of us
really noticed. I forgot about him entirely until my father
asked, 'what happened to that boy?' We were staying in his
cottage in Devon and we were getting ready to go and eat
with the family.

'Which boy?' I said.

'The one from your house who liked to go beagling.'
My father watched me. 'Remember. The men in our family
always look after the weak.'

I didn't go to the meal. Instead I walked away from the
house and out across the fields. The wind was cold and dark
clouds were being pushed towards our farm from the sea.
Birds called and rabbits ran for cover as I came close. Up
ahead of me was the pen where we kept the baby pheasants
that were reared for the shoot.

I opened the door and slipped in. There were a few
birds left and they scattered and ran head first into the
chicken wire fencing. A few more cowered in amongst
bales of hay. I caught one with my foot and picked it up.

It stretched its neck out as far as it could, desperate to get
away from me. I took out a piece of string from my pocket
and looped it around the feathered neck and pulled tight.
The bird's tongue showed out of its beak. I swung the bird
round and round on the piece of string until its neck broke
and the head fell off. The body fell into a corner with a
thud. I trapped another and pushed a bamboo cane through
its rib cage. Then I cornered one more and stamped hard on
it four or five times. I hid the bodies in the woods and then
left the pen and walked back towards the house, glad that
I had made up for the pheasants my father had missed.

Excerpt from a fantasy crime novel for 9–13 year olds. Set in Johannesburg.

KRISTIEN POTGIETER

✳

THE AZALEA FILES

I WAS IN ACCOUNTING when he came for me.
A chubby kid with a shiny Discipline Prefect's[1] badge on
his blazer to match the smug grin on his face. I knew both
the badge and the smirk, and they meant only one thing:
trouble. Big trouble. Then there was also that characteristic
delicious chocolate brownie smell that emanated from all
things dangerous[2] which trailed behind him.

'Excuse me, ma'am,' the kid said to Miss Crisp, who
was scribbling the usual pecuniary prattle on the whiteboard, perched atop her stool to reach to the top. Her
left eyebrow pinged up in annoyance. 'Official prefects'
business.' He handed her a note.

She frowned but as she read it a sickly smile oozed
across her pointy little meerkat-like face. I was familiar
with this smile and it, too, did not bode well. Miss Crisp
looked up. Straight at me.

'Azalea Zondo,' she said. 'Go with Khumalo to the
crypt. Come back at break to finish this.'

There were murmurs and gasps from the class, who'd
already had trouble concentrating on account of the
dramatic events of the morning.

'I did *not* say you could stop writing,' Miss Crisp
snapped at them. She narrowed her eyes at me. 'Well. It
seems Miss Kitty Kotze, our school's dearest culture cat,
has summoned you, Azalea. Of course, there's not much

1. DPs – prefects that were in charge of discipline. My
friend Kabelo called them the Hallway Police. They were
generally irritating but harmless overeager brownnosers
who craved teachers' approval, but occasionally there was
a member who became power-hungry and attempted
a whole evil-dictator-overthrowing-the-teachers thing.
They'd never succeeded, thank Eish.
2. Yes, I could smell danger and it smelled like chocolate
brownies. I had no idea why, OK, it just did. It was one
of my so-called 'superpowers', though thus far it's mostly
only put a real distrust of bakeries in me.

you can do. Now, thank Eish, her frivolous prancing
around in microscopic frocks will soon come to an end.
You see, children, the dangers of so called *artistic expression*? It leads down dangerous paths… Like murder. Kitty
would have done well to choose something sensible like
Accounting instead.'

I stopped listening to Miss Crisp's tirade and started
packing up my stuff, wondering what all this had to do with
me,[3] but my best friend Maggie Marmalade put a hand on
my arm.

'I'll do it,' she whispered. 'You better go.' The gleam
of adventure already shone ominously in her bright green
eyes, and her golden curls had come loose from her plait,
which meant she was gearing up for excitement. All this
despite my recent ban of adventures of *all kind*. She'd be
sending an SMS to Kabelo under the desk as soon as I left,
telling him to get ready for a possible next case.

The Mystery of the Vanishing Cupcakes was supposed
to have been our last case. It had nearly killed me, after
all. We got the job done in the end, but the stress of all the
villainy and danger and carbs we'd had to face had taken
its toll, and so at my urging Maggie, Kabelo and I had put
our mystery-solving/superheroing on hold to focus on
having sudden dramatic mood swings, squeezing pimples
in front of the mirror, responding to our parents' questions
in unintelligible grunts… You know, the usual teenagey
stuff. I didn't like to be reminded of Tumi Mosoane and
the Vanishing Cupcakes. I still had nightmares about it
sometimes. We'd seriously underestimated the severity

3. Though of course I should have known better than
to question it by now – trouble followed me wherever I
went since I'd acquired my 'powers' in that accident at the
ESKOM power plant a few years ago. Apparently that
was just what happened when you became a superhero/
detective/ballerina.

of Tumi's Macaron's Syndrome,[4] and what was supposed to be a pretty one-sided climactic showdown between me and him turned rather nasty when he went full cookie-dough monster and nearly bit my right arm off.[5]

I followed Khumalo out of the classroom. I'd been called out of class to the crypt[6] many times before, but I was still nervous. It's not like I ever got sent there for something nice like a tea party or a Liz Twizzle fan club meeting.

'I know where the crypt is, dude,' I said. 'You don't have to come with me.'

'I have strict orders straight from Prefect Tashura to escort you to the crypt,' he said. 'So, actually, I do.' He smirked.

I rolled my eyes.

As we passed other classrooms I saw kids turning their heads, peering out curiously and whispering to their friends. After what had happened at assembly there was a crackle of barely suppressed excitement in the air.

You see, in the middle of assembly Mr Runt, our preposterous excuse for a principal, had announced the winner of Horace Mbangeni High's annual art competition: Kitty Kotze. But then the stage curtains swung open to reveal *not* Kitty's nauseatingly politically correct painting featuring a group of multi-ethnic kids having a picnic of multicultural foods (biltong, samosas, koeksisters, bobotie, chesa nyama, etc.), but the corpse of Suki Sithole,

---

4. Macaron's Syndrome: named after the victim of the first reported case of the disease, the Frenchman François Macaron. Also known as Carbodehydration Disease or BGWS (Baked Goods Withdrawal Syndrome).
5. For a full report of this harrowing case, see CASE FILE #9: CODE RED VELVET.
6. It wasn't a real crypt, obviously. (There'd only been the one sarcophagus.) It was just what everyone called this particular area of the school because it happened to be underground and creepy.

Kitty's fiercest rival in practically everything,[7] swinging from a rope tied to an overhead beam. People had shrieked, screamed, fainted and all the rest which you'd expect.

Khumalo and I passed the hall, which was still barred by purple DP tape. As we went past, Mr Dinkelmann[8] came striding out from inside, ducking under the tape and getting his foot stuck in the process. He did a sort of fall-trip-stumble-dance into the hallway and his face reddened as he saw us.

'Ballroom lessons going well, then, sir?'

He ignored this. 'I'll take it from here, Khumalo. Back to class,' he said, 'and tuck in your shirt. You're supposed to set an example, for Eish's sake. All right, come, Zondo.' He set off down the hallway towards the crypt. As we walked, he frowned at me. 'Now look, Kotze may have asked to see you, Zondo,' he said, 'but I won't have you and your friends causing trouble again. The three of you are a – a bloody pebble in my shoe.'

'We just help where we can, sir,' I said sweetly.

'Well, you won't make a bloody gemors[9] of our investigation this time. And anyway, the evidence against Kotze is irrefutable. No one would have thought it,' he swallowed

---

7. Such as lead roles in school productions, scrapbooking competitions, and – most importantly – the race for next year's Head Girl.

8. First rugby team coach and teacher in charge of Discipline. Wore a Springbok rugby jersey to school nearly every day. Drank coffee out of a rugby ball-shaped mug. Had a rugby ball signed by Francois Pienaar in a glass case on his desk. Had his classes do a haka instead of a prayer at the end of the school day. Generally more interested in rugby than in the subject he taught (History).

9. Mess. I didn't point out that usually he and the rest of the DPs were the ones making a bloody gemors of their own investigations by always being completely wrong about everything.

nervously, 'but it's true. She murdered Suki.'

I nodded, though it was hard to think of Kitty as a murderer. 'Of course, sir. I just came to get out of Accounting, anyway.'

He narrowed his eyes, like he was trying to work out if I was mocking him or not. He pushed open a heavy wooden door to our left. Narrow stone steps led down – so far down you couldn't see where they ended.

The crypt had been shut up for decades due to its lack of ventilation and general air of spookiness, but, as the demand for more classroom space had recently increased, the school had been forced to crack it open and dust it off. Quite literally in this case, as the door had been stuck and it had been really dusty in there.

There'd been a few tiny little issues at first, like when a cleaner came across a sarcophagus, which happened to be all ancient and cursed and wreaked havoc for a little while.[10] Or when that treasure map from 1865 surfaced and sent the entire school into a treasure hunt frenzy for a few days.[11] But all that was sorted now.

They'd moved in some desks and chairs but were too lazy to get rid of the eerie atmosphere. So the walls were bare, the lighting was gloomy, water dripped from the ceiling and odd, unidentified noises startled you every few minutes.

As I followed Mr Dinkelmann down the steps, I got a very bad feeling. Not the doom and despair echoing from the crypt – I'd been there too many times before to be

---

10. I sorted out the sarcophagus's inhabitant – a mummified guy called Kevin – pretty easily. He can now be seen in a display case in the school foyer. Just don't tap on the glass, it really annoys him.

11. Sadly, it turned out to be merely the prank of an old student (the location of the 'treasure' was a toilet in the matric boys' bathroom).

squeamish anymore – but more of a superpower-choco-
late-brownie-smelling kind of bad feeling.

At the bottom of the stairs was a long hallway with
several doors on both sides. Mr Dinkelmann led me to the
door at the very end, which was closed. He knocked curtly
and opened it without waiting.

'Zondo's here,' he said. A petite Indian girl with black
hair long and shiny enough to belong to a Disney Princess
came to the doorway from inside.

'Azalea,' she said icily, and her DP Captain's badge
flashed just as coldly. '*Our famous detective.* Come to solve
the case for us, have you?'

Tashura Reddy wasn't a fan of my work. This was
totally normal, though, as she was the typical disgruntled
representative of the law who disapproved of my eccentric
methods and my meddling in her official duties. I wasn't
worried, because we'd eventually develop a grudging
respect for each other and even learn how to work together every now and again. Well, either that or we'd become
sworn enemies. I was hoping for the former, though it
didn't seem likely yet. In the meantime, though, it was my
job to torment her. It would ruin the dynamic otherwise.

'Tashie,' I said brightly, and her face darkened. She
hated that. 'Nice to see you. Good weekend? Crime never
sleeps, though, hey? Lovely day today, isn't it? Did you see
the jacarandas? Such a *vibrant* purple. And in *February*.
Just crazy.'

'Yes, yes, beautiful,' she grumbled. 'Go in now. There's
not much you can do this time to fudge it up for us, Azalea.
She's guilty, and you know it.'

'Don't worry, I'm just here for the free food. There is
free food, isn't there?'

She rolled her eyes. 'Fifteen minutes.'

I stepped inside and she slammed the door behind
her. I was relieved that she left us alone. I acted tough, but
secretly I was still shaken by the sight of Suki's lifeless body,

swinging over the stage like that, bloated and blue.

Kitty was sitting by a table, her blue eyes red and puffy. Her blonde ponytail drooped sadly down her back. It was a terrible shock to see Kitty's face, which was normally beaming with overenthusiasm and over-eagerness, so crumpled and blotchy.

I sat down opposite her.

'You have to help me,' she said, her chin wobbling. She leaned forward, gripping the edge of the table, a crazed look on her pretty face. 'I didn't kill Suki,' she said. '*The mutant cats did it.*'

Excerpt from a novel

RORY POWER

*

WILDERGIRLS

THE SCHOOL IS ON a big plot of land, on the tip of the island. Water on three sides, the gate on the fourth. And beyond it the woods, the same kind of live oak we have on the grounds, but tangled and thick, new trunks wrapping around the old ones. Animals grown sharp and angry. Whatever lived here before is different now.

Reese leads us to the old dock where it juts off the point above a steep stone drop-off. It's the one we used in Sailing class when this was school and the gate was open every day. Now we sit there side by side by side, Byatt in the middle, our feet dangling down. The water looks smooth and almost solid, like you could spread it on your toast.

'How's it feeling?' says Byatt. She's asking because two mornings ago the scar across my bad eye bloomed wide.

I make a face but I can feel my heartbeat throbbing in too many places. 'Can you stitch it for me?'

'That bad?'

'No,' I say, 'just –'

'Did you even clean it? It could be infected.'

Reese makes a satisfied sound. 'I told you not to leave it open.'

I look at Byatt, bite my bottom lip. 'Please? It's itching. I'd do it myself but I can't see it.'

'Yeah, OK,' she sighs. 'Come here.'

I shift around on the dock until she's kneeling up and my chin's lifted to her. She runs her fingers along the wound. Something in me flinches.

'Looks like it hurts,' she says, pulling a needle and thread from her pocket. She started carrying them every-where after Reese hurt her hand. 'OK. Stay still.'

She slips the needle in and there's pain but it's small enough. I try to wink at her, make her smile, but she shakes her head, a frown hanging on her brows.

'I said stay still, Hetty.'

And it's fine, Byatt and me, breathing together, and she's staring at me like I'm staring at her, until she digs the needle in too deep and I buckle, my whole body folding in. Hurt blinding and silver and everywhere and then it's over. I brace my hands on Byatt's knees. I can feel blood leaking down over my mouth.

'Shit,' she says. 'Shit, are you OK?'

'It's only stitches,' says Reese. She's lying back on the boards, her eyes closed, her shirt riding up so I can see a pale strip of stomach.

'Yeah,' I say. 'Keep going.'

Byatt starts to say something when there's a yell from somewhere else in the yard, back near the garden. We twist around to see if somebody's gone wrong. The youngest ones are thirteen now, and it's just starting to take them apart. After the winter's done, they'll crack open for spring, just like we did.

But there's nothing wrong, just one of the other girls in our year waiting by the end of the dock. 'Shooting,' she calls to us. 'Miss Welch says it's shooting time.'

'Come on.' Byatt gets up, holds out her hand to me. 'I'll do the rest of your eye after dinner.'

I remember I was out in the grove when it happened, in the tangle of low trunks and limbs, Reese and Byatt watching as I walked out on the lowest branch as far as I could go. And I fell, which wasn't strange. I fell all the time, we were all of us covered in scabs and nicks back then, some of us turning a corner too fast, some of us sewing our hems too short, some of us pressing sharp things into ourselves just to see what it would feel like. It was what came after.

I stood up, laughing, we were all laughing, but then blood started slipping out of my mouth. Slowly at first, and then faster and faster, running up my face and pooling in my eyes. Hot like it was about to boil, and I started to cry because I couldn't see.

Byatt grabbed my elbow and Reese grabbed the other, and they walked me back to the house. I kept my eyes closed, blood flowing onto my cheeks, and I could hear other girls in the years below us, hear them talking and giggling and falling silent as we passed by. Byatt tucked her body in close to mine. She was the only thing that kept me on my feet.

I finally opened my eyes in the main hall. Reese sat down with me on the staircase while Byatt ran to get the nurse. We sat there for a while, I don't know how long. Reese held my hand in both of hers while I leaned on her shoulder and bled on her shirt. When Byatt came back, she had Miss Welch with her, and they pressed gauze to my eyes until they dried. The nurse was gone. Everything was starting.

They evacuated the island the next morning. Trucks full of soldiers, plastic suits bright like fire. Built a buffer zone into the coast where nobody lives, set up a quarantine so rigid even calling home would break it. Tests and tests and no answers, just a sickness spreading through every one of us.

The first few months, they tried to keep it like school. Breakfast in the dining hall. Math, English, French. Lunch, then shooting. Tests and first aid, Miss Welch bandaging wounds and drawing tubes of blood. Back together for dinner and evening mass, and then locked inside to last the night.

By now shooting's the only class we still have. Every afternoon, as soon as the sun comes back to earth, one by one, firing away until you hit dead center. We practice out in the barn, near the point, with big sliding doors on each end that are always open so the stray shots fly into the ocean. There used to be horses, four of them, but early in the first season we noticed how the wildness was starting to get inside them, so we led them out to the water, prodded them deep until it closed over their necks. Shot them if they tried to come out before the water had finished. The stalls are empty, now, and we pile into them to wait our turn. You have to fire at the target and you're not allowed back to the house until you've hit the bullseye.

At some point the order was alphabetical but we've all lost things, eyes and hands and last names, so it's the oldest girls who stand up first. They nestle the rifle in the notch of their shoulder and they're done, one shot.

I hoist myself up onto the door of a stall and Byatt settles next to me. Reese slouches between our knees. She's not allowed to shoot because of her bad hand, but she's here every day, tense and quiet and watching the target.

'Hetty, you ready?'

I grin back at Byatt. 'Now, what kind of question is that?'

The rest of my year, they're near the middle, but somehow I jumped the order and I'm right after the oldest girl, even with my eye. I'm not better than any of them, and it always takes me three shots, moving closer each time until I hit the center, but I just kept going sooner and sooner and they kept letting me.

The same three shots, the rifle back on the table, and then I'm in the crowd with Reese and Byatt again. We'll wait until Byatt's had her turn to go back. We always do.

'Next,' calls Miss Welch. It's usually Julia who goes now but there's a little shuffle, and someone shoves Mona out into the middle. I don't know Mona that well, because she's the year ahead of me and even after everything that still matters, but I remember how her face steamed and cracked. They carried her to the infirmary with a sheet over her like she was already dead. A season later and she's still unsteady on her feet.

'Can I rest for today?' she says. There's a waxy calm on her face, but a fidget in her bones.

Miss Welch is waiting. 'Afraid not. Let's go.'

It looks like Mona says something else, but it's too low for anybody to hear, and she goes to the table. The gun is

laid out. I left it loaded. All Mona has to do is point and
shoot. She lifts it with three fingers, cradles it in the crook
of her arm like it's a doll.

'Any day now,' from Miss Welch.

Mona levels it at the target and sneaks a finger onto the
trigger. We're quiet now. You can tell her hands are shaking.
Somehow she's keeping the gun aimed right but the strain
is tearing at her.

'I can't,' she whimpers. 'I don't, I can't.' She drops
the rifle, looks my way.

And that's when they slice, three deep cuts down the
side of her neck like gills. No blood. Just a pulse in them
with every breath, the twitch of something moving under
her skin.

Mona doesn't scream. Doesn't make a noise. She just
drops. Flat on her back, mouth gasping open. She's still
looking at me, her chest rising slow.

'Hetty.' A hand on my shoulder, shaking it. 'Hetty, hey.'
It's Byatt. 'You OK?'

'Yeah.' I blink hard. 'Fine.'

Around us, the other girls are collecting in groups, and
Miss Welch is kneeling on the floor at Mona's feet. 'Let's
get her to the infirmary,' she says.

The oldest girls, Carson and Julia and Taylor, they step
away from the rest. Always them, and they take Mona's
arms. Haul her up, lead her away, back to the house.

Chatter, and a break as we all start to follow, but Miss
Welch claps her hands.

'Ladies,' she says, and she drags it out like she used
to do in Algebra. 'We'll start again from the top.'

There's no surprise in any of us. We left it someplace
and forgot where. We line up, we wait, and we take our
shots, and we feel the warmth, Mona's warmth, seeping
out of the rifle and into our hands.

Excerpt from a novel

SAMANTHA PURVIS

*

ARRIVALS

AFTER WHAT FELT like hours in a holding pattern, the plane at last began its descent. Marcus scrunched up his blanket and wedged it behind him. He'd only slept intermittently; his body was tired but his mind was awake. He'd flown the short hop from Abidjan to Accra yesterday afternoon and waited five hours for his connection to London. Every step of the journey had been plagued by setbacks, from the taxi that was late picking him up from his hotel, to the straggler who'd kept his plane waiting on the tarmac at Kotoka International. He imagined his wife Helen in the airport somewhere down below, watching the flight's ETA creep further and further into the future on the arrivals board.

The pilot announced that they were coming in to land at London Heathrow Terminal 3: local time 05.23 AM, temperature 7°C. In Abidjan the temperature had never dropped below 20°C and the dense air continually threatened rain that never arrived. One particularly close night he went to a bar in the city's downtown area and got talking to a local woman about the weather. 'I can't get used to it not raining,' he told her. 'We barely go a day without it back home.'

'And where is home?' she asked, poking the ice in her drink with the thin straw.

'London.'

'Why are you laughing?' she asked, sitting back from the table.

He placed a gentle hand on her elbow and said, 'No, I'm not laughing at you. It's just, people make fun of the English for always bringing up the weather.'

She relaxed again and asked, 'Business or pleasure?'

He hesitated and she looked around the bar, waiting for his answer.

'I'm doing a study of modernist architecture,' he said.

'Modernist,' she repeated, and he could tell the word was unfamiliar to her.

'It's a style of building… It doesn't matter.'

Shortly after, she excused herself to go to the bathroom. While she was gone he paid their bill and slipped
away. The next day, while he was sketching the cathedral,
he slapped his sketchbook on the ground in the middle
of ruling a line, turned on 3G, and booked an early
flight home.

The plane wheels caught the runway, adding the rum-
ble of tyres to the engine's whine, and Marcus got his first
ground-level look at England in almost two months: airport
flatlands, empty and dark. A text from Helen came through
the moment he turned off flight-safe mode: *In Costa, reading my book so don't rush.* He started to type, *Finally landed,
can't wait to,* but then he touched backspace until the words
were gone and wrote, *Landed, see you in a bit!*

The plane finished taxiing and there was a long pause
before the engines shut down. When they were allowed
to get up, Marcus sidestepped into the aisle and stretched;
aches and pains lurked in every corner of his body. Queues
were forming in the aisles, and there was no sign of movement up ahead. He checked his messages again, wondering if he should let Helen know things were going slowly.
Instead he drafted a text to Molly: *Landed safely! Hope uni
is going well. Call me when you get a chance? Lots of love Dad
xx.* He paused before sending it – it might wake her up –
but she most likely had her phone on silent. Message sent,
he tucked his phone away and looked up: all the other passengers were also texting as they began to shamble towards
the exit.

He cleared immigration and reached baggage claim
just as the bags were coming out. His suitcase was one of
the first to emerge from the plastic flaps. He'd wanted to
take Molly's Interrailing backpack, but Helen had said,
'You're not eighteen.' He would have been able to live
with the undignified gap year connotations, but he knew
his choice of luggage signified something darker to her:

a suitcase was appropriate for a research trip; backpacks were for 'travelling', and everything that went with it.

In the arrivals hall he didn't immediately see her. Then she was coming towards him. She was in his arms. She was a bundle of different textures: cold, silky hair; the itchy wool of her coat. He'd forgotten how neatly their bodies lined up. They held each other for a long time, and he was glad they hadn't tried to speak. The hug seemed to say everything. When they broke apart he was able to look her over properly: she had a good colour for this time of year, and was more well-groomed than he'd seen her in a long time. He met her eyes and saw that she had been appraising him too. It was so obvious that it made them both laugh. He pulled her in for another hug.

She said, 'Let's get you home,' into his chest.

By the time they made it onto the M4, the sun was coming up and there was traffic. Helen said, 'I was hoping to miss this.'

'I doubt it would have made much difference,' he said. 'If I'd landed on time, I mean.'

It only got worse as the motorway turned into the A4 in town. They got stuck on Earl's Court Road for a particularly long time and Helen lapsed into a grim silence. He was still adjusting to the particularly *London* sights on the pavement beside the car: office workers hurrying out of the Sainsbury's Local with orange plastic bags and hot drinks; a pigeon shaking a piece of croissant in its beak; commuters stooping to pick up copies of *City AM* from bales on the ground.

'It's so strange to be back,' he said.

Helen's eyes tracked a businessman in a trench coat as he stepped into the road and made his way through the gridlocked traffic to the other side of the street.

'Couldn't do that in Nairobi,' Marcus said.

'I can imagine,' she said.

'Spoken to Molly much recently?'

'Not really. I think she's been partying a lot.'

'Well, it is her first year.'

'No, I know,' Helen said. 'It wasn't a judgement.'

He turned his head to the window and watched the goings-on outside again. Helen nudged the car forward about a foot.

'Who's looking after the bakery this morning?' he asked after a while.

'Alex.'

'I didn't know he helped with the practical side of the operation.'

She glanced at him sidelong. 'He doesn't really, it's just for today. Georgina's there, anyway, she'll be serving the customers. Alex is just there to open up and sort of…'

'Oversee things?'

'Yeah,' Helen said, smiling briefly.

He paused, then said, 'I'm glad you found Alex. He's been a good partner so far.'

'Yeah, he's been great.'

'Do you see him much socially?'

'Now and again,' she said.

They swung towards the river. Although it was still manic, the road felt less claustrophobic with the water on one side. The tide was low, the Thames a strip of silver snaking along the wide flat riverbed. He glanced at her; she was driving with an air of absent concentration.

'Helen?'

She mouthed a swear word as a cyclist shot out in front of them, then said, 'Yeah?'

'Nothing.'

'What were you going to say?'

'I don't know.'

They crossed Vauxhall Bridge and were quiet for the rest of the drive to Peckham. Their street looked just as it always did, although leaves were out on the stripling trees,

which had been bare when he left. They got out and unload-
ed the luggage. Helen walked up the garden path in front
of him and unlocked the door. The house smelled of wood,
faint cooking odours, aired linen.

'It looks nice in here,' he said, tucking his suitcase
between the hall table and the coat rack.

'I tidied up for you,' she replied over her shoulder
as she made for the kitchen.

He followed her. 'What now?'

'Well, are you hungry?'

'A bit.'

'Scrambled eggs?'

She was already in motion, brewing coffee and tea,
opening and closing cupboards. He lingered behind her
while she fired the hob to make his eggs, grazing her hip
gently with a hand that he let drop when she didn't lean
back against him. He went over to the breakfast bar and
perched on one of the too-high stools, looking out of the
French doors. Their garden was brown, overgrown, and
the sky was a non-colour.

Once she'd made his breakfast, she leant against the
sideboard sipping tea and watching him eat. When he finished, she took his plate and made to start clearing up.

'Don't,' he said, hopping down from the stool and trailing her to the dishwasher. 'Do it later. Let's have a sleep,
you must've been up since, what, four?'

'I'm OK,' she said. 'I just need to do a few bits of paper-
work this morning. You go on up.'

He couldn't see her face, as she was leaning over
the dishwasher and he was standing behind her. 'Is
everything OK?'

She glanced at him between slotting dishes into
the rack. 'Of course. Why?'

'You seem…'

She straightened and – after only a second's hesitation – put her arms around his neck. He received the

hug passively, then gave himself a mental shake; he was
overanalysing.

'All right,' he said. 'Well, you know where I'll be.'
He kissed her cheek and she smiled. That was better.

As he mounted the stairs he realised how leaden
he felt; by the time he reached the bedroom he barely
had the wherewithal to drag his clothes off and crawl
into bed.

'Marcus.'

Suspended between sleep and wakefulness,
half-dreaming he was still in Abidjan, Marcus heard Helen
talking to him from beyond a blinding glare. With an effort
he pulled himself to the surface. It was feverish under the
covers and he wondered if he was getting ill. Helen was
sitting on the edge of the bed. He wrapped his arms
around her and pulled her down for a kiss.

After a moment she propped herself up again.
'Sleep well?'

'How long have I been out?'

'It's almost five,' she laughed. 'I just wanted to wake
you because I have to go out in a bit.'

He frowned and tried to pull her down again, but
she resisted.

'Why?'

'Louise's opening. I told you.'

He groaned. He hadn't known the date of the gallery
opening when he changed his flight.

'Is there any way you can skip it?'

'I'm sorry. It's really important to her. I'll be back
by eight, nine at the latest.'

When he didn't reply, she got up and went over to the
dresser. While she spritzed perfume and tinkled jewellery,
he lay there trying to absorb the fact of her going. She came
back to the bed one last time to say goodbye. When she
leaned over to kiss his cheek, he turned his mouth towards

hers and she pulled away, saying, 'You'll mess up my
lipstick.'

'Fine.'

She sighed, trailing her fingers over his hand. 'Marcus,
I'm really sorry.' She waited for him to reply, then went
on, 'Are you sure you don't want to just come with me?
Everyone will be there.'

He turned his hand palm-up and stroked her fingers
as they spidered over his. 'No, you go. I'm in no fit state,
really. Have fun, say hi for me.'

He didn't see her to the door; he lay in bed listening
to the soles of her ballet flats tap down the stairs. Her footsteps paused in the hallway. He knew that she was checking
her appearance one last time in the hall mirror. Then
she left.

Extract from a novel. Set in Dublin.

JENNIFER ROE

✳

TEMPLE LANE

I KNOCKED ONCE and let myself into the office. The blinds were still shut. The sun's heat hadn't worked its way inside yet so the place had a wintry feel. Dami had one hand hovering over the mousepad of his laptop. The light from the screen cast a faint glow across his face, catching underneath his high cheekbones. I didn't get much of a look at him on Friday, but he really hadn't changed much in four years. His hair was a little longer, though just as dark. Might've been a bit thinner, but his weight fluctuated so much. Even when we'd been going out I couldn't keep track.

'It's very fucking early to be meeting,' I said. Rush hour on the DART had nearly killed me. Hadn't done it in years.

Dami mumbled a good morning and pointed to a slick red coffee machine in the corner, the light green. 'Be quick James. I wanna talk to'ya.'

'Well you'd better have, dragging me into town this early.'

Dami gave me a filthy look and shooed me along.

Strange, being in here again. He'd rearranged, divided the room into two sections. Couches and TV closest to the door, desk and cabinets at the far end. Separating business and pleasure. His finest skill. I glanced down at the desk as I passed. Looked like he'd been here quite a while, judging from the mess of scattered paper. He always did work best in the morning.

Reminded me of that time we'd done it on the desk, when I shoved a heap of invoices onto the floor. Wasn't like I knew they'd been sorted. Though he hadn't minded much when we were doing it. Soundproof walls are a wonderful thing. Took ages to order the bloody things again. He'd restricted sex to the couch after that. Leather'd been easier to clean so it was grand.

Dami had the machine set up for me, cup poised and waiting, a capsule in the little slot. I pressed the blinking green button and it flashed white, before letting out a few grunts.

'So, where were you last night?' Dami asked, a hint of amusement in his voice. 'You didn't sound too happy when I called.'

'None of your business.' No way I was letting him know about Sarah.

'Just, it's not like you to let your clothes get wrinkled.'

I bit my tongue, ignoring the low chuckling from behind as a heavy stream of coffee began. It smelled so good, my eyelids felt lighter just getting a whiff. I straightened the cup so I didn't miss a drop. Took a moment to realise that it looked familiar, red and white little criss-cross shapes. Dami still had it. Sentimental fucker.

'What you working on?' I asked, turning to face him, setting my hip against the sideboard. He shifted the laptop so I couldn't get a clear view of the screen.

'Business,' Dami said, snapping me a quick glance.

'What business?'

'None of your business,' he quipped. Christ.

He looked back and forth between the screen and the pile of paper, his spindly fingers hovering over the sheets. The bones in his wrist jutted out from beneath his pale skin. It wasn't my place to worry anymore. Just had to trust Cáthal was looking after him. Bastard had better.

The machine beeped twice. I grabbed the cup and Dami shut his laptop before I even got close.

'Sit,' he ordered, a quick jab at the seat opposite him.

He began clearing the desktop, raking together the loose sheets. I caught the names of a few alcohol and shipping companies, a few invoices, lots of lists and figures, but a letter stood out, handwritten in heavy black ink. Dami flipped it before I could make out any of the words, giving a warning with his eyes and shoved everything into a folder. Fuck it, too early to be thinking properly. I should have left Sarah's house earlier really, just didn't think I'd get lost. If she found out she'd laugh her ass off.

Dami took a coaster from the pile on his right and slid

it across to me. Made me happy to know he was still taking care of the desk. Thing cost almost two weeks of our salary, and hardly anyone ever saw it. Bloody shame. I bet Cáthal hated seeing it every day, just a constant reminder of me. I ignored the coaster, instead holding the warm ceramic in my hands, smelling the steam.

'So, how's investigating going for'ya? Turned any good stones?'

Yeah, guess I shouldn't have expected any pleasantries. Could have waited a minute though. I blew across the top of the coffee, rushing away the coils of heat, pushing the traces of foam clinging to its surface to the edges of the cup. 'Got nothing.'

How badly I wished I could've lied, but he probably already knew. I waited for him to whip a snarky little jibe at me, but nothing else came. 'What, you call me over to rub salt in my wounds?' He said nothing, just looked over my shoulder. Fuck sakes.

I drank, glad for something to do while Dami helpfully stared off into space. It was good, real hot, but not burning. Just enough to hurt a little. Dami pushed back from the desk and opened a drawer. He tossed a brown A6 envelope across to me. Something shifted inside when I picked it up. I wedged my finger into the side and tore through the gummed seal. The hell? Took out a driver's licence with my picture, but the name in it was William O'Donoghue.

'What's this?'

'A fake ID,' he said, chin resting on his steepled fingers.

'Well thanks. I kinda got that. Why're you giving me a fake ID?' I put it back on the table with the ripped envelope and took a big fecking gulp of coffee.

'It's a strange system,' Dami said, closing the drawer with his foot. 'You have to download and print off a PAS1 form if you want to request a copy of a will, and then send it off to the probate office. Why they can't do it all online is beyond me. I mean, they don't do anything the simple way.

It's like with –'

'Get on with it, will ya?' I didn't need a rant about
the fucking government first thing in the morning. Already
had enough of them.

Dami scowled and gave me the finger for interrupting.

'Then you have to collect the copy of the will from the
probate office,' he continued. 'Pay for it too, though its only
€10. All the bloody loopholes. Pain in ass is that they need
to see your ID.'

'Dami!'

'I requested a copy of Marcus Leeson-Reid's will.
Peter's father.'

That gave me a start. We'd hardly looked at him in
the investigation. Was from one of the old families round
Killiney Hill. 'Right Dam. Whadaya know?'

Dami took a deep breath, holding it for a few seconds
before leaning back and releasing it towards the ceiling.
'I asked you not to get involved, but you're just so fucking
stubborn.' When he looked at me again his eyes were hard.
'There's no bowing out like last time.'

His words were like a slap. Neither of us had mentioned it on Friday. I thought he'd pass over it like it never
happened. The coffee suddenly didn't feel too good in my
stomach. I could feel my tongue bend around the words,
testing them. 'This time is different.'

'No it ain't. You screwed a lot of people over last time,
just up and running like that.'

I didn't need to hear the words to know that Dami was
right up the top of that list.

'This country's a tiny fucking place. Pretty quickly
people're gonna realise who you are, and that you've been
suspended from the Gardaí. You can't do this alone James.
You need my help.'

So, this was how much our past was worth. I'd hoped
for more. At least this time he gave me something to go on.
I left my half-finished coffee on the coaster. 'I can't afford

the kinda return you're looking for Dam.' Nothing was free with Dami. 'I didn't go straight just to get dragged back in at the slightest hint of trouble. Then trying to clear my name, it'd be for nothing.'

And Oisín. I couldn't let him down. I got two steps before Dami stopped me.

'This is a one-time offer,' he said real quiet. 'I owe you for not pressing charges. That time.' His eyes flickered to my left side, just underneath my ribs. Where Cáthal had stabbed me.

I sat down. Ran my thumb over the rim of the cup.

'If anyone follows up through the system they'll find that ID,' he said, pointing down at the pink licence. 'Though I can't help you if you're recognised. And if the Guardaí find out you're using that to investigate a case you've been told to back off of? Least you'll be worrying about is your job. Mountjoy is a fucked-up place.'

'What choice do I have?'

'You can work for me.'

That made me laugh. 'You think Cáthal'll go for that?' He balked and looked away. I knew Dami was doing his best to keep us from seeing each other. If Cáthal knew I had keys for the place he'd blow his top. 'If I don't do this then I'm right back where I started. If I do it and get caught, same difference.'

'You could quit.'

I gave him a half-smile, the one that used to drive him nuts. 'Same difference.' I held his gaze until his fingers twitched. This talk was going nowhere good.

'Who's,' I looked back at the licence, 'William O'Donoghue?'

'Marcus's illegitimate child.'

I nearly bolted out of the chair.

'As of two weeks ago.'

'Ah Dam, what're'ya playing at?'

Fucker had that glint in his eyes. 'You gotta be a family

member or a lawyer to request a will. Lawyers were a no-go, so, walla! Peter has a half-brother.'

Shit. Dami's people were skilled. On paper, William was real. 'This complicates things.'

'And not just for the Guardaí,' he said, reading my mind. 'There's a lot of people sitting up on their hind legs for this case. Someone's gonna have noticed a prodigal son.'

In other words someone'd probably be watching the probate office. Watching me. 'Can't I just get some random-mer to collect it?'

Dami raised an eyebrow. 'You want someone else involved in this? You want another Cian?'

The scene played behind my eyes again. I just couldn't get rid of it. The concrete wall, blood trailing to the floor where his wrists had been torn against the rough edge. Clumps of his skin had stuck to its surface. Forensics had to pull them off with tweezers.

'Yeah, thought not,' he said.

I downed the rest of my coffee, taking the ID and putting it into my back pocket. 'Right, where's the office?'

Dami's cocky little smile returned. 'Phoenix House.' His shoulders jerked with silent laughter.

Oh come on. 'Not –'

'Smithfield.'

'For feck sakes!'

'I'm not exactly rooting for you, ya know. Maybe this'll make you reconsider.'

Sakes. 'Anything else you wanna tell me? Anything I should look for in the will?'

'Hell no. I've given you a shitload more than you deserve. Go do your damn job, seeing as you're so keen to keep it.' Always with the dramatics. 'James. The will's not for keeps. Get it back to me tomorrow morning. If you manage to get it, that is.'

I didn't even bother looking at him. 'Thanks for

the coffee.'

I had the door open when Dami called out. 'I still expect something in return for this. Remember that.'

'You never did give unless you'd receive.'

'Oh fuck off,' Dami snapped. I couldn't stop myself from laughing. I left him with a little colour in his cheeks. It was so easy to rile him up.

RASHMEE ROSHAN LALL

✳

THE UNSAID

THE NEW YEAR BREAK is over. We're barely a
minute away from the house when we see the small crowd.

We walk faster. Our garden gate and front door
are wide open. All the lights are blazing, even the one
in the porch that's never switched on.

Zahid and I have been away little over an hour, buying
bread and butter for the shared larder. We dawdled in the
little market and, on the way home, I let him hold my hand.
In the darkness, we walked wedged into each other and
I could smell the Brut I had given him. The warmth of his
body has become a comforting night-time habit in dark
byways. I missed it during the holiday period at home.

A car sounds its horn behind us. We spring apart,
standing to one side, our backs against the bushes planted
by the householder on what should be pavement. We
watch the jeep pass.

'That's the police,' says Zahid.

We start to run when the vehicle stops outside our
house, forcing the solid knot of people to part. Three men
emerge and disappear through the gate.

We reach the crowd. It is a dozen or so men. I recognise a few of the faces. One of the men runs a tea stall in
the neighbourhood. There is a security guard from the
pink and white house at the corner. Our neighbour – a
Mr Yadav, who works in a bank – is there too, staring like
everyone else at our house, as if it were a television set.

'Please *bhaiyya*, please let us pass, we live here,' I plead
to the wall of backs.

'Side *deejiye bhai*, side *deejiye*,' says Zahid, taking my
arm and pulling me through. Narayan is on the porch
talking to the policemen. They stand aside to let us pass.
It is quiet in the Common Area.

The TV's sound is off, but on the screen *Udaan* is about
to start. I can see the birds wheeling in the clouds and the
little girl looking up into the blue sky dreaming that one
day she will become a police officer. All of India roots every

week for Kalyani Singh's *udaan*, her determined flight
of destiny.

Jaishree is sobbing noiselessly on the two-seater.
Sakina is rubbing her back.

I go up to them, dropping the bag of bread and butter
onto the side table. 'What's the matter? Why're you crying
Jaishree? Why are the police outside?'

'Oh, Indira,' she wails, clutching at me.

'There, there,' Sakina murmurs soothingly, 'it's OK.'

Revathi is sitting very still on the sofa, Parvathi's head
on her lap. Avijit stands next to them holding a glass of
water. Parvathi's face is wet.

Narayan leads the policemen into our bedroom. 'Yes,
Inspector, of course,' he says, closes the door behind them
and takes his usual chair near the TV. He switches Kalyani
Singh off. She is in uniform, so nothing too bad can happen
to her now.

'What's happened, Narayan? Why are the police in
our bedroom?' I ask.

'Oh, Indira,' says Jaishree and cries harder.

'Now, now, we have to be brave,' Sakina whispers,
patting Jaishree gently.

'You had better sit down Indira, we don't want any
more fainting,' Sakina says, nodding towards Parvathi.
Strands of hair are falling over Sakina's eyes and her lipstick
has faded. She looks younger but in charge.

I obediently perch next to Jaishree on the arm of the
two-seater. Zahid pulls over the chair with one short leg
and sits down near me.

Narayan's gaze flicks between us. He seems very grown
up all of a sudden. 'It's bad news I'm afraid. Happened
while you both were out. There's been an accident.'

I prepare to listen but, in my heart, I fear I already know.

*

'There's been an accident,' I tell Mummy on the phone.

We have spent the night distributed between the homes of our teachers. 'But don't worry. I'm safe,' I add.

'I'll come with Daddy and we'll bring you home,' Mummy says instantly. 'What a dreadful thing to happen to that poor girl.'

'No, it's fine. I'm fine. We've got class anyway, and right now I have to be here.'

It is the first time I haven't wanted her nor longed to be at home.

I don't tell her about the horror. How the police had Revathi and me go into the bathroom to 'verify' the objects in there. We squeezed into the familiar white-tiled bathroom with its speckled grey pebblewash floor and I stared at the narrow rust stain running from the lip of the toilet to the floor. Standing by the sink, I remembered the giant cockroach that had surprised me near the drain, that first day we arrived at the house. It seemed so long ago. Then, Aditi had been in the bedroom next door. She had been fanning herself profusely and talking about Delhi being so much hotter than Madras. Now, she lay on the floor. Someone had thrown a bedcover over Aditi but I could see part of her face and the Einstein Frizz. She lay spread-eagled near the door, at an angle between the toilet and the sink, as far away from the turquoise electric water heater as it was possible to get. I glanced at the heater, staring and squat, crouching on its three short legs. I couldn't believe Aditi wouldn't stand up and say, 'I swear, it's so funny how scared you look.'

The police had asked us to 'confirm' the details.

Yes, we had agreed, this bathroom was shared by the three of us, Revathi, Aditi and Indira.

Yes, we all knew that we had to switch off the free-standing electric heater at the wall, just outside the bathroom, and unplug it before we dipped the plastic mug into the water. But it was easy to forget.

Yes, Aditi must have forgotten.

No, there is 'no unusual object' that we can see in the bathroom.

I tried not to look at her, focusing instead on the cake of soap lying near where I thought Aditi's poor hand must be under the blue and white bedcover. It was a usual object in an unusual position, on the floor when it should have been in the white scallop-shaped ceramic soap dish mounted on the wall. Her blue plastic mug stood upside down in the corner. That made it an unusual object. It should have been in her blue bucket, which was half full of water. She must have been on the point of adding hot water from the heater to the cold in the bucket. The smell of shit was strong. She must have dipped her hand into the water by mistake and when the bolts of current hit her body, she was flung across the room, losing control along the way. Perhaps she had been lost in thought. Perhaps she was dreaming of the journal.

'A rural-urban interface magazine, what do you think Indy? Good idea don't you think? They're doing it abroad but not here. Not yet. I want to have real stories, the farmer talking of his crops, the village schoolmaster about dunder-heads and Dante. I swear, it'll be so exciting, so much more fun than being at *The Times* in Madras.' I could hear her in my head. I wished she would get up.

We had to give a statement. The police officer looked at me suspiciously when I said I had been away during the 'incident', buying provisions for tomorrow's breakfast with another student, Zahid Ahmed.

'What's your connection with this Zahid Ahmed?' he asked.

'He's a housemate, a fellow student and a friend,' I said.

'Why did you go with him, not with another girl?'

'It was my turn to buy stuff. It was night and I didn't want to go alone. Everyone else was busy so Zahid came with me, as a favour.'

Revathi and I were not allowed to remove our toiletries from the bathroom but Sakina said we could share hers and it was two o'clock when we went into the cold clear night with Professor Krishnan and his wife and Namita and Sudhir.

I couldn't bear to think of Aditi in the house alone, with only a policeman outside the gate.

'They've promised they'll hand the house back tomorrow,' Professor Krishnan said grimly, 'but I don't think you all should return for a few days.'

'At least a week, *jani*,' corrected his wife. Then to us, huddled in the back of the car. 'You poor things, I can't even begin to imagine how you must feel.'

'How do you feel? Are you OK?' Mummy is asking on the phone.

I don't feel anything. 'I'm fine. Everything's fine,' I say.

'I hope you're eating all right, Indy?'

Not eating won't kill. Electricity does.

Pulao versus Curd Rice. North Indian food versus South Indian.

'You northerners eat such heavy food, Indy,' I can hear Aditi say, 'but it's *dosas* that are good for the *doshas*, the three energies that circulate in the body.'

'What a line,' I exclaimed. 'I bet you've been practising that for days. Come now, just admit it, Miss Aditi Iyer.'

'I haven't, I haven't, I swear… OK, I did think about it once or twice and roll it around on my tongue.' Her eyes were bright, she was smiling and slightly sweaty as always, whatever the weather.

We laughed so hard I had to give her my hanky for the tears.

'I'll bring back some of my mother's *dosa* mix the next time I go home,' she'd said when we stopped laughing. 'I swear it's the best. You'll love it.'

Now, it will never happen.

'Indy,' came Mummy's voice, tinny, urgent, 'are you

still there? Say something, darling.'

'I'm here, Mummy.'

'I asked if you were eating all right?'

'Yes.'

'What did you have today? Did you have some breakfast at Professor Krishnan's?'

'No, I'll get an omelette-slice or something at the
canteen.'

'Good, do that right away. And Indy?'

'Yes?'

'There are times in one's life when we think, I really
can't bear this, it's just too horrible for words. But my
darling, you'll find that things change, nothing remains
the same. Everything passes. Both the good and the bad.
This too shall pass.'

'Yes.'

It is passing.

Time. Or, at least the hours.

The funeral at the electric crematorium.

Meeting Mr and Mrs Iyer, who flew in from Madras,
their faces crumpled with grief. Aditi is their only child.
Was.

*

'I can't bear this, I've got to go,' I whisper to Jaishree,
who is sitting cross-legged on the *dhurrie* next to me at
the memorial service. It is crowded though Aditi's aunt
has a large house.

The cremation was held, as is customary, within
twenty-four hours of death. Today's service is thick
with incense and a sorrow so solid it cannot be liquefied
into tears.

The service is meant to bring together the family's
friends in Delhi and everyone else who knew her. This
means mainly her aunt and uncle's connections, the

Institute faculty and students, and *The Times*'s editor and
managing director. There is a three-paragraph story in
today's *Times*. It describes Aditi Iyer as a gifted student
of the Times Journalism Institute, which is 'sponsored by
this paper.' That's it. She will never again have a mention
in a newspaper.

I leave the house unnoticed and walk along the rows
of Jatropha that edge the road, the flowers a waxy pink.
Their long dark fiddle-shaped leaves will remain glossy
until summer when the dry hot wind breathes dust over
everything. Then, the monsoon will wash them clean.
I had never known Aditi at the height of summer or in
the season of rain. Now, I never will. Darkness blooms
inside me, where the sunshine cannot reach.

Opening extract of a novel

VANDANA SARAS

$*$

THE LAST PLACE

Twinkle twinkle little star
How I wonder what you are
Up above the world so high
Like a diamond in the sky

Twinkle twinkle little star
How I wonder what you are …

Coal tar   inside of the womb   onyx   punched eye
deserted moonlit street   swollen knocked knees
   carbon   dried menstrual blood   the opposite of
day?   At the mouth of daybreak   basket of tiger
cowries   colour of horizon line   field of Gossypium
Arboreum bulbs   lint sunlit swan-wings   walls of
chess boards   pink inside of the mouth after a savage
kiss   dandelion florets in flight   final drop skyful of
unfolding reams of organza   last flight   sandpaper
hand-stroke on the spine   down the blur of superspeed
and clouds   Freight Dump Racer falling   gauze
   'Plug in parachute.' Blue monitor beeps and displays.
   I am the first in line so I reach for the cable on my back
and hook my chute to the release panel. The man behind
me is struggling, weighted down and wheezing in short
rhythms. He looks like an out-of-shape sumo wrestler, a
museum piece, since wrestling is now banned due to the
new decency and propriety codes. He raises his arm with
the cable but it doesn't go all the way to the panel and
drops to the side, and the swaying arm-flesh flaps against
the wall. His forehead lines are filling with sweat. Circles
around the eyes resemble black curtains gathered to the
sides. He strains his nostrils open to draw in air but gets
interrupted by a cough. His teeth are outlined by what can
only be blood. Whatever he has, he won't last more than
a week. The person behind him pokes his head out and
upon meeting my eyes disappears right back, in a cobra-like
movement. I want to hook the cable for the man but I don't

know what germ family he has on his hands and I want
to stay healthy till my last moment.

I glance at the monitor – still too high – and look back
to discover that there are tears on the man's cheek. I'm
ashamed of my selfishness. There was a time when I was
a good person. I used to open doors for people, I used to
stop when someone sat lonely in the park to engage them
and listen to their stories, collecting five good deeds a day.

'You want me to hook you?' I ask.

'Huh yes uhh' – he looks down, coughing into his
chest – 'yes, please.'

I put on my gloves, take his cable and hook him to
the panel.

The monitor display beeps: 'On standby. Next stop,
Diestan.'

The last place – my soles tingling, pin-pricked, receding
inward – peace finally. I am so close.

The Racer stabilises. The monitor beeps continuously
and flashes, 'Platform opening in 3, 2, 1.' The wall sucks
in the black metal door, I step forward and a massive cloud
takes a bite out of my face. I let out an inappropriate yelp
and jump into the sky – the colour of lightning, slate and
melancholia. The sun is not visible yet and it's the perfect twilight, moist and painted with anticipation, like an
aroused body, taut and limber, pliant and singular. *'You're
so perfect. Fuck. Oh fuck!'*

I have settled into free fall: face down, hands up, arms
and legs splayed out to the sides, like an active spider, like
a flying frog, jolted and stroked by wind thrusts. The sky
has its own music and it beats on me – hissing, rustling,
thumping, slapping, shoving – from all directions. Like
when I was a baby and Mother used to lay me face down on
the towel and pour coconut oil on my back, sometimes the
buttocks, drop by drop, and then slap it all over me making
loud hollows. I used to respond with 'wa wa wa wan wa wa
wan' to each slap and rub. Sometimes, she would hum and

sing; other times she would talk to me and ask questions like, 'Do you like your rubby rubs?', 'Are you a good baby?', 'How did you become so precious, my googoooo?'

She lies in a coma now. I said goodbye but I will not go until I get the news. I am of the old world and believe that children shouldn't die before their parents. She is mostly just a–

I am tugged into a vertical position as the parachute opens in response to the timer. I look up – no entangle-ments – just smooth waves of fuchsia and peacock-green, like a kite. I pull on the strings to change direction and get a full view of the approaching ground. I want to avoid ending up in water. The entire landscape looks the same, brownish yellow: the colour of puke, or sand. Could it be? Maybe just a barren patch. I pull on the strings in the direction of a charcoal spot in the distance.

I am pulling on the strings of my kite, for the fourth straight afternoon. I have cut forty-eight kites just this week. I have discovered that there is beauty to cutting a kite and not just maths – the moment you make contact with someone's kite in the right spot, feel the tug, and seize the moment of exact pressure and speed in harmony with the wind, and cut the kite free, its owner throwing his arms down and looking in your direction, looking at his kite, roaming loose and unbound, in gentle zigzags. My hands are cut but I have the gauze on really tight, bloody in spots.

And there in the sky is the designer kite. My heart punches my chest and I am unable to blink. The kite has a shocking yellow base filled out with a pair of three-dimen-sional parrots touching beaks at the spine, which turns into two branches at the bottom for parrots' feet. It has many tails of varying lengths and colours, languishing in the sky this way and that. The kite is triple the size of an ordinary kite, mine. I want to look at the parrots kite close and hold it. I track it and see that it's coming from the rooftop of the palace house. At first, I just want to touch it with my kite so I reel in the line and bring my kite down to the plane of the designer kite. When they're close, I run backwards so it feels like my small pink kite is running past and saying hello to the regal parrots kite. But halfway through, I step on a Coca-Cola bottle and fall down, dropping the handle. The handle rolls away and sends my kite higher and farther, and by the time I grab it back, the parrots kite has crossed over and it's blocking my kite. Its owner, a boy, brings it down and I feel the contact on my string. He is heavy, choppy and blundering – like he is beating on a drum. I could come in super fast and smash into his kite, but I don't want to destroy the parrots. It would be marvellous to watch his kite for a little while as it ascends and swings down across the crisp sky at different angles to the sun, and changes its colours, and to see the tails flip up and out, like an aerated rainbow frock bottom. I wonder how it would feel to have this kite in my room.

I am hovering over the charcoal area and close to landing. It looks like the ground has been burnt. I start to paddle in the air so I won't land hard and break my ankle, an often-repeated instruction in training. In unison with the breeze, it's a smooth and flowy landing, just like I have practised many times. The chute heaves on the ground like a heap of warm paints, the only bright colours as far as the eye can see. Keeping to a habit, I move to pack the chute even though I will never need it again.

The boy releases his kite to chase mine. If they tangle, I know how it will end. I don't want that, at least not yet anyway. I drop my kite lower; if I can flatten out enough without getting caught by the wind or any of the surrounding kites, I can bring it home for a while. But the boy is determined to tussle: he comes down beastlike to stay with my line and lets his kite drop low; he's hoping for an upward wind that would loop his string around mine, tying us at the hips, which would force us to fight till death, by cutting. There are other boys with the designer kite flyer and they are prodding, laughing and jeering. Their echoes reach me through the flying oblongs of colours and hues, and expressive birds in the sky.

The sun has not appeared and the twilight seems to stretch on – dense and overbearing – like a low silvery dome on a flat stretch of wet desert. I tell my wrist computer to locate me on the map and strangely it shows that I'm surrounded by water, which I would have to cross first to get a bus to the house. I will have to blow up my umbrella into a boat. I have to leave behind my packed parachute bag after all, the bag I have carried for over 150 years. I rest it on its back and consider leaving a note, a poem perhaps. But to whom? All those dying from incurable diseases and the punishments of the Supreme State of the Religion of Peace? What would I write – A happy death to all! Or, hope you meet your maker today, or later, if that's what you want! Enjoy your death! – really, what would a dying person want to hear, what would they want? I think as I chew on a pancake pill, Masala Berry. I know what I want to hear. I don't have the right words for a note so I take one last look at the worn khaki bag with the embroidered red pockets and head towards the water.

I pace forward and almost lean over the ledge as I lower my line but I have to pull back swiftly as two kites are rising up too close from the fields. The boy pulls in and for a moment I am clear, and I am reeling in hard, but there is a brisk crosswind and with it I have looped myself around the parrots kite. The boy hammers in with laughable force, accompanied by the shouts and calls of his group. I soften the loop; he cannot cut me if I provide no resistance. The boy keeps reeling in, attempting to cut my line – the more he does that, the closer my string is to looping like a noose around the neck of his kite. He is running into it. The wind has blown my kite into a second loop and now I just want to get it over with. I get close to where his flying string connects to the bridle string and cut him.

'Ooooooh aaaaaaa aaaaaaaeeeeeeeee aayyyyyeee!'
The boys' sighs pile up in a chorus.

Their heads turn to me and go back to the parrots kite,
snaking away and away and down to land in the hands of
some lucky person. Peacocks are screaming to each other.
The kite owner runs to the rooftop ledge, huffing in my
direction. The other boys join him. The boy at the edge says
something in a low cool tone. The other boys climb onto
the ledge and crane their necks forward towards me.

'What?'

'Girl?'

'A girl!'

'Ooooh sisterfucker!'

'Cunt. Whore. Motherfucker!' the kite owner shouts,
as he beats the air down with his fists.

Opening from a novel

LEIGHTON SEER

✳

THE ANGLER'S EDGE

CHAPTER ONE

Forceps, chipped scalpel, hydrogen peroxide. Cotton pads, a needle. Sutures. Scott checked his implements, lined them up in careful right angles on the dusty metal tray. If he was going to die, he wanted to make damn sure it wasn't from an infection. The implant was just beneath the surface. Running his fingertips over the soft flesh of his inner arm he could feel it there, three inches above the crook of his elbow. Just where it always had been.

Warm light poured between the broken blinds of the room's only window. Golden hour. Soon the hospital would be washed in darkness, but he hoped to be long gone by then. He pulled the cart on rusting wheels toward the window and tried to draw courage from the light. He was sapped already. The sky had still been black when he'd left that morning. Hours of walking red-soil back roads had left him drained, and now his tongue was sticking to the roof of his mouth. He could've used some water. Hell, he could've used a Jack and Coke and a little siesta, but it wasn't like he had a whole lot of time. Two more days and he'd be dead.

He sank onto a stool, air hissing through the seat's cracked vinyl cover. First things first. He poured peroxide over a cotton pad. The chemical stench of it filled the room – one whiff and, nostrils stinging, he felt sharper, more awake. Resting his forearm veins-up against his knee, he pressed the soaked cotton to his skin and swiped downward. He straightened out his leg, leaning to the right to fish in his pocket. Steel rattled against steel as he slammed the crumpled scrap of paper down beside his scavenged instruments. From the shadows, someone grunted beneath a pile of unwashed sheets. Scott spared a brief glance. It was a squatter, bedraggled and grey. He cursed Scott and turned over on the examination table. Let him be bothered, Scott thought. Squatters had set up camp in every corner of the building – there was no place else.

With his left hand Scott tried to flatten the paper. He had read the instructions twenty times already, but could afford no mistakes. Torn from the back of an old employee handbook, the scrap had small, crowded scratches of dark ink. Hunched over it, he read:

1-inch incisions. Peel the skin back – need to see. Lift bottom end – DO NOT PULL – cut wire close to casing. Grasp with forceps – GENTLY – DO NOT CRUSH – 5 sec. before release.

No room for failure. First Genners had developed the process through fatal trial and error. Casualties were nine out of ten. Success rates had seen modest growth for implant-dodgers in the intervening Generations. As a Fifth Genner, Scott figured he had a one-in-four shot. Low odds, but if things didn't go well he was only losing two days. That was almost a comfort.

He had hoped to find some topical anaesthetic in one of the drawers, but anything that might help with the pain had been picked over and pocketed long ago. He counted himself damn lucky to have found the peroxide and poured out a generous measure to clean the scalpel. And then there was nothing left to do but get on with it. The implant had to come out today. When the collectors showed up to take his body to the Disposal Centre and didn't find him, they would come looking. He needed to get to the docks and onto *The Angler's Edge* before the authorities got involved.

Palms slick with sweat, he adjusted his grip on the scalpel and poised it above his flesh. Muscles tight, eyes unblinking, he brought down the blade to make the first incision – across, clean but painful. Blood flowered from the cut, thick and fresh. He realised he'd been holding his breath when he gasped and choked on a great lungful. Heartbeat in his ears, a persistent thrum, he set his jaw, tried to steady his hand.

'Two more,' he growled through his molars. 'Just two.'

But when the blade didn't come down, he lifted his hand to wipe away the anxiety beaded on his forehead. It was one thing to make plans, to imagine taking control. It was another thing entirely to be there, really there, ripping his arm open and going on the run. But if the alternative was dying 'peacefully' at home against his will, he had to take the chance.

Neither of his parents had any faith in his escape. His father believed in the programme, thought thirty years on this earth was time enough. Most people who felt that way were just like his father, too old to be affected. The old man was closing in on seventy-six, now – he'd been forty years old when the programme had gone into effect. Scott's mother at least understood his need to try. Still, she would've preferred to hold her only son in her arms the morning the toxins were released. A grim celebration. As it stood, he'd be spending his birthday huddled with strangers in a cargo hold. Strangers like him, born the unlucky baby in three, the wrong number in the queue. Strangers who had managed to cut out their own implants and run.

Or he might end up another dead man in a disused hospital.

He brought the scalpel down quick, hoping to make the next cut before his brain had time to react. But he wasn't left-handed and in white-knuckled haste his downward slice had gone too deep. Too long. Jagged. A strangled groan tore through his throat. Pain blossomed in his mind like something precious and tender. Blinded by misery, he found the final cut easier to make.

Lifting the skin – peeling it back – was worse still. He was soft. Not like his father, who still worked every day repairing heavy machinery. Scott had spent his entire adult life in a phone bank with an auto-dialler and a multi-step script for slinging diet pills. People – a lucky two-thirds of them, anyway – might be living past a hundred, but they were still vain. Fourteen billion people clogging up the earth and they were worrying about the same old shit. So maybe the worst he had to deal with was a dissatisfied customer, or a high-pitched rant about being interrupted during dinner. Nothing like this.

Loose skin, too much blood, and worst of all the exposed tissue. He retched, eyes shut so tightly they began to water. Not for the first time, he wondered if he would be able to pull this off. His father hadn't thought so. *There are worse things than knowing when you're gonna die*, he'd said. *Like dying alone miles from home.*

With all the willpower he could muster, Scott forced himself to look at his arm and assess the situation. The implant was easier to see and smaller than he'd expected. A centimetre long and less than half that across.

In the early days, when the programme was only a proposal, the International Committee on the Crisis of Overpopulation had put the focus on the humane process by which they would 'release' individuals selected randomly for implantation at birth. The toxins would be completely painless – like going to sleep, they said. Even the hard core of religious conservatives, so strong in the States, had posed no opposition. After all, no one was being asked to kill his or her children. Every infant would be given a chance. One in three would simply be given a much shorter chance.

Placing the tip of the scalpel against the bottom of the implant, Scott willed his hand not to shake. A steady breath, a count to three, and he pressed the tip down at an angle. If it stung he didn't know it. With a layer of his flesh peeled back like the tart skin of an apple, all pain melted together. Even the moist, heavy hospital air dug into the wound, unbearable. Behind thinly pressed lips he gave a low whine. The moment he lifted the bottom of the implant he could feel the wire attached to the back of its casing. It tugged deep within his arm, as though a part of his muscle.

He lifted his finger off the handle and used it to hold up the end of the implant. Once the wire was cut, he would have five seconds to remove the implant before the toxins released. After that, game over. He needed to do this quickly. *Bite the bullet*, already, his father would've said.

From the corner came a dry, ear-splitting cough. Scott's shoulders jumped. His eyes snapped shut, every nerve stretched taut. Instinctively, he gripped tighter to the scalpel. The wire snagged on a chip in the blade and twinged within, all the way down to his elbow. One swift jerk of the wrist and the wire snapped. He felt the tension release and his stomach turn to water.

There wasn't enough time to panic. The blade fell from his grasp and skittered across the floor. Left hand scrabbling blindly around the tray, he snatched up the forceps. How many seconds had passed? Two? Three? His hands trembled so violently he missed the first pass at the implant and pinched the exposed tissue. High and clear, ringing off the linoleum floor, the scream seemed too distant to be his own.

'Christ almighty! Get on with it, would you?' the squatter grumbled, kicking his legs under the mountain of piss-soaked sheets.

Scott fumbled with the forceps, realigning the clamps. Three seconds? Four? His entire body shook – with nerves or from poison, he didn't know. A quick pinch and he caught the implant, yanked it upward. All the fanfare he received for the effort was a milky squelch.

His anxious grasp had been too firm. Held over his mangled arm, the implant cracked and began to weep. One toxic bead, crystalline, beautiful in its way, fell into the open wound. Raw terror ripped through his gut. He hurled the forceps over his shoulder, heard them shatter the window. Glass rained down his back, the implant lost among the shards.

He sprang to his feet. Blood rushed to his head, stars

erupting in his eyes. He swiped at the tray, groping for the peroxide. Maybe he could wash the toxins out. Flicking the cap off with his thumb, he upended the bottle. A river of agony flowed from its mouth, white bubbles fizzing on the wound. It had only been a drop, just one drop.

But you're so soft.

Erratic, racing, his heart threatened to crack open his sternum. He forced himself to breathe. He seemed no worse off than he'd been a minute ago. Not yet. Casting aside the empty bottle, he lifted the dangling flap of skin barehanded and, with a rasping groan, flipped it back into place. It would have to be sewn shut, but he needed a moment. Just a moment to catch his breath. To think.

Carving himself open like a honeyed ham had been difficult enough. How was he going to stitch himself up left-handed? His fingers weren't that nimble, and he didn't think his grimy companion in the corner would do much better. Scott plucked the needle from the tray and held it up, the dying sun glittering off the point. It began to bend and sway before his eyes.

Warmth spread through his blood. He thought the pain was finally ebbing. In fact, he could hardly feel a thing. His entire body was like static, tingling, his limbs curiously light. His head began to spin, the edges of his vision blurring.

'No... N-no...' The words clung to his lips like syrup. Scott threw his hands out, grabbing for the cart. Its wheels gave a half-hearted whine and rolled out from under him. He knew it was over. His father had been right, dying alone was worse. He crashed into something warm and musty. It pushed back. His knees buckled.

AVANI SHAH

✳

WE ARE THOSE LIONS

THE OTHERS FOLLOW Papa through the gravestones towards the crematorium. Their tunics billow around their ankles. As I squint in the glaring sunlight, their figures flicker in my vision, half here, half somewhere else, like they're made of shadow.

'Hurry up!' Namisha shouts. She and Neha wait for me while MamaPapa go ahead.

When I fall into step, Namisha points at a large shell-pink headstone with three roses in a small vase at its base. 'Look at the dates.'

I peer at the letters:

IN

LOVING MEMORY

OF

ELIZABETH MARTHA BANKS
02.07.1968 – 04.04.1974
*
AMY MAUD BANKS
23.06.1970 – 04.04.1974
*
SARAH SHIRLEY BANKS
07.12.1972 – 04.04.1974
*

BELOVED DAUGHTERS
STOLEN TOO SOON

'What do you think happened to them?' I ask.

Namisha spins around to look at me. The beginning of a smirk plays on the corners of her lips. 'Maybe,' she says, 'maybe they were *murdered*.'

'God. What's wrong with you?' Neha scrunches the end of her dupatta in her hand.

Namisha can't hide the smirk any longer. 'How else do you explain the fact they all died on the same day?'

'A hundred ways! A fire. A car crash.'

'Drowning,' I offer.

'Exactly. It could have been any number of terrible accidents.'

'Say what you want. You know I'm right.' Namisha winks at me. 'You know what probably happened, Neha? Their mother probably smothered them in their sleep – no, wait! She probably strangled them with their own braids. Just imagine it. Your own mother is brushing your lovely long hair for you, twisting it into beautiful blonde braids and then –!'

Neha shoves her. 'Shut up!' She shudders and marches ahead.

'Hey Neha,' Namisha calls. Neha doesn't turn but I can tell she's heard because she stiffens. 'Neha! See that chimney? That's where the smoke comes out when they burn the bodies. You're not just walking on dead people, you're probably breathing them in too.'

Neha starts walking even faster.

The area around the crematorium is fenced off and on the other side there are rows of shrubs instead of graves. On some of the plant pots, metal plaques glint in the sunshine. I look back for the pink headstone: the inside-of-shell colour, the gold lettering, the three roses. I wonder what actually *did* happen to those little girls. The air is full of sound: the rustle of leaves in the breeze, buzzing insects, birds whistling and squawking out of sight somewhere. A blade of grass that's got caught in my chappal prickles against my little toe. A grey squirrel hops from one headstone to the next. I didn't expect this place to be so alive.

'Come on.' Namisha pulls me by the elbow.

Inside, there's an overwhelming floral smell, like someone has tried to mask something much worse. Mama is waiting on a brown settee while Neha hovers in front of a large noticeboard and looks at the overlapping leaflets. Papa paces. After a while, he stops in front of the only door, lifts his fist to knock, and then changes his mind. He looks at his watch.

Eventually, we hear footsteps, then voices. A man in a tweed jacket slopes out.

'Excuse me!' Namisha jumps up before anyone else can speak. She's using her most-English English accent, her voice much higher than when she talks to us. 'Is there a lavatory I could use?'

'Of course,' the man says. He points through the door behind him.

Neha gets to her feet too. 'Coming?' she asks me.

I shake my head and she narrows her eyes for some reason, then shrugs.

'I'm Mr Thompson,' the man says when they've gone. He extends a hand to Papa, who shakes it. 'My deepest sympathies for your loss.'

I wait for MamaPapa to reply, but neither of them do. They just stand there awkwardly, shuffling from one foot to the other, staring at their chappals. And now Neha's narrowed eyes make sense. She was trying to warn me. Because how many times has this happened before? I imagine her and Namisha giggling away over the sinks, running the taps to cover their conversation:

'It's not as if MamaPapa don't speak English.'

'And anyway ours is just as bad as theirs.'

'Plus how do they expect to get any better if they don't ever practise? Even at the factory, it's Gujarati Gujarati Gujarati all day long. Imagine if I did that at school.'

I consider changing my mind, saying, 'Actually I think I *will* go to the lav' in my best English accent and waiting to see what MamaPapa do, see if they'll just stand there in silence until one of us comes back. But before I can, Papa says, 'Naina, ask him how this is going to work,' and then Mr Thompson veers round to look at me too, and I watch his eyes change – widen for a second – as the penny drops.

'Oh,' he says, his voice slower, which makes sense, but also louder, which doesn't. 'I understand. No English, right? NO ENGLISH.'

'My father says thank you for your condolences.' I'm not sure if I've pronounced the word properly but Mr Thompson doesn't comment. 'My parents are wondering what –'

'Not to worry, not to worry,' he says. 'I'll show you what's what, and then you can pass it on to them, yes? And I'm sorry about your grandma, love,' he adds. I don't bother to correct him.

In the next room, there are three rows of benches, separated down the middle by an aisle. There must be space for about fifty people, sixty at a push – if we were in Eldoret, people would have to stand, they would end up spilling out onto the gravestones. On the other side of the room, a younger man moves from window to window opening all the curtains. He smiles when he sees me looking at him. I wish I wasn't wearing this stupid outfit.

'We're getting more and more services like this, you know?' Mr Thompson tells me. I nod vaguely and watch the younger man finish with the curtains and begin dragging a broom across the wooden floor. 'Two or three so far this year, can you believe it?' Mr Thompson continues. 'I'll show you the layout of the place, and then once everyone arrives, and it all gets started, we'll leave you alone for half an hour or so, so you can do your prayers and whatnot. And then, when you're ready, Charlie –' he points at the young man, who waves '– Charlie over there'll come through and see to the cremation, OK?'

I relay the information back to MamaPapa.

'Are we allowed to be there when the body goes in?' Papa asks.

I'm umming and erring, trying to work out what the English word for 'furnace' is and wondering how long a fake wee can possibly take, when Mama – in English – calls, 'No, wait!' She moves towards Charlie, who's now at the front of the room lifting a large gold crucifix from a long table covered with a green cloth. 'Please, stop.'

Charlie holds up the cross to see if it's what Mama's talking about. She gestures for him to put it back down.

'All gods deserve respect,' Mama says to me in Gujarati. Savitaauntie's mantra.

Tears pool in her eyes and as I watch her blink them back, the corners of my eyes prickle too. I list Savitaauntie's other favourite sayings in my head: 'There's no such thing as yours and mine. Family and community first. Show respect to young and old alike.'

Charlie looks at us like we're crazy. I think about staring him straight in the eye, with a hand on my hip, and saying, 'Jesus was Indian, didn't you know?' like my old schoolfriend Puja's uncle used to shout at people in the street whenever he'd had too many whiskys. But then Charlie just nods and puts the cross back down, and he doesn't mutter anything under his breath. Not like people usually do.

*

We all wait for the coffin in that rare kind of not-quite silence where no one wants to say anything or even has anything to say. The men are on one side of the aisle and the women on the other, except the white couple who sit together on the men's side. Everyone fidgets.

The clock on the back wall seems to tick louder and louder with every second. I don't know what to expect, how funerals are supposed to go. The only thing I remember from when Dadi died is how Puja's uncle kept burping during Navkar Mantra and everyone pretended not to notice.

Too-loud thoughts rattle about in my head. Not full thoughts, but strange half-formed what-ifs with horrible endings. I try to focus on the clock, but the ticking seems to be speeding up. My thoughts rattle faster with it.

I force myself to notice how the green tablecloth hangs lower on one side of the table than on the other, how it's bunched up in five, six, seven creases that ripple out from around the gold crucifix. My neck begins to itch. I want to look behind me, see what the white couple are doing, what they make of all this. Namisha's words from this morning ring in my head: *Why are there so many people we don't know here?*

The electric lights are too bright. I wipe my forehead with my dupatta. The benches creak as people sit down.

Savitaauntie's supposed to be ours, not theirs. She's the one who looked after us when MamaPapa were busy at the shop. She's the one who planted the guava tree with us after Dadi died. She's the one who tied Namisha and Neha together until they stopped fighting.

People start standing up. My legs move automatically. Jayanuncle and Papa lead the procession, carrying the coffin on either side. Three uncles I recognise from earlier follow, and then right at the back, balancing the weight, is a white man in a suit. Charlie.

The coffin looks smaller now that it's closed. I don't quite believe Savitaauntie's inside. What if she can't breathe? What if she wants to get out? What if this is all a terrible mistake and we're about to burn her alive? I bow my head so I don't have to look anymore.

Then, to my surprise, Neha steps out into the aisle. Everyone stops. What is she doing? I try to catch her eye. Namisha reaches out for her hand. 'It's OK,' we silently tell her, 'we're here for you. We'll get through this together.' But she doesn't come back.

Everyone is staring at her. Even Jayanuncle looks confused.

'Neha,' Mama whispers, a mixture of worry and embarrassment knotting in her eyebrows. 'Beta?'

Neha takes a deep breath, swallows, and then walks back up the aisle towards the coffin.

Namisha looks at me, her lip between her teeth. I know she's wondering if she should leave too, if she should skirt around the room and check that Neha is OK. But then we realise what's happening. Neha isn't fleeing at all. She whispers something to Charlie, who moves out of the way, and then she – Neha of all people – takes his place.

I wait for something to happen. For someone, MamaPapa, Jayanuncle, for *anyone* to object, but no one does. Neha holds her chin up high, and stares straight ahead. For a few seconds no one even breathes. Then Jayanuncle nods and they all step forward together.

Behind me, a wobbly voice starts singing Navkar Mantra, then another one joins in, and then Namisha, who's refused to sing prayers since we left Eldoret, begins singing the loudest of all.

Opening of a novel set in
a future virtual reality

RADHA SMITH

✳

VALLEY RESURRECT

IT'S SUNDOWN HERE, in the desert ranges beyond Mortal's Leap. I'm camping in the lee of a dune, done for the day. Same as always, nothing found, and trekking's got me beat. I've got my old canvas slung on its poles and my blanket spread over the sand. Not that it makes a difference: in seven weeks the desert's settled in every crease of my skin and crimp of my braids.

And still, no sign of Sass. Every day just like the last. Searching from dawn, westward with the wind that tells me nothing, and erases my trail as I go. It's only the tracker on my portaterm screen that tells me I'm not moving in circles. I'm tracing a grid, deeper and deeper into empty land. Each day it gets harder to believe I'll actually find her, but easier to imagine I'm seeing her: off in the distance, striding on the ridge of some dune, falling away over the lip when the sun shifts in the sky. And her voice, grazing me in gusts: scraps of a song that's familiar, that I can never catch. I know those illusions now; know not to let them throw me off my course.

But when I stop for the day I wonder – would I recognise her now if she were really there? Would I know her from a trick of the heat?

I take a handful of sand and let it fall onto my blanket in a mound.

The heat swimming over the desert like a fever. Warping my thoughts, making me doubt and forget. My shelter's scant shade does nothing to ease it. Only the night gives some relief, and I'm desperate for it to spill.

But it's not coming as it should.

The sun's not sinking. It's jamming on its way down. Blazing brighter and brighter, smearing a red zig-zag as it jerks and skates over the horizon. All around it the whole sky's pixelating yellow and black. Everything's wrecking and flickering, making me squint.

I take my slingshot and put a stone in the elastic; let fire. It flies fast, arcs over the slope of the next dune, and then snags and stalls: just hangs there in mid-air, doesn't budge. I fire another stone; it does the same. Another and another. A constellation of puny, thwarted missiles pinned under the ruining sky.

Yesterday's sunset came broken, too. I didn't report it; put it down to a random glitch. This far out in the wild-lands, that sort of thing can happen. But this business with the stones – it's new. I've never seen anything like it. I doubt Jojo has either, and I hope he doesn't detect it now. I stare at my portaterm: will it not to buzz.

Of course it goes just as I'm looking. The screen blink-ing green for the first time in days.

[19:36] <Mission Command> *G, how's the search?*

I let the text flash for a minute, send another stone flying, watch it lodge in the air just beyond the others.

The usual, I type. *Zilch.*

[19:43] <Mission Command> *You getting any limb freezes, mind freezes? How's your power feeling?*

Here it comes. I put my slingshot back in my belt. Get ready to calm him down.

[19:44] <GoblenGirl> *No, I'm fine.*

[19:45] <Mission Command> *Because the charts for your zone are going haywire.*

If there's one thing that Jojo can't take, it's the charts going haywire.

[19:45] <GoblenGirl> *I'm OK, thanks for checking.*

[19:46] <Mission Command> *Good, but listen, I'm getting some major malfunction alerts.*

[19:46] <Mission Command> *I'm recalling you.*

[19:47] <GoblenGirl> *What?*

[19:47] <Mission Command> *Right now.*

Sin of a mortal.

[19:48] <GoblenGirl> *No need to overreact, Jojo. Just a couple of little glitches out here.*

[19:48] <Mission Command> *So you can see it?*

[19:48] <GoblenGirl> *Sunset's being a bit jumpy is all.*

Happened last night and today was fine.

[19:48] <Mission Command> *It happened last night and you didn't report it?*

I realise my miscalculation.

[19:50] <Mission Command> *It happened last night and you didn't report it?*

[19:53] <GoblenGirl> *Like I said, everything was fine today.*

[19:53] <Mission Command> *It's part of your assignment to report these things. This is serious, Goblen.*

[19:53] <Mission Command> *We can't have you out there when things are freezing and malfunctioning. What if you corrupted?*

[19:53] <Mission Command> *We're going to talk about this when you get back.*

[19:53] <GoblenGirl> *I'm not ditching Sass, Jojo.*

[19:53] <Mission Command> *Yes, you are.*

[19:54] <Mission Command> *I've let you stay out there way too long.*

[19:54] <Mission Command> *From what I'm seeing on the charts, even if Sass is still out there, she's probably corrupted.*

[19:54] <Mission Command> *And I'm not letting the same thing happen to you.*

I chuck my portaterm into the sand.

It buzzes at me.

Buzzes again.

[19:55] <Mission Command> *Do I have to remind you who's in charge here? Don't think you have special privileges.*

[19:58] <GoblenGirl> *You're actually giving me that line?*

[19:59] <Mission Command> *Really don't push it, Goblen.*

[20:00] <Mission Command> *Also the situation's changing in the Valley. I need you back here on something else.*

The sky flickers and I look up; see the stones I launched thumping down on the slope of the next dune. Night finally flashes in, black and cool. My portaterm flashes again, too: the recall command, and Jojo's sign-off.

I walk out from under my shelter, yank the canvas off its poles, and hold it to my chest with both hands. Up above in the sky, neither the stars nor the moon have appeared. The only light's the green glow of my portaterm screen. It illuminates just the small patch of sand where it's lying, and about half of my canvas, and half of my body. I watch the seconds on the recall command tick down:

15-14-13-

I curse this desert that's given me nothing.

Curse my twin brother being Mission Commander.

Curse myself not finding her.

The seconds go to 1.

And I feel myself disintegrate.

An excerpt from a short story

TAYMOUR SOOMRO

＊

A SUBLIME PORT

I START FORGETTING things. I think at least I
remember that I'm forgetting but sometimes I don't so I
keep a list. I note the consequences because I think that may
provide an incentive for me to remember in the future. So:

Forgot: to wear sash.
Consequence: beaten on soles of feet and pay docked for
three days as couldn't work.
Forgot: to salute the Valide Sultan when she returned to
the palace after an excursion to the Sweet Waters of Asia.
Consequence: beaten on the backs of knees with cane and
pay docked for two days for insolence.
Forgot: words and motions of midday prayer.
Consequence: no one noticed as initially forgot prayer
time and so was at back of congregation. Punishment in
afterlife of course – beg forgiveness from Almighty.

The man who sleeps beside me – an Assyrian with sad
eyes and a handsome face that condemns him to the most
menial jobs in the palace – provides me with useful prompts
when he sees me.

'What should you be remembering right now?'

'To have lunch.'

'To deliver the note in your hand –' (here he taps the
package by my side) 'to the Sultana that the Master of the
Robes gave you only minutes ago. Then lunch.'

I never forget lunch I think. Especially on the days
we have aubergine and pilav.

An important doctor comes to see one of the Sultan's
mistresses, a Venetian princess who was abducted by
a corsair when a child, and sold to the Sultan.

On such a visit, procedure requires us to assemble in
rows between which the doctor may pass into the harem
without seeing the sick woman. She inserts a hand through
a gap between two of us for the doctor to inspect. He is
not permitted to speak in her presence and so, outside the
Chamber of Favoured Women, he provides her prescription – invariably a sherbet of some sort.

On this occasion, in error I wear a ceremonial hat in place of a turban. The doctor assumes I am senior and gives me the Venetian's prescription. I take the opportunity to tell him about my forgetting.

'Impossibly common,' he says squinting into his eye-glasses. 'Of course, I remember everything. Seven almonds with breakfast every morning. And a sherbet of roses and another ingredient.'

The Assyrian continues in his efforts to help me. He whispers as we lie on our mats looking up at the tiled ceiling in the dim light of the moon and stars late at night.

'What is your name?'

'They gave me the name of a flower,' I say.

'Rosebud,' he says. 'What is my name, Rosebud?'

'You are the Assyrian with the sad eyes.'

'I am Egyptian,' he says. 'Do I have sad eyes?'

On another occasion, 'What is the year?'

'1087.'

'1089!'

'What is the name of the Sultan?' This question very softly.

'His Sacred and Imperial Majesty, Sovereign of the Sublime House of Osman, Sultan of Sultans, Khan of Khans, Commander of the Faithful and Successor of the Prophet of the Lord of the Universe –'

'Mehmet the Fourth,' he says.

He asks me about my life before the palace and when I can't remember a moment, I ask about his. 'I've told you,' he says. 'How many times we lay beneath this starry ceiling, and talked of our villages, our parents, our livestock, our journeys here.'

A bird sings outside and I say suddenly, 'I remember that!'

'What?' he says.

But there are no trees and the bird flies away. 'I don't know,' I say.

He continues, 'My name before I came here was
Kekkol. I was the seventh child in my family and my
father sold me for what would be twenty Aspers today,
not enough to buy a barren goat. I went by boat up the Nile
and then from Grand Cairo to Alexandria at the back of
a camel train. I was auctioned to a man who brought me
to the Sublime Porte and here they paid three hundred
Aspers for me.'

'But what do you remember?' I ask him.

'I remember the smell of a man who was sick and died
in our boat. It was a smell that knotted itself deep down the
back of the throat. And when they tossed his body out, he
floated away on the currents, not even food for crocodiles.
I remember,' he continues, 'that the sand when they buried
me up to my neck burned at the surface but was cold beneath. I remember a dish my sister made of curdled camel's
milk sweetened with the sap from a date palm. It coated
the tongue like a fur.' He makes a noise – *tchanp* – with his
tongue against the roof of his mouth. 'I remember the heat
of my mother's stomach against my forehead.'

My problem becomes public knowledge in our community of servants. Nonetheless, I am promoted. My face
is my fortune – 'The ugliest in the Kingdom,' the Master
of the Robes says when he tells me I'll be moving from the
Carriage Gate to the Baths.

'But the women,' I say, 'they're cunning and clever.'

'If they ask for gourds or radishes, slice them before
serving.' He has a cruel laugh and dark gums slick with spit.
'There's only one Sultan and he's too few to service
them all.'

I have a new uniform – a sash of stiff red silk with
a waistcoat in the same fabric over my tunic and trousers.
My hat is of green velvet embroidered with birds and vines
in golden thread.

I serve in the final room of the Baths, where the women
come after they have been steamed and washed and

a lump of dead skin the size of a pomelo has been scrubbed off their blushing bodies in the tepidarium. Then they emerge into a bright, carpeted room with a vaulted ceiling. Cushioned divans are arranged around it and a fountain of spurting marble pinecones gurgles in the centre. It is said that the water cascading from one basin to the next masks the sounds of voices so the women may gossip freely. Some of them sing, some dance and some play the flute or tanbur. They drink coffee perfumed with cloves and cinnamon, and sherbet made of violets and scented with ambergris, and eat sesame halva and talk. I am the only servant of my kind there and spend my days running between the kitchens and the Baths, without time to forget.

One afternoon, the room empties and only one woman remains. She is a Circassian with breasts that swell like full skins of wine and a complexion as smooth as feta.

She kicks off her high pattens and sprawls across the divan. Her muslin chemise barely covers her. In the tremulous curve of her lips and set of her jaw there is something desperate and familiar. At intervals, she reaches across to a crystal narghile and puffs at its mouthpiece. A Nubian girl behind her braids her hair with pearls.

I stand to attention by the cascading fountain. The light through the wrought-iron grilles over the high windows casts a shadow of scrolls and curlicues across her legs, which are thick like marrows.

'There was a comet last night,' she says to her girl. 'It left a trail in the sky the shape of a sword.'

The girl nods and says, removing a sharp hairpin from her mouth, 'The Sultan's enemies will be cut down.'

At one point, I realise the Circassian is signalling to me. 'You don't see me or hear me,' she says as I come closer. 'As though I'm nothing.'

'I'm old and forgetful,' I say.

'Who knows how old you people are. You could be ancient or a child.' She asks for coffee and melon and after

I set a tray beside her, she says, 'Don't stand so far,' and waves at a place by her Nubian, close enough that a plait of her hair falls across my hand as her girl flicks it into an arrangement.

The Circassian pays no attention to the tray I have set down and the snow scattered across the slices of melon melts into a soup that wobbles at the rim of the dish. From the steaming finjan of coffee, the fragrance of cloves and cinnamon creeps across her body, dips between the darting fingers of her servant and curls about my head. She enters into a discussion with the Nubian about a perfume that should be applied to her and her servant girl disappears into a side chamber.

The glass in the windows of the vaulted ceiling is stained amber and softens the light in the room. I hear someone singing a song I know about a beautiful boy who becomes a fish. The scales of the fish are silken but the fishboy can't find a mate because there are no others like him. The tune takes me to a yellow field of trees and I see red goats sitting in the branches.

She whips around, the heel of her hand pushing mine away. 'What did you do?' She jabs one knee into the divan and props the other foot against the ground.

'Nothing,' I say. 'I did nothing,'

'You put your hand on me.' She pulls her chemise closed.

I look at my hand and then at her and at my hand again.

'You touched me,' she says and raises a pointed finger. 'You touched me.' She taps with that finger against the swell of her breast. 'They will hang you from the hooks in Eminonu.' Her mouth glows crimson when she speaks and she sprays flecks of spit like crystals.

'No,' I say. 'No no no.'

'They will break the joints of your body with a hammer. They will strangle you and toss you into the Bosphorus.'

She looks at me and I think, *this is it. This is really it.*

I think, *this is it and I don't remember any of it.* I want suddenly to go home but I don't know where that is.

She is shaking her head and pursing her lips. 'People like you. The Sultan trusts you with what's most valuable.'

'Forgive me,' I say. 'Princess –' though of course she isn't one '– forgive me.'

'It's not for me to forgive,' she says.

My legs give way and I fall against the back of the divan.

Then she says, and her tone has changed, 'If you did something for me, I might.'

'What can I do?' I say.

'For something simple, I could forget,' she says.

I think, *This is nothing. This is a game. This is the snake and the civet.* My skin becomes hot and it seems as though a long time is passing. I look up and see that the Circassian's servant has returned with a cloth bag. She takes the bag from her servant and speaks some words softly, whereupon the girl leaves again. The Circassian removes from the bag a letter wrapped in an embroidered cloth. She gives the letter to me and then describes to me an area in the palace grounds. I tell her I may not go there without the Sultana's permission, and she says, 'Everyone knows you forget things. You could have forgotten.'

She walks away and I say, 'I could forget to deliver your letter.' I am only speaking my fears aloud.

She pauses and, with her back to me, says, 'Think of the hooks in Eminonu. Think of the Bostanci's hammer.' Then she taps her sharp nail against a marble column several times and leaves.

I stop in the walkway outside and lean against the gritty marble baluster. The sun slices through the arches, piercing the shade with hot blades of light. *I might as well be dead,* I think, *for the fool I've become.* Then, *What is death but another room in this house?* Then, *Can I remember being held?*

LAURA TOPHAM

✳

THE RED CASTLE

MARY STRODE DOWN the dirt path, her long skirt
swinging in time with her step. The steep descent of the
gardens quickened her feet until she was almost running
away from the house, stopped only by the sudden flatness
of the sunlit bottom lawn. Once beyond the water fountain,
Mary lay down on the grass. Cold seeped into her head and
wet leaves tickled her cheeks. The ground smelled damp
and fresh; she inhaled it like a curative.

When her breathing had quietened she propped herself
up on her elbows and surveyed her home: *Y castell coch*. The
red castle. It sat above her on a small hill, its windows rows
of glinting mirrors, the bricks between the panes like bars
across them. From here, the lowest part of the gardens, the
building was one vast crimson wall erupting into the sky,
a defiance in brick daring someone to come, to conquer.

She wished someone would come. They needn't even
scale the sides; she would open the gates for them. Not
the king of course, never Charles; not on anyone would
she wish that. Mary lay back, squinting in the bright April
sunshine but determined to look at the sky. If she could see
only a blank expanse of blue, she could be anywhere. Beside
her, water gurgled up through the stone fountain and fell
over the sides, an endless patter of droplets smashing back
into the pond. Mary could hear nothing else over the noise;
she would never hear them calling from here – and couldn't
be blamed if she didn't know she was needed.

She studied the top of the bank to see if anyone was out
looking for her and it was then that she noticed her younger
sister. Lucy was standing at the top of the cliff, to the left
of the house, with her hands together. She appeared to
be praying.

Even from where she lay, Mary could make out Lucy's
body, flat and little despite the wide pleats of her sleeves
and the full expanse of her long gown. She was five years
younger than Mary, having only just turned eleven, and still
had a child's shape. Her long blonde hair, which she always

insisted be plaited, was pulled back into a knot, and her salmon-pink gown was open over her stays and petticoat.

As Mary watched, Lucy lifted her hem and kneeled down on the muddy path that ran along the top of the hill. A sharp incline dropped away from the path. On one side, down which Mary had just come, terraces had recently been hewn into the rock. The other side, directly below Lucy, remained dirt and weeds. It was more a steep mound than a cliff, though they used to call it a cliff when they played, when they told each other frightening stories of what might happen if they ever slipped over the edge. From her spot on the bottom lawn Mary could discern the full extent of the drop, that it matched the height of all four storeys of the castle, including its turrets and crenellations.

Mary sat up so that she could see her sister more clearly. Lucy had her head bowed, though she kept glancing back over her shoulder at the arched entrance to the courtyard. Lucy should not be out of the house, not be kneeling in the mud, not away from her nurse – and her agitated turns told Mary that she knew it. Yet here she was, Mary's perversely polite and rule-abiding little sister, run away from her room. This was, thought Mary, possibly the first naughty thing Lucy had ever done in her life – and it was a sad indictment of her personality that this disobedience only amounted to praying outside.

Transfixed, Mary left her hiding place behind the fountain and began to creep forwards for a better view. She kept close to the laurel bushes that bordered the lawn, though the triumph of seeing Lucy get told off would certainly be worth her own discovery. Mary had travelled not half the length of the hedge when Lucy suddenly flung her head back, stood up and stepped closer to the edge. She seemed to be testing the ground with her shoe, pressing down tentatively then taking another step forwards.

Mary went to shout but realised she had both hands clasped across her mouth. She stared upwards, motionless, too fearful to move or speak lest she startle her sister into slipping. For a moment she thought she felt Lucy's terror, felt an affinity for her strange, severe sibling for the first time.

Then Lucy jumped.

Her tiny body tumbled down the bank, bouncing on uneven ground, slowing in the longer grass then rolling like a log on the sheared greenery. Her head was a blur of peach and cream. The bun unfastened and the braid flapped around her skull like a rope. Mary saw one mule come off; it skipped a few feet then stopped on a rock, its gold brocade a jewel among the stones. But Lucy continued down the hill, her one white stockinged foot now a recurring flash of light at the end of her tiny turning frame.

Only when the body stopped at the bottom of the slope did Mary find she could move again. She ran across the lawn towards her sister, shouting 'Lucy, Lucy, Lucy,' almost crying, as close to crying as she ever came, and it was the sound of her own voice that awoke her to what terrified her most: the silence, the lack of screams, that Lucy hadn't uttered one wail of complaint.

'Lucy! Lucy!' Mary screamed, but the heap of material did not move.

She dived onto her knees next to her sister and pulled Lucy's shift and petticoats back down and her hair away from her face. One cheek was grazed, a rash of pink lines and peeling white skin, and long scratches ran along her jawline.

'Lucy?' Mary shook her shoulders.

Lucy's eyes opened.

'Are you hurt?' said Mary.

Lucy smiled.

'Lucy?' said Mary. 'Speak to me. Have you been hurt?'

When she still made no sound Mary slapped her un-grazed cheek.

'Stop it!' squealed Lucy. 'What are you doing? Leave

me alone, I need to be on my own.'

Mary crouched back onto her ankles, trying to understand. 'Aren't you injured? You fell off the cliff!'

'You would think I was, wouldn't you?' said Lucy. 'Did you see how I tumbled?'

'I was terrified. You fell like a little doll.'

'But look, all of my limbs are intact.' She slid her arms and legs back and forth along the ground. 'I survived. I'm not hurt at all. I fell off the cliff and here I am, alive.'

'You must be concussed.' Mary moved her hand over Lucy's head, feeling for swelling. 'Your gown is a mess. You've lost a shoe. You could have been killed. What happened? It looked... it looked like you jumped.'

'I did jump, Mary.' She sounded almost excited.

'You jumped? Why? You could have been killed!'

'But I wasn't, was I? I knew I wouldn't be hurt because God would look after me – and He did.'

'God?' Mary stared at her sister.

'It's a miracle isn't it?' said Lucy.

'You tested God?'

'Say it, Mary.' Lucy sat up. 'Say it's a miracle.'

'You know you should never test God.'

'You don't know anything about God. You wouldn't understand.'

'I know more than you. You're just a child.'

'No you don't. You don't listen in chapel, you don't pray, I know you don't pray. You say you do but I know you don't. I can hear what you say and that's not praying.'

'You listen to my praying? That's private!' Mary stood and stepped away from her sister.

'It isn't private because it isn't praying. You can't say things like that. It's wrong, the things you ask for. You should be thanking God.'

'How do you know?'

'I know everything. God tells it all to me.'

'And God told you to jump?'

'No, I decided to jump, because I knew He would save me and He did.'

'LUCY! What on earth are you doing down there? What are you doing out of the house? Come in, come in at once!' Winifred, the nursemaid, was hurrying down the path from the house, the gardener behind her. 'Mary! What have you done to your sister? Lucy dear, oh dear, dear Lucy.'

Lucy pulled herself up from the ground and tried to smooth her gown where the fabric had ripped. She examined her mud-strewn pink sleeves and picked off pieces of grass.

'You've gone mad,' said Mary. 'You are mad.'

'No, you are mad to wrong a faith that Father is imprisoned for,' said Lucy. 'He suffers so we can serve God in the right way yet still you don't do it. You should listen in chapel. You should repent. God saved me but He won't save you unless you turn to Him.'

'Maybe I don't want to be saved,' said Mary.

'You do,' said Lucy, dropping the volume of her voice so she was almost hissing. 'You say it over and over when you're asleep. But you won't be saved, you will be damned. God won't save you because you are not gracious to Him and I won't save you either.'

Lucy turned and started walking towards the house.

Mary squeezed her fists and swallowed down on a tightness in her chest, then followed her sister.

*

Lucy knew there was only one place that could quieten her thoughts, the only place she ever felt at peace, but Winifred was insisting on a wash, fussing and fussing, blustering about her, chattering on and on about her fall.

'If your Lady mother could see you, if she had found you as I did, you would be scrubbed down right now, Lucy, hard and cold,' said Winifred.

'I would rather be cold than have to wait for the water to be warmed,' said Lucy.

'Cold! You must have hurt your head. I had better send for the physician. It's excessive humours, spread to the flesh.'

'No!' said Lucy. 'I keep telling you I am perfectly well. Please, Wini, let me be.'

'Perfectly well she says! Look at the state of you. If Lady Elizabeth could see you now, let me tell you –'

'I don't see what is quite so terrible.' Lucy picked up a hand mirror, peering into it at the scratches along her chin and neck.

A maid entered the room with an iron kettle and poured hot water into a large bowl. At the sight of it Lucy started to weep, desperate to be alone so she could pray, could make sense of her salvation.

'Oh Lucy,' said Winifred. 'I told you there was trouble inside. You've hurt yourself, likely caught a chill. Only hot water and dry clothes will cure that.'

Two hours later Lucy was at last free. She walked through the house, sniffing at the pungent smell of ash and rosemary soap now emanating from her skin.

The chapel was in the far corner of the second floor, darker than the other rooms despite its six windows as these were predominantly deep blue. The stained glass depicted Christ and the cross at different stages: Jesus being judged alongside it, standing upright and confident as Pontius Pilate spoke to the crowd; bowed, staggering with the huge cross crushing his back as he carried it uphill; nailed onto it, bloody holes in his hands and ankles, his head lolling on his jutting collarbone. Lucy didn't need to look at them, she could see them when she closed her eyes at night, private messages meant for her. Judgement, suffering, pain: these were to be borne by her in service to God.

There were eight wooden pews in two rows and a wide aisle between them. The floor was a mosaic of tiny dots that displayed again and again her family's coat of arms, an azure and gules shield with three lions rampant. She passed the small wooden table on which sat the Book of Common Prayer, a nod to the king, and sidled into the second row. In front of her the altar was draped in plain white linen, and on it stood a black ebony cross on which hung Christ, crucified and gilded.

The beginning of a novel

LAUREN VAN SCHAIK SMITH

✳

JOPLIN

I MET MY HUSBAND'S MOTHER on the first day
that promised rain all spring, when she tracked us down
from the two-year-old Joplin postmark on the wedding in-
vitation I'd made Clair send. She arrived on our porch with
luggage for a long stay – a steamer, three raffia suitcases,
a ziggurat of hatboxes – and pushed a handshake at us. The
humid charge of the air had flattened her permed hair into
waffled ridges and set her mohair coat springing with static. When she shrugged it off and bundled it into my arms,
I felt like I was trying to wrangle a cat. There was a fine car
down the road, scabbed with red dirt, and a bottlebrush
man cranking at its engine. She squinted back at him: her
lover, P Holmes Madigan, she said, bringing her here to die.

   Clair took off down the road to prise free the car, and
Horace and I eyed each other under the electric light in
the kitchen. She was thin like a woman a third her age, in
a supple, stylish way, not the dry shrinking of seventy and
her reported illness, and she was dressed to match that
sleekness. A fox melted across her shoulder and gawped
with glass bead eyes. Her own eyes were tight and unyield-
ing, but she kept smoothing my hand in hers. She made me
feel ragged, graceless in the way I only ever felt with a Sears
catalogue on my knee or the time Clair and I went to a St
Louis hotel and slept on the chenille bedspread to keep
the linens neat.

   I knew Horace from Clair's sloe stories, sadness ginned
up after he'd burned through his rail journeys, the ragged
cliffs of California, and the time he'd cut his finger to bone
on a bowie knife. She had been as fit as a cat to be a mother,
forgetful of meals and impatient that he was a child for so
many years. 'Mrs Horace Hale' was a relic from her first
husband, varnish over a Polish name, but it had stuck so
firmly not even familiarity and three successive marriages
could dislodge it. Sinclair was a mistake of her forties, two
decades after Horace Hale widowed her, and he had 'Hale'
on his birth certificate. I use it too, although it still gums

in my mouth. I've thought, perversely, about giving it to
the baby.

*

In the kitchen Horace stroked the stitched mouth of her
fox and jogged his paw at me. 'You can have him when I die,
with my clothes,' she said, 'but it'll break my heart if no one
sees them out here.' She flicked her hands over them: lemon
suit with wide nacre buttons and puckers like dimples at
the hips, still standing starchily in the wet heat. We would
bury her in that suit, and in such hurry I wouldn't have time
to iron the tucks right. But I couldn't look at it curdling,
unworn, in my closet. I was sun-faded, boiled and flat in
the way everything is on the plains, like a well-beaten rug.
I'd look bloodless in yellow, and I'd have to curl my hair to
wear the hat. But when I first saw Horace in it, yellow as
cake, she seemed too glamorous to ever die.

Working at my hand, she drew me in so close I could
smell the diner grease in her hair.

'It's good you're here,' she said. 'Men are helpless with
this dying shit. Madigan's been making love to me with the
lamp off.' She exhaled, fluttering flaccid curls. 'It's the scar.
I'll show you.' She hitched her purse up to her elbow so she
could unbutton her jacket, wiggle down her brassiere and
flop out a breast.

I couldn't look away. It was small, little more than
cushioning around a nipple, but that was wide as a half-
dollar and brown as a penny. 'I had to keep something
for myself.' She twisted the brassiere and showed me the
straight-mouthed scar where another breast had been, the
empty bagging of skin. 'The rot is here now.' She snatched
my hand and pressed it to the flat of her chest, then to the
doubling of fat at her armpit. Her skin there was roomy
and flecked blue with age. Her hands had skin so slack they
looked webbed; they were the only other marks of her age.

She tucked my hand back at my side and ranged in her
purse for a cigarette and made no move to button her jacket.

'My mother died in this house.' I offered it as
feminine credentials. Horace didn't want comfort and
I was clumsy with sympathy anyway. I would chew my
mouth bloody at wakes and sickbeds for want of anything
to say. I fumbled now with the kettle, but my eyes kept
twitching to her chest. Lenore Thackery had once shim-
mied down her skirt to show me her Caesarean scar, and
it was like Frankenstein stitching: violet and crooked and
creased where her skin had been folded together. Horace's
scar was gristly and white and shined like those nacre buttons, but her breast was stranger. Separated from its pair
it was animal, awry. My aunt Mill's cousin Beauregard had
lost an eye under murky circumstances, and I could never
stop looking at the one that remained. That eye was wet,
blue, and it rolled after me, following the hem of my skirt
as Beau tongued chicken grease out of his moustache and
pretended to read the newspaper.

Horace seemed to enjoy my discomfort. She spoke like
we were confidantes, but she smiled gamily when my hand
trembled and coffee sloshed out of the mug I passed her.
'You seem very young, Faye,' she said.

'Only three years younger than Clair.' I was surprised
to hear myself say it. When we first married Clair had to
teach me everything, to smoke without coughing and kiss
with my eyes closed, and I sometimes still felt like a child
around him.

'Clair is younger than he should be,' Horace said. 'And
I'm antique. I can't remember what my mother looked like
or the middle name she gave me. So I'm not so upset to die.'
She shrugged. 'I just have a lot to straighten up with God.'
She pointed a finger to the ceiling and spun it, and, as if
chastened, buttoned her jacket.

Horace was all jangling nerves, not uneasy but hurried.
She'd released me but her hands kept rippling, at her purse

clasp, the mug she barely sipped. She reminded me of
Clair, sitting in my aunt's parlour, legs jostling dangerously
near the china, hurrying through a romance. He kissed
me flat on the mouth the second time he sat on that fiddly
Davenport, so suddenly he caught my teeth. When he set
his mind to something, marriage or a farm, he couldn't
sit still. He'd be tense and thrumming like a rubber band
until I went to bed with him, even in the middle of the day.
He said he got that restlessness from his mother, the lust
too. When he was small she'd had a series of projects, he
said: theatre, digestion, a menu of lovers. She'd trained him
as a ballet dancer in the kitchen at their boarding house
and then dragged him to the public library every day for a
month so she could pronounce French words from the dic-
tionary at him. And then she'd forgotten that all in a craze
for vegetarianism. His father had been a butcher's delivery
boy – seventeen, Clair thought. Horace had set herself to
teaching him about women.

*

When Clair came in Horace stood him on the hearthrug
in the parlour and plied her hands at him. He was skinned
in red dirt, sweated away in rings at his neck and hands, but
Horace didn't mind. She'd hardly noticed Madigan when
he'd followed Clair in. She seemed thrilled with the new
size of her son, his height, the late ranging of his shoulders. He'd been a boy when she left him with a cousin in
Kentucky and so small for his age he could shut himself in
her suitcase.

'Can you believe I'm a mother?' Horace said. Behind
her, Madigan whistled, low and obliging. He was fifty,
maybe, and neat and pressed as linen, with just a tinge of
Missouri dust on his trouser hems and knees. He'd claimed
the best chair in the room, after a quick assessment of
the evenness of their legs, and produced a newspaper,

accordion-folded, from his jacket.

As Horace embraced Clair I looked away and flattened myself to the wallpaper. It seemed like a moment I shouldn't interrupt, although Clair was tense and squirming under her hands, shifting from foot to foot.

'Get off, Ma.' He peeled her hands from his shirt and slumped on the couch. He ran his own through the hair she'd mussed. 'Jesus,' he said and looked for me. When they met mine, his eyes were wild and ashamed.

Horace settled beside him, legs plaited, hands kneading his arm. 'Do you know that until I saw Clair here I'd for-gotten how his father looked?' she said. She and Clair were very alike, I thought: vulpine faces, colourless eyes, that skin that turns up moles, like blood spots in eggs, but never freckles. I couldn't see space for another person. Madigan still didn't lower his newspaper but I couldn't prise my eyes away from them.

'I'm ages older than that, Ma,' Clair said.

She acted like she didn't hear him. 'How lucky you are, Faye,' she said, but she grinned at Clair and wider than she'd done for me. I saw her teeth then: milky and nubbed, like a girl's. Clair had told me that nursing him had made her teeth rot, that when he was older she'd make him tap their husks: a mouthful of blight and all his fault, so he couldn't say she hadn't loved him. Weeks later, when she hadn't died as quickly as she promised, I found her mouth, shrieking, in a glass at her bedside: an inch of pink acrylic gum and strand of pretty, raw teeth. She told me they were 'genuine' – a gift from Madigan, pulled from the mouth of a fourteen-year-old niece who was struck by a car. He'd offered the girl's parents fifty dollars for them and 'with money like it is now, they couldn't refuse.' That's how much Madigan loved her, she said.

In the parlour that day they barely looked at each other.

Clair was looking at Madigan though, at his frontage of newspaper – the *Minneapolis Daily Star*, three days old.

'Isn't our drought in your papers?' he said.

It was supposed to rain that day but Clair had forgotten. When we'd woken that morning, we'd tasted it, the iron tang in the air, like a mouthful of pennies. Now, crammed beside Horace on the couch, he looked desperate again, thirsty and too thin.

He pointed at Madigan. 'I thought at least it'd be in your papers.'

'Don't be dramatic,' Horace said. 'It feels like rain. Doesn't it feel like rain?' She walked to the parlour window. Faraway, over the corn, the clouds were curdled and green. As she looked, lightning, like a hairline crack, flashed, and faded. 'There.' Horace turned back to us, gloating as if she'd conjured it.

'It's heat lightning,' Clair said.

'Well, maybe you should pray for rain.'

'We'd get a damn flood,' Clair said.

Horace kept smiling, only tighter now. 'Madigan,' she said, 'did you know the Mormons think Missouri is Eden?'

'Faye, Ma thinks you're from paradise,' Clair said.

'Don't joke,' she said. 'I want to tell you something.' She rummaged in her purse and wiggled a book, pocket-sized and pebble-leathered, past its Bakelite jaws. She flapped it and its onion-skin pages shivered. 'The nuns used to say I was incorrigible, but I think I can make it stick this time.' She tossed the book at Clair. It landed with a leathery slap on his knees: a Bible. He handled it like he'd handle a potato pulled blistering from the grate.

A short story

ZAKIA UDDIN

*

WALKING THE DOG

JEN&TONIC44'S HEART was trailing its way through
central London. Ed's spatulate thumb had hovered over
her face before. She was online all the time and he felt
compelled to meet her. The familiarity of her picture
(selfie, mirror, pensive) had become a placeholder for
greater intimacy. Sitting in the pub, staring at his phone,
he watched the streets of Soho populate with desiring
emoji. He seized the opportunity when the gap between
her messages grew shorter and her non-virtual body drew
closer: *Meeting some friends at Nin's. Come along!* He
googled Nin's – a new cocktail bar – and followed the
glowing dot.

He had only taken his first sip of Porn Star Martini
when she walked in, heels thumping on the artfully thread-
bare carpet. Ed's mouth went itchy, dry. Jen&Tonic44,
Jenafova: a colossus in fishnets. He got off the banquette
and moved to kiss her on the cheek, a reciprocal hand on
her shoulder. There was an awful lot of her – the heavy
coat, the marshy scent, hair mounted above her head like
a lacquered obelisk. He submitted to the aphrodisiac of
possibility: she was in his league.

She squeezed herself in next to him, and ordered drinks
from a passing waitress. They watched a tall woman in
black introduce herself as Madame X before circling the
room and greeting customers. A man with synthetic angel
wings scuttled over to drop a menu on their table.

'Busy night?' Ed eyed Jenafova's short skirt to indicate
that he knew he was a bit of fun. A man of the world.

'Just got ready and came here. People always make out
they had other plans, as if they'll look desperate otherwise.
Seems like you're the busy one, Ed.'

He hesitated, remembered not to move his eyes to the
left. *Body language.*

'I like to take my time so I can do things properly. Get
the timing right. Don't want to… get my feelings hurt. Or
anyone else's.'

'Oh, definitely. You meet all these men – especially in our forties – and you think, get a grip. I suppose you must think that too. Of women.'

'You've got to live your life the way you want. Meet a strange man near midnight, have a drink, no pressure,' Ed said. The Eurodisco hit had been incrementally turned up, so he shouted: 'Have some fun before you die!' as the song came to a breathy post-coital end.

She looked at him closely. 'You're not that strange.'

'I didn't mean I was strange. I meant... the other men.'

'Ed: officially never been strange.' She sucked a drop of drink from her little finger. Her stockinged ankles were generating static against his nylon mix trousers. 'My friends will be here soon. Lucy's a children's illustrator. Greg's in tech. Very cool couple. They're in an open relationship.'

'That the kind of thing you're into?'

'I don't like to close myself off to things. I'm a bit of a handful.'

She stood, threw her arms open before he could answer.

'Lucy, Greg!'

A couple much younger than Jenafova approached them.

'Hey, man, you're Ed, right? So good to meet the mystery man!' Greg, abstractly handsome, did a full body hug, transferring his sweat onto Ed's face. He then laughed a long one-sided laugh that induced the same sense of uselessness in Ed as watching someone cry. He pounded Ed on the back before sitting down, and said: 'All good, man! All good.'

Lucy, short and in a polka-dot dress, smiled at him across the table, her glasses slipping down her nose. The giant fish tank lining the wall made everyone's faces green.

'You've been to a munch before, Ed?' Lucy asked.

'What, they do food here?'

Jenafova handed the menu to Ed. In ornate script, it

had four items without any description:

Treats

Madame X Special

Pass the Slipper

Last Night in Paris

Greg and Lucy giggled, and then pointed out items to each other on the menu. Ed whispered to Jenafova: 'What are these? Cocktails?'

'They're games.'

*

Jenafova left to go to the ladies' room. Lucy and Greg slowly inched towards the empty seat, as if to make the most of the free space. They began kissing, their arms sifting between layers of clothing. No one in the room paid attention. Ed moved closer. Lucy's hand was roaming up Greg's twitching thigh. Ed saw the dress, her prolonged eye contact when they met. Jenafova's lashes flaring open with the words 'open relationship'.

He reached across the banquette and planted a stiff hand on Lucy's back. She fell back, so that Ed's fingers were crushed. He lurched at her, over her, gesturing with his other arm that he was trapped. They all watched the freed hand move away and return to the table.

'What the fuck was that?' Lucy asked. 'If I wanted you to join in, I would have given you a sign.'

'It doesn't work that way,' added Greg. 'We're not swingers.'

'I thought that's why we're all here?' Ed's voice came out squeakily. He stared at the tank opposite him. A lone fish swam past, hid behind a tower. He wished he could devolve into something with no need to be attractive to other creatures.

Lucy edged away from him, just as Jenafova approached.

'For future reference, keep your creepy little paws to yourself,' she said under her breath.

Jenafova sat down, her phone flashing in her hand. Had they texted her? Had he ruined his date with her without her even being there? Lucy's mobile was turned downwards on the table. She and Greg pointedly talked only to each other. Ed grabbed Jenafova's fingers, entwined them with his to make them notice. He was annoyed that he'd left it so long to make a claim on her.

'I've never met anyone like you before.' He meant this but he didn't want her to think it was meaningful.

'That's funny. I've been told that all my life and it's just starting to feel like a compliment.'

'Anyone make you feel otherwise?' He wanted the conversation to go back to a manageable level.

She ignored his question. 'I feel unafraid. I've already got what I *need*. I want big feelings in my life, even the bad ones. Just to know that I really cared. I hate all the belittling, the petty emotional manipulation in relationships. Is that mad?'

Ed tried to smile. Her mojito was untouched. He could tell that she'd never made this speech before; something in the pauses, the way she glanced at him for reassurance before catching herself and looking at the mirrored back of her phone. His upper lip was stuck to his gums. He discreetly unglued it.

'Funny we met. I like to take things easy,' he said. Silence, ambient disappointment. 'But not that easy. What will you do to me? I mean, what do you want from me?'

'I want you to feel the same. Free. In love with possibility. I want everyone to feel the same!'

Ed wanted to show her that he was ready for anything, at least for the next six or seven hours. He picked up the menu, decided that he wouldn't ask what any of the games involved. Jenafova huddled against him, watched him underline *Treats* with her ruby-encrusted pen.

'Are you sure, Ed? That's a weird one.'

'I'm just going to go with it. It can't be that bad.'

'Let me buy it for you. It's my gift to you.'

Ed double-checked the price. It said £40.

'OK. That's lovely. We do this together, right?' he asked.

'No, it's just you. You on your own.'

She called Madame X to the table. The woman tucked the rolled up twenties into her leather corset belt.

'What's your name?' She towered above Ed, so he had to wrench his neck back to see her properly. He had tried not to look at her when she introduced herself because he didn't know if she was meant to be looked at.

'I'm going to name you Scruffy!' Her voice was rich and deep.

'This is my best outfit!'

'Quiet down, Scruffy!'

The music stopped playing and the other customers stared at their table. Ed laughed, as if he knew exactly what was about to happen. He wasn't just a membrane with feelings. His anxiety wasn't visible. The woman reached inside the purse and pulled out a leash and collar. Feeling the blood pulsing in his ears, he let her clip it around his neck.

'I'm going to take you for a walk. Get on your knees.'

Ed scrambled off the sofa. He put his hands on the floor first so that he wouldn't injure himself as he dropped down. If he followed instructions, he would be fine. Jenafova clapped as he moved away. Lucy and Greg kissed. Madame X gently yanked the leash and Ed followed on all fours, his hands on the rough surface of the carpet, his best Camper shoes squeaking as he dragged them.

'Bark, Scruffy!'

Ed opened his parched mouth. A whimper followed. Woofs lodged in his larynx. He felt a coursing shame countered by a determination to carry on. He barked aggressively, determinedly. Madame X bent down to pat him.

She carried on walking him around the room, stopping at each table. Fingers ruffled his hair. A forest of legs, heels, trousers swayed before him. This was role play. He was role-playing and he was doing it so well that strangers were patting him on the back.

A peanut landed in front of him. He ignored it.

'Good boy, Scruffy,' Madame X's voice hovered above him.

'Thanks,' said Ed, forgetting he was supposed to be a dog.

'Why don't you do some panting?' she whispered.

He slackened his jaw, breathing heavily and without rhythm.

'Maybe you need some water. You sound very thirsty.'

She led Ed to the bar, and he waited while she reached for something. A bowl appeared next to him on the floor. It was full of yellow liquid. He stared into the bowl. It was deep. He was a dog wishing he was a fish.

He stuck his tongue out and swilled it in the hoppy beer.

His chin was wet. His neck ached. She pulled the collar and walked him around the room once more. He felt strangely tearful as he realised the music was over and the tune had changed.

'Sniff this lady's crotch, Scruffy.'

The legs were thin and inelegantly far apart. The unfamiliar shins snapped together, levered up. He thought of Jenafova's encased thighs, the tanned flesh impressed with diamonds. He heard laughter, scuffling.

'No. I don't want to.'

'Scruffy, you're a terrible dog. So badly behaved.'

She dragged him towards another pair of disembodied legs.

Ed reared back and stood as the lead fell from her hand – it must have only taken seconds but he tottered, uncoordinated, before he ran through the door and back onto the street. The leash swung around his neck, and the doorman swivelled away, embarrassed. His trembling fingers couldn't prise the thin leather strap away from his skin. Behind him, he could hear the urgent tap of heels.

'Ed! Ed! You didn't have to do that! You could have said no!'

She waited for him to stop.

'I feel terrible! I'm so sorry!' she shouted.

He carried on walking, before turning at the end of the street. Jenafova's face was pallid in the neon of the shop window next to her. She began walking towards him hurriedly. Ed felt the first communion between them. A painful hot white connection. She felt sorry for him. He would wait for her. Romance, thought Ed. He didn't know how to show her that he was fine – he was now fine – so he got on his hands and knees and barked loudly until she reached him.

Excerpt from a novel

SAM WEST

✳

WATER MEMORY

IN THE YEAR AFTER the king died, amid the national
displays of mourning, Frederick Norman quietly entered
Jarwada at its western border and proceeded overland to
the capital city of Bankali. He made the trip in the back
of a Nissan pickup fitted with two benches running from
the cab to the tailgate and an overhead tarpaulin zip-tied
to a frame of steel pipe. A woman with thick, sun-cracked
cheeks and gray eyes breathed through a piece of dirty
T-shirt for the first few hundred miles before falling asleep
on Frederick's shoulder. She sat with a woven basket
between her feet. When she began to snore Frederick lifted
the rattan top and saw the basket was full of tamarind.

At dusk the driver pulled off the highway and parked in
a track of dried mud beside a tin awning. As the passengers
unpacked themselves from the truck bed, a boy appeared
and ran a length of PVC tubing into the truck's fuel tank.
He leaned against a 55-gallon drum while he spun the rota-
ry pump's handle and a glass globe hanging from the edge
of the awning filled with pale yellow gasoline. When the
globe was full, the boy flipped a valve and the gas ran down
the clear tube and into the tank. He turned the valve back
and started the process again.

Frederick walked a little way off from the road and
passed water between two stones, their surfaces flecked
with mica and quartz. The smell of woodsmoke came from
far off, and the low mountains in the west were rimmed
with vermilion light. In the east, evening stars shone in the
gradations of blue above the horizon. The driver topped
off the radiator from a corrugated water bottle and spoke
to the boy's mother as she leaned against the corner of
the mason-block wall smoking a cheroot. They exchanged
bleak predictions for Jarwada now the king was dead. Bells
were sewn onto the woman's cuffs and rang whenever she
moved her hands.

As the seventeen passengers settled back in their places
on the truck, the driver caught Frederick by the elbow and

offered to kick the two women out of the cab if he would
pay a little extra – he brought his shoulder blades together
in an exaggerated stretch. Frederick smiled and pretended
not to understand, then asked if he could arrange him long-
term accommodations in the capital. The driver's eyebrows
lifted and Frederick watched him change out his SIM card
as he flicked his cigarette into the roadside grass. The driver's door slammed and the engine roared under the hood as
Frederick squeezed back into his place on the bench beside
the tamarind woman.

The room the driver arranged for Frederick was the
third floor spare in a shophouse in the southeast of the old
city. A grated window with a wire mesh screen ran along
the far wall behind an orange and gold polyester curtain.
The heavy screen and grating prevented all but filtered day-
light and street noise from getting in. The room's floor was
unfinished concrete covered by a thin layer of adhesive vinyl
printed to mimic woodgrain. The masonry walls radiated
heat stored from the afternoon, causing the vinyl flooring
in one corner to bubble up like blistered skin. A particle-
board wardrobe with the ghosts of children's stickers on its
door stood across from a matching bedframe holding a thin
grey mattress. Frederick gave 200J to the driver and 400J
plus 20 USD to the man who owned the house, Der
Nag-Paakshim. The driver and Der Nag-Paakshim argued
in fast Jarwee as Frederick herded them backwards through
the door and onto the top of the stairs. He pushed the
warped door shut and stuck a rusted woodscrew hanging
from the door frame in front of the hasp. The voices faded
down the stairs. Frederick finished the water he had in his
bag and lay back on the mattress. That first night he dreamt
of walking barefoot through the tall grass at the edge of
a lake while passing clouds obscured and then revealed
a silver moon.

The Nag-Paakshims ran their businesses on the ground
floor, Jaan Der selling and servicing satellite receivers

across a hinged wooden desk, while Pim Swarti, his wife, cut and colored hair in a tile-floored room that opened onto the street. The most they saw of their boarder was in the early afternoons when he returned to the house with his rucksack hanging from his shoulders. They would hear his slow footsteps on the stairs and sidetrack their conversation. 'Khe param,' God's peace, they exchanged as Frederick circled the kitchen landing and started the next flight up. Not knowing when he ate, Swarti took to leaving plates of mangosteen and creamed rice outside Frederick's door, which he replaced empty the next morning. Even so, Pim Swarti often brought up the increasing angularity of Frederick's face in talks with her husband.

Bankali was blue at dawn, the pale concrete walls cold and pockmarked in the heavy shadows. Dogs slept curled into their tails outside the bus station as the stationmaster unchained the painted gates. Attenuated morning sun lifted the curtain of mist hung through the narrow streets while women set up folding tables outside the shuttered markets and lit propane burners for their pots of rice porridge. The thin whirr of small engines echoed from the underpasses on the superhighway. Monks draped in blue wool carried alms bowls as they stepped barefoot through the dusty streets, stopping to receive dried noodles and rose apples from housewives kneeling outside their gardens.

Even with a bhikku haircut and clothes from the walking street, Frederick still drew suspicious looks from the back rows of the 6:10 towards Lampang. Their eyes followed him until he stepped off the bus on a dusty stretch of road between two bleak townships, the closest any route came to the monastery on Soon Dai Kow.

The road to the monastery ran in switchbacks up Soon Dai's south face, the slabs fissured and peeling from the mountainside as they doubled back and continued in graded ascent further up the slope. Frederick walked quietly in

the shoulder carrying his sutras folded into a dry shirt
and tied with a length of gray cord.

The head monk isolated him from the other novices.
After morning session, while the monastery came together to tend the temple grounds, Frederick was taken to a
sweltering annex where he was left for hours to fold yellow
envelopes and pack them into crates. While the other
novices ate their group meal, Frederick received instruction
from a majjhima who spoke an unfamiliar northern dialect.
He was never permitted to stay past second session. After
a rushed recitation of his dharma, Frederick tied up his
sutras and started back down the broken road in the searing
azimuth of afternoon sun. Back on the highway, he waited
in the shade of a stunted dillenia to flag down the bus back
to Bankali.

The routine provided distraction. His joints hardened
to long sitting; the memorization of Pali scripture
exhausted his mind. The mesmeric intonation of the
dharma allowed momentary glimpses of a life unburdened
by guilt. Back in his room at the Nag-Paakshims', Frederick
meditated on the enlightenment of Sengtsan by the master
Huike in *The Transmission of the Lamp*:

> Sengstan asked Huike, saying, 'I am diseased: I implore
> you to cleanse me of my sin.' Huike said, 'Bring me
> your sin and I will cleanse you of it.' Sengtsan thought
> awhile; then said, 'I cannot get at it.' Huike replied,
> 'Then I have cleansed you of it.'

The light faded from the window curtain, and Frederick
reopened his eyes in darkness.

After fourteen months of his immutable routine,
Frederick arrived one morning to find an envelope tacked
to the monastery gate with 'ktchu', foreigner, written on it.
Inside was a letter instructing that he would no longer be
permitted to practice at Soon Dai Kow. He waited outside
the locked gate until sundown, hoping someone would be
sent to explain the letter. Under a moonless sky he made

his way back down the mountain road, the distant lights
of Bankali scattered across the horizon.

On the second anniversary of the king's death, Frederick
sat on the edge of his mattress in the arc of an oscillating
fan. It was early evening and the orange window curtain
beside him was lit up like a paper lantern. He was rereading
an email on his phone from a photographer he had known
in Africa – Eric Johansson had been working in Nigeria
under contract with Agence France-Presse when Frederick
first arrived in Lagos. Typical of Eric, his email raised more
questions than it answered. Yet the last lines were perfectly
clear: 'My apologies for interrupting your exile, old friend,
but I'm in Bankali on assignment. Meet me somewhere.
You'll still be anonymous.' Frederick studied the email
signature, a London address and a phone number with
a Cyprian country code.

    'Predil,' came Jaan Der's voice through the door. The
fan swung slowly across Frederick's face as he waited to
hear Der's footsteps descending the stairs. 'Predil,' the
voice came again. Frederick fingered the button on the top
of his phone and tucked it under the corner of the mattress.
Soft brown knuckles knocked on the hollow door. Predil
was Jaan Der's way of calling Frederick, a colloquialism
meaning oldest son. Frederick unstuck the soles of his
feet from the plastic flooring and went to the door. Der
Nag-Paakshim stood on the other side in a shirt turned the
color of manila rope from sweat and longan pollen, unbut-
toned and parted on either side of his smooth brown belly.
'Shwara. Soup. Pim Swarti wants you to eat soup tonight.
She is worried you are wasting away up here. Doi agrees it's
a good idea,' said Jaan Der. He clipped his sentences into
fragmented jokes when he spoke to Frederick. 'It is cooler
downstairs. You're not a cake, you won't collapse if you
leave your oven.'

    'Taaqil. Thank you, please tell Pim Swarti and Doi

they are very kind.'

'Me tell them? They want to hear it from you. We won't force you to eat, but you must help us with something, only tonight.'

'Taaqil, Jaan Der, but I would like to be alone.'

'And soon you may well be, Predil Fareck, but tonight,' Der took Frederick's knobby wrist in his swollen fingers and pulled him gently through the doorframe. 'You will join us. Doi has a question and thinks her father is too old and stupid to be of any use. Perhaps the foreigner who lives like a monk above us knows better. "He has seen the world," my daughter said. "He'll know how to step on the Radhim's toes. Go Jaan, fetch him from upstairs so he can tell us."'

At the second floor landing Frederick asked Jaan Der for time to wash his face. Der nodded then motioned for him to come down to the kitchen when he finished. He took a half-smoked cigarette from his shirt pocket and continued plodding down the stairs.

In the bathroom, weak gray light filtered in from the pebbled glass window above the toilet. Frederick locked eyes with himself in the tiny sink mirror while the hot water ran out of the house pipes and was replaced with cooler water from underground. There were shadows in his cheeks and his eyes were sunk in their sockets. He lifted his lip and inspected his gums in the mirror. He tried to pull the hair behind his ears into the rubber band at the back of his head, but it had become too knotted and tangled to undo. At the edge of the sink he found a sliver of pink soap and a blue cloth stippled with bleach stains. He ran them under the tap and began scrubbing the dust from his face.

The beginning of a novel

J Y YANG

*

THE STORYTELLER'S WIFE

SHEILA HAD WARNED Muse about the state of Arthur's room. 'A total nuclear clusterfuck,' she had said. 'Shit stacked from wall to wall like an alcoholic Santa Claus just moved in. One of those crazy ones. You know. *Hoarders*.'

A stark sentiment, but no Sheila pronouncement was complete without a bright embroidering of profanity, and this rant had been mild by her standards. Sheila was Arthur's publicist, manager and agent rolled into one, a one-woman force of nature with a New York drive to succeed and Los Angeles propensity to overinflate the importance of everything. Muse survived by taking whatever she said and dialling the severity down by a factor of ten.

So when Sheila told her that Arthur's fans had mailed in so much stuff it looked like Chernobyl had gone off, Muse thought that the situation, on the disaster scale, was probably more like burning the morning toast.

But when Muse stepped into her husband's hospital room, she discovered that every one of Sheila's four-letter words had been well earned. Overnight, the small trickle of get well cards had fungused into piles of stuffed animals, bouquets, hampers, DHL boxes, FedEx boxes, suspiciously plain brown boxes, handicrafts, hand-knitted scarves, hand-knitted sweaters, hand-knitted tchotchkes, a large and fantastically ugly painted sculpture of a stag. A shoal of helium balloons clustered by the ceiling, aggressively cheerful, restrained by the fishing lines tethering them to Arthur's bed. In the middle of it all lay Arthur, annotated by oxygen lines and ECG feelers and saline drips, blissfully and unresponsively unaware of the chaos that had accrued around him.

The fans had truly outdone themselves this time. When Muse opened her mouth the words 'oh, my, God' tumbled from it one by one with the weight of anchors.

'They called it a *lovebomb*,' Sheila said, as Muse picked her way through the room with a goldfish jaw. She was leaning in the doorway, smelling of Kenzo Flower sprayed over notes of tobacco. '*Bomb*'s about right. This is a fucking act of terrorism.'

'You knew about this?' Muse stopped to examine a small amigurumi of Lady Eithwen – with the blonde hair from the TV series – that had been propped up on the bedside table.

'Someone texted me about it at fucking midnight. What was the point, when all this shit was already in the post?'

The fans had divined Arthur's room number a week ago, but they had waited to strike all at once. Sheila had suspected loose lips among the hospital staff the likely source of the leak, an offhand comment to a cousin at a dinner party that fell into the tarpit of the Internet and got stuck there for the masses to excavate and parade around.

Eyebags had precipitated on Sheila's face over the two weeks since Arthur's heart attack as she fended off media query after media query. 'Give me the days when tabloids were the worst I had to deal with,' she had said earlier that morning, Revlon lips pursing around a cigarette as they stood in an empty parking lot. 'Now any half-literate idiot with a functioning keyboard can shit out a website and expect me to treat them like they're the fucking *New York Times*.'

In the middle of the cluttered room, Muse put her hands on her hips, feeling more at sea than at any point since the night of the heart attack. 'This is a disaster,' she said. 'What are we – can we just stop people from sending him anything?'

'Sure, if you want to stop legit gifts from getting through as well. Like that one.' The offending item was an expensively-appointed hamper taking up half an armchair. 'His German publishers sent it by this morning.'

Muse moved around the bed to take a closer look. Red wine, fancy cereal, fruits, and a card that said 'Best wishes for your recovery!' 'Are those oranges? Art's allergic to oranges.'

Sheila shrugged. 'How do you say *anaphylactic shock* in Deutsch?'

Muse scratched the back of her neck. 'I mean, it's your call,' Sheila said. 'But surely he has adoring family and friends who want to send round a fruit basket too.'

Muse snuck a look at Arthur and his bank of machines softly keeping time, as if she might find answers there. But she couldn't keep on his face for too long, because then she started imagining his eyes moving, like they were in a version of reality where she would be half a second away from leaning over and whispering, 'Wake up sleepyhead, you've got words to commit today' in his ear.

She sucked a breath in through her nose, pushed it out through her mouth, and turned away to look at another fragment of the lovebomb.

'Trist called again this morning,' Sheila said. Tristan was Art's editor at Arrow Wound Books, and one of the bigwigs at the imprint.

'What did he say?'

'Bupkiss. Just checking up on Art's condition, blah fucking blah. He's panicking. Can't say I blame him.'

Trist was a six-foot-four brick wall of a man, lumberjack-sturdy. He had a story he liked to tell at award parties, about shooting wasps' nests with a BB gun. 'The trick is to stay still,' he'd say. 'Wasps don't know guns make gunshots, so just make like a damn tree and they'll leave you alone.' Muse wondered what he looked like panicked.

'What did you tell him?'

'What did I tell him? Same thing the doctor told me. No change, wait and see, et cetera.'

'That didn't help him much, did it?'

Sheila spat laughter like machine gun bullets. 'He can join the fucking club, there's plenty of space for us here.'

Muse picked a sweater out of the lovebomb and held

it up. It was a virulent shade of chartreuse – how was this colour not outlawed from shops yet? – and declared in awkward grey lettering GET WELL MR A M CARVER. The kerning on the knit letters made her eyes hurt. 'How's a sweater supposed to help a man in a coma?'

'How's a cut-rate Rudolf from Etsy supposed to help?'

Muse excavated under the tape-mummified top of one of the brown boxes. Coils of shaving spilled intestinally as the cardboard tore. 'You'll regret that when you need to move it later,' Sheila warned.

There was something rattling around in the box and she couldn't prise a big enough hole in the cardboard to see. Muse dug in her coat pocket for her keys and started sawing through packing tape with a chain-grinding sound.

'I'll get you a cutter,' Sheila said.

'I've got it.' The key came free from the box flaps with a jerk, and Muse was in. The shavings crunched as she pushed them aside. 'Oh Jesus.'

'What is it?'

'It's a sheep's skull. Or is it an antelope? It's got antlers. Jesus.' She lifted the thing out of the box, cold and smooth and shedding spirals of packing. Beads had been strung between the elegant pointed horns. The thing had a sourish smell to it, not the gutsy tang of rot, but something damp and organic, like meat broth.

'That's a deer, dumbass. Antelopes live in Africa.' Sheila had crossed the room and she plucked the skull from Muse's hands. 'Who does this shit? Mailing skulls to strangers puts you in the same category as serial killers, con-fucking-gratulations.'

There was a letter, ribbon-fastened, hiding among the shavings. Muse unrolled its creamy Hallmark weight and read aloud: 'Dear Mr Carver, you don't know me, but I know you. I've been an avid fan of yours since *Circle Of Bone And Roses* came out. Your books helped me get through some pretty tough times during my first divorce, and I'll always be indebted to you for that. I know it sounds silly to say, but I identify a lot with Lady Halamar. My family has been hunters for generations too. I'm a bow hunter, I shoot a recurve. She's my favorite character. Thank you so much for writing her.

'You must be wondering what this gift is all about. Two weeks ago we tagged this beautiful buck on one of my cousin's properties in Portland. That was the day we found out about your heart attack, and strange as it may sound, I felt like it was a sign. As I dressed the buck, I wove its lifewind into its skull and blessed it in the Name of the Lady. May it bring you strength and fortune for healing. Goddess smile upon you, Elizabeth Harding.'

'Can't have been a very lucky deer if it got shot by a bow hunter, can it?' Sheila bent over the box and her face wrinkled as she examined it. 'Portland. Must have driven here to deliver it herself. Figures. Write a bestselling series about a bunch of secret society witches, wind up with a bunch of weird witchy fans.'

Muse took the skull back from her and replaced it in the ruined box. 'You don't have to be so sarcastic. She meant well.'

'You don't think it's even a tiny little bit weird? Sending someone a skull in a box?'

'I don't know. Hunters keep trophies, don't they?'

'Yeah. You know who else keeps trophies? Serial killers.'

One of the duty nurses helped Muse cart some of the lovebomb to the trunk of her car. She took the boxes and parcels and things that could be easily stacked in the garage. They had a storage unit where Art kept fan gifts gathered from his signing tours, an ever-accumulating mountain of adoration he didn't quite know what to do with. I'll move these there after he gets better, Muse told herself. Because of course he would.

Sheila was surprised when she announced her

intention to head back. 'Taylor and the kids are in the house,' she reminded her.

'Ah fuck. I forgot – you told me. When did they arrive? Last night?'

'Their flight landed at eleven. They're still jetlagged.'

'What's the time difference with London? Eight hours?'

'I think it's seven. They've just ended summer there. The kids will be by later to see their dad, probably.'

'You driving them? Or their mother? She hasn't got a car, has she?'

'She's got a rental. We'll sort it out.'

The trunk of her Accord was only large enough for a fifth of the lovebomb. Fully laden, the rear end sagged over the wheels. The nurse called her Mrs Carver, and she corrected him: 'It's Carver-Li.' They had both changed their names – it was only fair –but Trist didn't want the hyphenate marring book covers. Besides, at that point ten years ago, Art was already a modestly midlist author of sword and sorcery novels, and Trist had hoped that the mild name recognition might nudge sales for the first book in the entirely new, but somewhat promising, Elderflower Chronicles series.

He had no idea. None of them had any idea.

Muse put the skull and its mangled box on the front seat. Elizabeth Harding had left a return address, and she wondered if she should write something to thank her for the thoughtful gift. What would she say, though?

Take that, Sheila. You know who doesn't leave return addresses? Serial killers.

NON-FICTION

INTRODUCTION

*

HELEN SMITH

ONE OF THE NOTABLE features of the anthology
this year is the inclusion of writing by students from the
MA in both Prose Fiction and Biography and Creative
Non-Fiction. This seems particularly appropriate given
the increasingly porous and contested boundaries between
fiction and non-fiction; indeed there is some debate as to
whether such boundaries should and do exist at all. As a
recent newspaper article pointed out, there is no equivalent
word for 'non-fiction' in many languages and the whole
concept of a distinction between 'real' and 'imagined'
narratives is alien to a number of cultures. The divide, it
seems, is something that especially vexes Anglo-American
minds. The reason, for this are undoubtedly complex and
go back a long way, but what is generally agreed is that
nowadays categorisation has much to do with bookshop
shelving and reader expectation and that, for good or ill,
it is here to stay.

The demands made of the novelist and the non-fiction
writer are obviously different in some respects – as Virginia
Woolf once said, 'The novelist is free; the biographer is
tied.' The non-fiction writer can never entirely shake off
the heavy burden of fact, but freedom can be onerous
too – the ready-made narratives of 'real life' can seem very
attractive to the novelist who sits down to a blank screen
day after day. The truth of course is that much is shared in
both forms of writing: many novels require some degree
of research, and the qualities that are vital to the novelist –
a sense of pace, form, and the ability to bring a character
to life on a page – are just as important for the writer of
non-fiction. The contributions by this year's students of
the MA in Biography and Creative Non-Fiction demonstrate just such an awareness.

The situation described in 'White Dress' by Katherine
Allen could have come straight from the pages of Somerset
Maugham. A group of expatriates lounge lazily by a lake-
side in sweltering heat but soon find themselves involved

in a tense encounter with the local community. The reader is made to feel the debilitating heat of that April day in Thailand in this evocative account in which travel writing meets personal reportage.

It was also Spring when the painter Laura Knight returned to her Cornish home and discovered the artist's model Dolly Henry there. Henry had materialised in Knight's garden unknown and unannounced, but immediately Knight asked Dolly to sit for her. Her rather romantic portrait of Henry makes her look as if she were 'part of the beauty' of her surroundings. Yet as Justine Ashford's piece makes clear, everything in the garden is far from lovely. Jealousy and violence stalk Henry's relationship with her lover, the talented young artist John Currie, and as this compelling narrative suggests, Henry's story is not going to have a happy ending.

Another relationship is at the centre of Lisa Eveleigh's sprightly tale of the machinations of the early nineteenth-century marriage market. Lord Granville Leveson Gower's gambling habits meant that he was in need of a wealthy wife, but finding one turned out to be less than straightforward and involved a delicate set of diplomatic manoeuvres between Granville's mistress – Harriet, Lady Bessborough – and his mother, Susannah, Lady Stafford. The letters between the various parties reproduced here are a reminder of how one aspect of the biographer's archival skill is the ability to 'read between the lines'.

Lady Stafford felt she had an important role to play in ensuring her son's future prosperity (although one can't help wondering how much she worried about his future happiness…). In 'Eulogy for a Mother' Sally Fox recalls her own mother trying to teach her to dance through life as she looks down at the now lifeless figure she hardly recognises in the funeral parlour. The interconnectedness of dancing, breathing and death is deftly and memorably sketched, as in the closing paragraph, when the breath of wind sways the trees and the narrator senses her mother rumba-ing her way down the street to her own funeral.

Daring to breathe a word against popular opinion has painful consequences in 'That Yellow Car' by Odrán Waldron. When a coachload of young Irish hurlers spot a yellow sports car on a roundabout, they all insist that the colour is an abomination and that it should be resprayed; all, that is, but the narrator – and it isn't the car that's black and blue at the end of a darkly humorous episode. This boyhood incident, recalled in the author's distinctive and engaging voice, has much to say about both the cruelty and kindness of children – the real hero of the piece is surely Fiachra, whose wordless loyalty is still gratefully remembered years later.

These five short pieces, which take us from Thailand to Ireland via rural and metropolitan England ably demonstrate how 'truth' can be as strange, entertaining and thought-provoking as fiction.

Helen Smith
Director
MA Biography and Creative Non-Fiction

KATHERINE ALLEN

✳

WHITE DRESS

IT HAD BEEN A SCORCHING April, even by
the standards of Thailand's hottest month. I was in
Sangkhlaburi, a small town about 300 km north-west of
Bangkok, deep in the jungle near the Burmese border. I was
here with Laura, an old school friend, and we were part of
a small group of Europeans and Australians either teaching
in the local school or helping to build new classrooms.

It was nearing 40° C every day. The nearby jungle
added a thick layer of moisture to the air and the combined
heat and humidity had brought most activity to a standstill.
All of the locals retreated inside as the sun reached its peak,
leaving the stray dogs panting in the dust as the only
signs of life.

Some of us *farang*[1] were coping better than others.
Sleep had been almost impossible for the first week. The air
conditioning was broken in most rooms and the replace-
ment fans simply pushed hot air onto our bodies. I had
been having unusually vivid dreams as I hovered between
sleep and consciousness most nights. I'd got heatstroke in
the first few days and after some long hours shivering in the
dark with the fans on full trying to soothe a raging headache I'd learnt my lesson. I had slowed everything down,
tried to emulate our Thai hosts and moved between areas
of shade. I found the trick was not to resist; to allow it to
wash over you and move through it gently.

The discomfort was exacerbated by the fact that we
were staying in a strict Buddhist community and had to
wear clothes that covered most of our bodies. Research
before the trip had described the more relaxed attitude
towards clothing in Bangkok and most of us had packed
inappropriately for a rural and traditional town. We had
bought new clothes from the local markets that went down
to ankles and elbows and added to the heat.

1. Thai word for foreigner.

Since we'd left the capital, much of what we'd brought from home had stayed packed in our rucksacks but one of the girls had carefully hung up her dresses in her room. There was no wardrobe so Sarah had suspended them from the beams that ran along the ceiling and they moved with the air blown by the fans. They were all too revealing to be worn in public and she would talk about how much she missed wearing them as she put on trousers and long sleeved tops every morning.

There was one place in the town where we could get away with breaking the rules about clothing. There was a hotel used mostly by Western visitors which lay next to a vast lake that marked the edge of Sangkhlaburi. Their property was bordered by a high fence and we could wear what we liked inside this boundary. We would spend much of our free time lying on a wooden pier that went out into the lake.

This is where most of us had headed one morning when we were given an unexpected day off. We had been there for several hours and I had fitted my body into the shadow of a kayak that was suspended on a rack between me and the midday sun. Occasionally I would roll off the pier into the cool, dark water before hauling myself back out of the sun and into my slowly migrating patch of shade. The heat had rendered the last few hours to nothing more than hot wood, cold water and the occasional splash as someone jumped into the water. The pace of my thoughts had slowed to almost nothing.

The shouts of children suddenly penetrated my reverie. I could also hear an engine. It would grow louder, was suddenly accompanied by a splashing sound, which was immediately followed by a fresh round of shrieks and high-pitched laughter. I could visualise what was happening. A truck with an open back would have about a dozen bucket- or water pistol-wielding children clinging onto it. They would be spraying those on either side as it drove up and down the road.

It was Songkran, Thai New Year, and these water-fights were happening all over the country. It was a modern muta-tion of an old Buddhist tradition. Respect is paid to elders or friends with the sprinkling of scented water on shoulders or hands. The water symbolises the washing off of the misfortunes of the past year in preparation for the next. These gentle and respectful traditions have become fierce, nationwide water-fights in recent years.

I glanced across the pier at Laura who had also looked up at the noise. 'Do you want to see what the kids are up to?'

She nodded and moved to stand up carefully. Though we had both been applying factor fifty sunscreen every few hours, she had missed two small patches on either side of her neck and the burns had blistered, making movement painful.

We put trousers and long-sleeved tops back on and walked slowly up the steps from the water, through the hotel and out onto the street. Water was flying everywhere. Armed with anything that could hold liquid, the children were spraying each other, people walking down the streets, or passing cars and mopeds. We stopped to watch but were quickly spotted by some of our students who ran down the hill towards us shouting, 'Teacher, Teacher!' Laura took an entire bucketful to the face and I doubled over laughing but immediately straightened up again from the cold shock of an equal measure being poured down my back. I grabbed a discarded bucket and raced to the tap.

After about half an hour the kids decided to move further down towards the lake where the supply of water would be never-ending and we decided to head back into town and stock up on drinking water at the 7-Eleven. Our clothes were soaked through and we decided that this would keep us cool enough on the half-hour walk up the hill to the shop so we didn't look for a lift.

The jungle crept right up to the edge of town and

between the buildings on the outskirts creating wild gardens for the little white houses. The fences lining the road were made mostly of their repairs and the houses slouched unevenly as though beaten down by the sun. We could see some locals lounging in hammocks in the shade. They were joined by a couple of stray dogs whose whole bodies rocked back and forth as they panted, tongues hanging out of open jaws. They heaved themselves off the floor to come and sniff us and our bags as we passed.

'Oh, I really don't like them,' Laura complained as she sped up to get away from the dogs. Though friendly enough to humans, these dogs would form gangs and square up to each other at night, when we hear the barking and yelping. I wondered if they became more agitated in the heat like us.

Fabrics were draped over the fences and hanging from the rafters of the weaving shop. The huge wooden looms were visible through the doorway. We'd been welcomed in and shown how the machines worked a few days before. We watched the well-practised hands at work and the wooden components flashed back and forth, too quickly for me to decipher quite how each thread was woven into the pattern.

We saw very few of the Thai people actually wearing the beautiful fabrics these women produced. They were sold to us or to tourists. Instead they wore things they described as 'Western clothes'. There was a feeling that we were playing the role of *farang*; wearing 'traditional' clothes that not even the locals wore while they wore what we might back at home.

As we passed 'Garden House', the town's only bar, I began to reflect that walking might not have been such a great idea. The temperature seemed to rise the further up the hill we went. The mid-afternoon heat caught in the back of my throat and made the road and tin roofs shimmer. The town seemed to be melting around us. Our clothes hadn't dried before we'd begun to sweat. I tugged repeatedly at my collar trying to fan myself with my shirt and unstick my clothes from my body. I began looking out for a tuk-tuk or a pick-up to jump in the back of to take us the rest of the way up the hill.

'Let's stop in the shade for a bit.'

We leaned against a fence and drank some water in the shade of the trees that had grown over the top.

A couple of mopeds, each with three people on the back, zipped past us up the hill. No doubt room could have been found for us on one of these two but we decided to wait for a tuk-tuk or someone we knew. As the whine of the overworked scooters faded up the hill the deeper sound of a bigger engine announced the arrival of an old Toyota chugging its way to a halt next to us. One of our Thai colleagues from the summer school leaned out of the window.

'Why you walk?' he laughed and motioned towards the back of the truck. 'Where you want to go?'

'The 7-Eleven please. Thanks Kamon.'

Sitting on the edge of the truck-bed I leaned out beyond the cab and savoured the rare breeze on my face as Laura sat drinking the last of the water in our bottles. I held on as well as I could while not touching any of the truck's metal and was jerked around as we hit potholes and rocks in the road.

We jumped off the truck at the shop, waved our thanks to Kamon as he drove off again and headed towards the door. I was keen to get inside and to stand next to the fridges for a bit. I walked into Laura as she stopped on the top step, 'What the fuck is she doing?' I followed her gaze and saw Sarah striding towards the shop. She was wearing a tight white strapless dress that didn't even reach halfway down her thighs and a pair of wedge sandals that added about four inches to her height.

'She's cracked,' I muttered back.

There were about a dozen locals in the street and all of them were watching her. A couple of women walked out of the shade of their stalls, hands on hips. A young boy who'd just started up his moped killed the engine to watch. The silence expanded down the road.

I tugged at Laura's sleeve and tried to pull her into the shop before we were spotted too. Even though we were doing nothing wrong I felt guilty somehow. But Sarah had seen us. She waved and called out a greeting. Faces flashed from her to us on the shop steps and then back again.

The whole demeanour of the town changed immediately. I felt blood rushing to my face as embarrassment rose up inside me. I knew this would mean trouble for all of us. A shop door that Sarah had just passed banged open. An older man strode out and started shouting in Thai and gesticulating angrily at Sarah. His voice cut through the air and the shock seemed to hit me. This was the first time I'd heard one of the people here shout in anger.

In response she simply raised her head a little higher and smiled as she continued to approach us. Then the man pointed at us as well and though we couldn't understand anything he shouted it was clear that we were no longer welcome. I fixed my eyes on the ground, nudged Laura and said, 'Come on, let's get out of here.'

NOTE: *Speech is not verbatim and names have been changed.*

JUSTINE ASHFORD

*

THE MANY FACES OF
DOLLY HENRY

IN JULY 1914 THE artist Laura Knight returns to her house above Lamorna Cove after a camping expedition with friends. She and her husband Harold have passed an idyllic month on Bodmin Moor at a place called Dozmary Pool. Here they have lived simply, painting and sketching in the woods, swimming naked in rivers (Laura, not Harold), walking for miles and living in harmony with several other couples. They only hear of the threat of war at Plymouth on their way home and pay it little attention. Laura is looking forward to getting back to work, spending her days painting at her hut on the cliffs above Lamorna. Frequently she ends the working day there having seen no one other than a lone fisherman prospecting for mullet along the coastline.

Cornwall enchants the Knights. When Laura and Harold first arrived, they were disappointed by its dullness after the vigour of Staithes on the North Yorkshire coast, where the women wore hobnail boots and carried loads on their heads. 'I hated leaving the moorland,' said Laura, 'the struggle that made you strong, the wild race of fisher people.'[1] But time and familiarity have bred a deep love for the Cornish fishermen, the tropical plants that thrive in the microclimate and the steep streets ablaze in Spring with narcissus and daffodils. The Knights lead the artistic community and its thriving party scene. They are friends with Stanhope Forbes, who runs his famous painting school in a series of huts in a wild meadow on a hill slope, surrounded by fishermen's cottages.[2] And they have recently moved into Stanhope Forbes's old house, Trewarveneth Farm.

Laura steps into the garden at Trewarveneth to find

1. Laura Knight, *Oil Paint and Grease Paint*, (London, 1936), p. 167.
2. Stanhope Forbes had begun, with his wife, Elizabeth, the Newlyn School of Art in 1899 with the emphasis on local subjects, good draughtsmanship and painting in the open air.

a young woman waiting for her there. There is no explanation for her arrival: it is as if nature has conjured her up.
Much later the artist will recall that 'she looked a sunflower
herself among the sunflowers.'[3] With professional interest,
Laura assesses the girl's features, taking in the bold, direct
stare, the high colour in the cheeks, the plump flesh of the
face. The girl's expression is hard to gauge. How old is she?
Perhaps seventeen, maybe a little more. Somewhere on the
cusp of girlhood and maturity. She is tall. She already has
the stamp of London on her, a certain opaqueness. The
lips are full and sensuous, like a pre-Raphaelite beauty. In
a further echo of Rossetti's muse Lizzie Siddal, her hair is
a wild frizz of bright red. Laura will render it redder still
by dashing streaks of scarlet paint among the auburn. Now
the girl's hair catches the sun and is a burnished thing full
of vigorous life, set against the hectic colours of the shrubs.
Without considering further, Laura Knight immediately
engages her as a model. Her name is Dolly Henry.

Over the next few weeks Dolly tells Laura details about
her life as she poses for her portrait. She is part-Irish: her
father comes from Roscommon and is a travelling salesman
of clothes. Born in Colchester, she moved to London three
years ago and first worked in a draper's in Regent Street before falling in with a group of young artists from the Slade
School. She has never been to Cornwall before.

Laura paints Dolly *en plein air*, a favourite way of
working and one that enables her to capture the play of
light on her subject. Most of the Newlyn artists paint in
the open, away from the restrictions of the studio. It is
one of the cornerstones of Stanhope Forbes's teaching.
And the Cornish light is extraordinary, a light so clean it
appears rinsed, capable of turning 'grey Penzance… into
a pearly city.'[4] Laura stretches a canvas twenty inches by

3. Knight, *Oil Paint and Grease Paint*, p. 209.
4. Knight, p. 170.

twenty-four, cleans it with turps and treats it with linseed oil. Then she paints Dolly as if she is part of the beauty of the garden, capturing their first meeting.[5] Dolly wears a simple dress with a modest neckline, the front of which is patterned so it seems the flowers have crept from the background to nestle on her breast. Her throat is emphasised by a smudge of yellow under the chin. This is the throat that – as Dolly tells Laura during one of their sittings – John Currie has threatened to cut.[6] Who is John Currie? Laura is not familiar with the name, even though Currie is an artist. He is staying at Newlyn nearby, where many artists reside. He paints the coastline in thick angular lines and blocks of dirty brown paint. He is a passionate man, full of energy, but jealous. He reads Dostoevsky aloud. He loves her, Dolly says, but they fight. He accuses her of seeing other men. And has she seen other men? The girl is defiant: what if she has? He's married, isn't he? Laura listens as she paints. In a few weeks' time, Currie will send a series of curt notes to Laura and Harold, demanding information about Dolly's whereabouts after she leaves Cornwall in a panic. He will follow Dolly back to London and corner her in her apartment in Paulton Square in Chelsea.

But that is for the future. For now, none of this turbulence is evident in the pretty studies of Dolly that Laura Knight completes. In *Marsh Mallows*, Dolly is in profile, looking down at a pink blossom in her hand. The mood is contemplative and Dolly looks very young and fresh. Her right hand is raised to her chin, the slender fingers resting at her jawline. Bright light comes in from the side bathing her elbow, cheek and neck in radiance and lighting on her lips. Her dress is a simple, belted style, her waist evidently

5. This is *Rose and Gold* (1914), a picture Laura Knight held onto until her death.
6. David Boyd Haycock, *A Crisis of Brilliance,* (London, 2009), p. 174.

slim. Laura paints her as an innocent on the edge of life with a palette of soft pastel tones. It is Dolly's hair that catches the eye again: shingled, sitting high off her neck, with a neat fringe falling to her eyebrows. She would be noticed in a group: she is eye-catching.

Dolly knows how to sit for her portrait. She is a professional, having already sat several times for Currie and his friends from the Slade, obeying their instructions. Currie's first portrait of her was flattering, a soft study of her head and shoulders, executed in oils.[7] In this painting Dolly's auburn hair contrasts with the pretty *eau-de-nil* of the background and she wears a medieval-style headband with a single green stone at the middle parting. How different from Currie's last portrait of her, *The Witch*. This does not seem like the same girl. Here the light has hardened to a hard-edged white, sharpening the shadows of her cheekbones and giving her red hair the gingery tone of a fox's brush. Her lips are pinched, her expression assessing and fault-finding. Her left hand is raised, holding a tress of her hair as if she is fully aware of her own artfulness. She is a femme fatale, looking upon somebody she disdains. She can do nothing about how he perceives her. First he sees her one way, then another. It is the lot of an artist's model. She is merely a vehicle for ideas about the application of paint or the magic of a line.[8] If the art is experimental, she becomes part of the experiment, liable to bend to whatever novel purpose the artist sees fit to put her form.

Laura relishes the female body and, unlike some of her contemporaries, wants to present it realistically. She photographs her neighbour – and fellow artist – Ella Naper, reclining naked on the grass. Female art students are not

7. This is *Head of a Girl* (1912), now in the Potteries Museum and Art Gallery.
8. The title of Laura Knight's autobiography, published in 1965.

permitted access to nude models – Laura had to learn from plaster casts – yet Mrs Knight is frequently to be seen painting from life while her models stretch out naked on the rocks by the sea. After war breaks out, rules will be tightened prohibiting any activity along the coast that could conceal espionage and the artists will have to return inside. No more will the locals happen upon unclothed women lounging in the dark gold meadow grass above Lamorna Cove. It is possible that one of those unclothed women is Dolly Henry; for a few months she becomes part of Laura's professionally confident world.

Indeed, Laura is experiencing an acute sense of *joie de vivre*: 'An ebullient vitality made me want to paint the whole world and say how glorious it was to be young and strong.'[9] She feels a surge of confidence in her eye, saying triumphantly of her painting *The Green Feather* (1911), 'Let there be Knight and there was Knight!'[10] She prepares canvases at speed and paints all day in the open air, not letting the wind or the threat of rain keep her from her vision. The images she creates of Dolly Henry in *Marsh Mallows* and *Rose and Gold* are optimistic, vigorous, handsome, romantic, giving no hint of the dissonance of Dolly's life, nor of the sexual power of which she stands accused by Currie. Looking at the paintings, you would be more likely to side with Currie's friend Adrian Allinson[11] who saw Currie as the aggressor: 'Violent jealousy continually drove Currie to threats of murder,' he wrote.[12]

Laura Knight is sceptical about Dolly's stories of John Currie. If he is so threatening, why, during these few weeks when she sits for her portraits, does Dolly return to Currie

9. Ibid.
10. Knight, p. 192.
11. Founder member of the Camden Group; he graduated from the Slade School at the same time as Currie.
12. Haycock, *A Crisis of Brilliance*, p. 112.

in the evenings? Dolly lets on that she and Currie argue continually, as they have argued in London and in Brittany where he painted the peasants while she longed to be back in Soho. He has threatened her with physical violence and she is frightened of what he might do. 'I know he is going to try and kill me again,' she tells Laura, who dismisses this as sensational nonsense.[13] Nonetheless, Currie sounds pretty unpleasant. When he and Dolly are walking on a clifftop path, apparently he says he will push her over the edge. He blames her for fatally distracting him from his work, for leading him on and then toying with him. Yet he says he loves her, adores her, cannot be without her. But then he claims he is losing his talent and it is all her fault. His friends call Dolly uneducated, possessive, dangerous.[14] He would be better rid of her, they hint.

Dolly is a marked woman.

13. Knight, p. 209.
14. This was the verdict of Currie's friend and patron, Michael Sadleir.

LISA EVELEIGH

*

AN UNLIKELY ALLIANCE

ON MARCH 23RD 1803, the elderly Susannah, Lady
Stafford, opened a parcel containing a stylish French coat.
Though religious, a strict moralist and interested in domes-
tic rather than fashionable life, she was feminine enough
to be pleased with the garment. Yet she was uneasy about
accepting such a present because it had been purchased
in Paris by her son's mistress.

Her anxiety showed in a letter she wrote to
him immediately:

> This evening my pelisse arrived; it is exactly what I like,
> and not one Bit too large. Pray thank Lady Bes. a thousand
> Times and tell her how much I like it, and pray take
> Money in your Pocket to pay it without Delay.[1]

To offer to pay for a gift could be construed as an insult
then but 'Lady Bes.' was Harriet, Lady Bessborough,
a woman of great beauty and charm, and the lover of
Susannah's adored son Granville, Lord Leveson Gower.
Belatedly realising she might cause offence, she returned to
the subject in a postscript to the same letter, with a clumsy
attempt at humour:

> Do not forget to pay the Pelisse, with my best
> Acknowledgements. It was very, very Good in Lady Bes to
> trouble herself to conduce to make my old Carcass warm
> and comfortable.

Susannah's ambivalence is understandable. She was
both hostile to – and frightened of – Harriet. She believed
– with good reason – that Harriet was preventing Granville
from settling down and marrying. He was thirty years old,
and Harriet was a married woman of forty-two. They had
been lovers for at least six years, and she had secretly borne
him a daughter (and would go on to have a son by him).

Harriet had a particular reason for sending Susannah
an expensive gift. Highly perceptive, she was aware of

1. *Private Correspondence of Lord Granville Leveson Gower,
Vol 1*, p. 416.

Susannah's suspicion of her, and had deliberately set out to disarm her. Susannah and her husband were upright Tories, who disapproved of the sexual freedom and extravagances that Harriet and her sister Georgiana, Duchess of Devonshire, allowed themselves. Yet the social and political influence of the sisters and their Whig friends could not be entirely discounted; they were close to the Prince of Wales, Charles James Fox and Sheridan.

Since she was unwilling to divorce Lord Bessborough, and risk losing custody of her legitimate children,[2] Harriet realised that it would be unrealistic for Granville to remain single. She steeled herself to encourage his efforts to find a bride in the hope that Susannah would think more kindly of her, and accept her role in Granville's life. She could not bear to lose his friendship entirely and hoped to remain on affectionate – if no longer intimate – terms with him, should a future wife forbid further dalliance. By flattering his mother, she hoped to establish herself as a friend of the wider family.

As his swagger portrait by Sir Thomas Lawrence shows, Granville was startlingly handsome, with abundant dark curling hair and azure blue eyes. Though many women admired his face and elegant figure, he needed to marry money. He was a second son with no estate to inherit, and like Harriet and Georgiana, gambled recklessly, once losing £23,000 in one night.[3]

During the 1803 season the most sought after *debutante* in London was eighteen-year-old Lady Sarah Fane, sole heiress to the immense Child banking fortune.[4] Granville had commented on her 'great beauty' to his mother in a letter written the previous year.[5] Now he was

2. Her daughter Caroline Ponsonby was fragile; we know her as Lady Caroline Lamb.
3. £740,000 today.
4. Approximately £4 million today.
5. Ibid. p 332.

one of several young men pursuing her; his rivals included Lord Craven, Lord Villiers and the playwright Sheridan's indigent but witty son Tom. But since Granville was both vain and accustomed to adoration from his mother, Harriet, his three sisters and other women, Sarah's failure to show a clear preference for him irked him.

It also greatly concerned Susannah, who constantly advised him. Perhaps she sensed that a proud man would be unlikely to relish this interference for in the same letter, after a paragraph of tame political gossip, she hesitated before mentioning Lady Sarah:

> *I thought not to mention what I have so much at Heart, fearing to worry you; but upon second Thoughts, I believe it must be the most pleasing Subject to you, for I know you are attached to her; and though sometimes Jealousy may make you see things in a false Medium, yet you must feel that you have Cause to hope, and you cannot but be pleased to read or to hear anything of the Object of your Affections…*

As if taking a deep breath, she continued:

> *…and I do hear that though there is not any Certainty, yet Spectators fancy you the favor'd lover, and take Occasion to report how much Lord Villiers is to be pitied, for that he is really and truly in Love with her, and scruples not to own himself miserable, but that you are attach'd elsewhere and follow her for her Fortune.*

A key phrase is 'attach'd elsewhere'; Susannah is obliquely referring to Harriet. And though Sarah was lovely to look at, Susannah and other ambitious mothers were certainly interested in her immense wealth. She plunged on with more advice:

> *This very ill natured, false Report, though it provokes me, yet to me it proves that his Aiders and abettors think you have the Preference in her affection, and so I trust you have.*
> *Do not allow a Dash of jealousy to poison your Mind,*

*but go on in following her, talking to her, and paying her
every Attention in your Power. You may be agitated with
Hopes, Fears, and anxious Doubts – all who truly love
experience these contending Plagues; you are therefore
as well off as any of your Sex ever were whilst in that
State of Uncertainty.*

So Good Night, my beloved Granville.[6]

Susannah was trying to convince herself, as well as her son,
that he was genuinely attached to Sarah: 'all who truly love
experience these contending Plagues'. Clearly reflecting
the values and preoccupations of the upper classes in the
early nineteenth century, beneath the affectionate tone
and overt advice, there was much left unsaid in this letter.
Superficially a mix of maternal concern, worldly advice and
hope, it was also self-deceiving.

Susannah did not name 'the aiders and abettors' but
Granville's chief rival Villiers was the son of a wily and
rapacious woman, Frances, Lady Jersey. A former mistress
of the Prince of Wales, she was determined to achieve
brilliant marriages for her ten children now that her
career as a *femme fatale* was over. Harriet's own eldest son,
Viscount Duncannon, had narrowly avoided being caught
by Frances's flirtatious daughter Lady Elizabeth Villiers the
previous year, much to Harriet's relief. She thought he was
too young to marry, and additionally did not want a connection with the Jersey family. A vengeful Frances would
not have hesitated to remind Lord and Lady Westmorland,
Sarah's parents, of Granville's affair with Harriet.

But Harriet was also lobbying for Sarah and had written to Granville from Paris, using Sarah's nickname:

*I wish you could have heard what a fine character and
description I gave of Sally last night…upon a less favoura-
ble one having been given. You could not have prais'd
her more.*[7]

6. Ibid. p. 416.
7. Ibid. p. 389.

When she returned to Britain she continued to take a close interest in the progress of the courtship, writing:

> ...if she thinks at all about you she cannot be much in love with Ld. Villiers. Real serious love completely roots out every vestige of Coquettery [sic]. She would scarcely know whether you exist, much less whether you follow her or not, and if she is not in love with him you have full as good a chance as he has – I should think better...[8]

And revealingly, in the same letter, she included a humbly expressed message for Susannah, who had been persuaded to accept the *pelisse*:

> Will you give a message for me to your Mother? Thank her a thousand times for her letter, and for indulging me about the Pelisse. Tell her she never can appear to me in any light but that of a Person for whom I feel the highest degree of respect and affection...I am far from expecting that she should trouble herself to answer any nonsensical letter I may happen to write when you are away, if I can pick up any news which I think will amuse her.[9]

So Susannah's desire to pay for the fashionable French garment was ultimately overcome. Even she – based in Staffordshire – could not resist the offer of 'nonsensical' society gossip from one of its leading participants. Harriet's charm had won her over.

However, a courtship which required quite so much advice cannot have been a very ardent one. Granville needed employment and was sent to Russia as Ambassador before he had been nagged into proposing by either his mother or his mistress. Sarah eventually made her choice; she married Lord Villiers in May 1804. Harriet was to retain the chief place in Granville's heart for another six years, though he flirted with many Russian beauties. As she had desired, she established a respectful friendship with Susannah and they

8. Ibid. p .417.
9. Ibid. p. 418.

took mutual comfort in his absence by corresponding regularly, quoting snippets from his letters that might interest the other.

Sadly, Susannah did not live to see her beloved son marry; she died in August 1805, when Granville was still abroad. Harriet wrote to him at once:

> *I have scarcely heart to write to you, dearest G. No words can tell you how much I regret being from you at this moment – how deeply I feel your loss, and let me say, my own, for I can never think without gratitude and affection of her kindness to me.*[10]

This reads sincerely. Due to the resumption of the Napoleonic wars, letters from England took a long time to reach Russia and, sadly, Granville first learnt about the death of his mother in a newspaper.

When he returned, his hunt for a wife resumed. One can only speculate how his mother would have reacted to his eventual choice of bride; in 1809, he married Lady Harriet Cavendish (known as Harryo), Georgiana's daughter and Harriet's niece. It was to be a happy marriage. Harriet faced the end of their long relationship bravely, writing generously:

> *I think only of your happiness – yours and Harriet's. God bless and preserve you both.*[11]

Harriet and Granville remained friends and exchanged letters until her death in 1821, partly about their two illegitimate children, George and Harriette Stewart. Because he wished it, Harryo and Granville took them from their foster parents and brought them up with their own children.

This must have been torturing for Harriet to witness; but she was always a pragmatist.

10. *Private Correspondence of Lord Granville Leveson Gower, Vol 2*, p. 106.
11. Ibid. p. 348.

SALLY FOX

*

EULOGY FOR A MOTHER

IT'S SUNDAY AND THE rain pounds relentlessly against the walls of the house, beats on the windowpanes. My mother, who is determined to teach me to dance, pushes the kitchen table back against the wall, switches the record player on and tosses her shoes carelessly to the side. I sit and watch as she jigs and shuffles around the room, showing me the steps. *This is the rumba,* she explains. *Aahh, there's nothing like the rumba. It's lovely when it's danced well. It's slow, you see, you circle around your partner. Like this. . . . And this is the foxtrot. One slow, two quick: slow, quick, quick; slow, quick, quick.* She holds her body tall, taut. *And this is the jive,* she says, pulling me up out of my chair. Swinging and twirling me around, she pushes me back and forth to a scratchy rendition of Joe Loss singing *In The Mood. Loosen up; let yourself go; get some movement in those hips,* she urges. Afterwards, panting and out of breath, we collapse on the sofa and she tells me that if she hadn't had us, her children, she would have made something of her life. She would have been a dancer.

This scene with my mother runs throughout my life like a worn-out home movie. The screen is faded; the black-and-white images, no longer distinct, are grey. The words, and the meaning behind the words, are sketchy, broken, distorted from the constant replaying. More so, now that she is no longer alive.

She died in March, early one Monday morning, in the middle of a rainstorm, in a hospital bed with only a nurse sitting beside her to count down the spaces between each last dying breath. She went so quickly that my sisters and I had not been able to get there in time. The nurse told me she was brave at the end. She slipped out of this world like she slipped along the hospital corridor in her wheelchair, fast and focused. I think the slipping metaphor might have been more accurately applied to one of her wild swing dance routines. *Pace your breathing,* she'd tell me when, in the space of our small kitchen, her feet tapped and slid across the linoed floor. Breathe, breathe. *That's it. Time it . . . breathe. Ahhh. Now, let go . . . aaahhhh.*

The viewing is at Finch's Funeral Home in Northampton, a large town in the centre of England that is renowned for its shoe factories and its puritan, working-class mindset. It is the place where my mother was born, where she lived and died. She might have been working class, but she was no puritan, and she would have hated this sterile, dull place. The coffin, which sits in the middle of the room, is black and imposing. It is surrounded by four round tables that bear flowers – lilies, tulips, orchids, irises – and funeral directory leaflets (for future reference, of course). The walls are white and bare. There is not a television in sight. No radio blaring out the war-time oldies, no Glen Miller, foot tapping, finger clicking, voice wavering to *That Old Black Magic* that was always under my mother's skin. No, not my mother's room at all.

Not my mother's body either. This body is plump, stout, the face swollen, puffy. I can't see her for the swelling and the make-up. Somewhere, underneath the rouge that covers her white skin (hard now in death), the baby-blue eye shadow (a colour she would never wear), and the painted red lips (thinner than I remembered them) is the woman, the mother, I knew. She was a beautiful woman, full of life. Not plump and stout, but slim and fine. Her limbs were the limbs of a dancer, her hands delicate, her features high and bold. Similar to Klimt's women, she was sensuous, all wrapped up in colour and soft paint and soft fabrics and soft music caressing her. Always.

As a small child, I would sit on her bed and watch as she dressed in front of her full-length closet mirror. I remember how she would pull her dress over her head, then turn and twist, this way and then that, watching as her skirt swirled and flowed around her. Finally, with an appreciative smile, she would pose one leg in front of the other, run her hands down the length of her body, and ask, *Not bad, eh Sal?*

Not bad at all, I repeated, nodding my head. It was expected.

But now, I would hardly know her if it wasn't for the green wool suit she is wearing. She made it the summer she was first diagnosed with lung cancer. I'd been living in Canada at the time and I'd flown back to England to spend the summer with her. The holiday consisted of long, lazy days spent making and drinking copious amounts of tea. Hour after hour, I watched her cut out the pattern, cut the material, pin and sew it together. She had liked that suit: the slim-line pencil skirt and the fitted jacket. She had worn it when I took her to one of her first hospital appointments. Looking at the X-ray, we saw the long tentacles of the tumour already wrapping itself around my mother's wind-pipe. The doctor pointed it out: *Look, this grey area here. That's where it is.* Neither of us talked about it afterwards, refusing to give credence to this stranger, this unwelcome intruder, inside her.

I have a romantic image of my mother, made up from what I know about her and what she herself has told me. She is young, maybe fifteen, and she is lit up by the strange, wavering gaslight of a streetlamp, its silver aura falling on her as she clutches the post with one hand; with the other, she leans out, reaching into thin air, and swings around and around. She has the poise, the graceful ease of a dancer. As I watch, a man – a Fred Astaire lookalike – walks towards her, holds out his hand. She takes it and they glide across the pavement, spinning and leaping to the music of the imaginary band.

But with the outbreak of World War II and the call for women to enter the factories, the music was soon replaced by the insistent drone of industrial machines, the dancing restricted to the repetitive punch, burrow, countersink, and clenching of the rivets she drilled into the wings of planes. Anything to reduce turbulence, unnecessary drag. The man she married (my father) was no Fred Astaire. He was a navy signalman, a communications specialist. He spent his days writing to her and staring out to sea, mentally sending her love messages in Morse code. After the war, he, too, became a factory worker. Unlike my mother, though, his feet were firmly on the ground, and life became reduced to Saturday night football, fish and chips on Fridays, and a holiday to Heacham once a year.

Standing here now above my mother's prone body, her eyes tightly closed, arms crossed, feet together, I tentatively reach out and run my fingers over the back of her hand. I am surprised at the coldness, the hardness of skin that had once nursed me, held me. Hard to think of her here, dressed up, as she would say, with nowhere to go. And I think of how she died: grasping for breath, the cancer in her lungs wrapping itself around her windpipe like some parasitic, suicidal beast.

I bend, kiss her softly on the crease between her eyebrows, and leave, returning to the house where she lived most of her adult life, the house in which I was born. My sisters, Toni, Maureen and Pat, come with me. We go to her bedroom, the room in which I sat and watched her dress as a child, and we sort through her things. I am shocked by how little she had. A few bits of old make-up, a few bottles of stale perfume, a fake pearl necklace, and a few rings: her wedding ring, an amethyst set in silver, and a gold ring that says 'Mum' on it. My oldest sister, Maureen, takes her wedding ring and slides it on her finger, next to her own wedding band. I take the ring that says 'Mum,' even though it doesn't fit any of my fingers, and I put it on a chain around my neck. My sister, Pat, takes a scarf she had always wanted. She folds it around her shoulders. *Mum had great taste*, she says, *such style*, and we all agree. Ghosts of Mum remain and we take these parts, these fragments of her, these things, to carry with us. Always.

Look at this, my sister, Toni, says as she pulls a long

fifties-style silk dress out of the closet, the skirt flowing wide and free as she holds it against her body and swirls around in a circle. Maureen swirls too, her head held high, her arm extended out and around an imaginary dance partner. Pat and I, the more conservative sisters, do not swirl, but we do move our hips a little and laugh. I think if Mum could talk now, she wouldn't reminisce about what she didn't have or couldn't do. She would tell us to dance. *Dance like your life depends on it. Dance around the small spaces of your house like the small spaces of your life. Swing those hips, shuffle those feet, step to the side, step forward and back and do it over and over again. Aaahh …*

On the day of the funeral, it is overcast. My sisters and I are dressed up to the nines. *None of this feels real*, I say to my sister. *A whole life spent on this small red-brick, working-class street. And for what?* I smile, though, when Mum arrives in all her splendid magnificence, riding horizontally in the back of the hearse. She always liked to make a grand entry. And now a grand departure, all stuffed and dressed up and ready for the next gig.

The neighbours come out to see her off when the hearse arrives. It is a ritual. They look suitably sorrowful. The woman from next door, the scruffy one with the six kids, tells us that she is sorry for our loss. *A wonderful woman, your mother*, she says. Everyone, as they do on these occasions, is either crying or trying to cry. My sister Maureen is sobbing loudly, as is her way. My sister Pat, stoic, poised, wipes away a tear that has slid unbidden down her cheek. I don't know where I, the youngest of them, fit. I try to cry, but I am numb inside.

I expect to get in the limousine and drive, albeit slowly, to the crematorium, but this doesn't happen. Instead, the funeral director, dressed in black with top hat and tails, begins very slowly, step by slow step, to walk in front of the hearse. *Why is he doing this?* I ask Pat.

It's a sign of respect, she whispers, reaching for my hand and squeezing it gently. It takes him twenty minutes to walk the hundred yards or so that it takes for us to leave the street where Mum walked and sang and danced and slept and cried and loved her life away. By the time we get out of the street, an involuntary sob escapes my throat, and, try as I might, I can't stop the slow fall of tears that slide down my face.

As we drive away, a wind picks up and sways the newly green trees, shaking a few tender leaves loose and spraying them, like flowers, on the street ahead of us. I sense her now, not in the back of the hearse, but all around us. She is dancing – dancing on her coffin, dancing on the roof of the hearse, dancing in the street – leading us in a soft shoe sliding, sweet slipping rumba to her own funeral. *Watch my feet*, she says, *this way. Follow me.* And we do.

ODRÁN WALDRON

＊

THAT YELLOW CAR

WE WERE ON A ROUNDABOUT in Newry when
it appeared; a sports car, I can't remember the make. The
manufacturer wasn't important, but apparently the colour
was. All the boys on the bus said it was a really nice car, but
it was an awful colour; this sentiment got passed down one
row of seats and made its way back up the other. Nobody
could abide that bright yellow. If anyone on the bus were in
possession of the car, they would have resprayed it. Maybe
they'd spray it blue, or black. Anything other than the
eyesore of a colour the car currently sported; it was almost
unanimous. 'It's not that bad,' my newly cracked voice said
as everyone leaned towards the back window to gaze in disgust at the car ruined by its bright exterior. Heads turned
away from the window and soon there was a group of casti-
gators asking what my problem was, what was wrong with
me and how it was possible that I didn't consider the car's
colour to be among humanity's gravest offences. It wasn't
that I loved the car's colour; I just didn't think it was as bad
as everyone was making it out to be.

Unlike most of my childhood friends, I wasn't obsessed
with cars and their aesthetics. I maintained a strict 'I hate
body kits' policy, but I knew an attractive car when I saw
one. All I was trying to say was that, for me, the colour
of the car, while not appealing to look at per se, didn't
destroy the attractiveness of the car's shape. A hurl wasn't
deemed bad if someone put a stupid grip on it; I assumed
we adhered to the same principles with cars. Maybe this
was lost in translation; maybe it was lost in my sentences
that were stopped in the middle of the first word as I was
shouted over and derided for my lack of critical eye. Then
again, I did put pink grips on my hurls, so maybe I was just
wrong all the time. Long after the car had passed out of our
lives, its presence hung on the bus as anything I said was
met with a reminder that I thought that the car's colour
hadn't been that bad; my opinion on the Irish soccer team
was devalued because I thought that the car's yellow colour

wasn't that bad.

'Yeah, but you thought the colour on the car was nice, so what the fuck would you know?' was a sentence that was repeated often over the course of the weekend. Chief among those who sought to discredit the worth of my views were Jay, who would go on to become one of my best friends in Goldfields, and a boy nicknamed Mash. Jay and I weren't friends at the time; neither were we childhood enemies or anything along those lines. Our relationship was pretty much non-existent, but he was two years older than me and, as does happen at that age, he liked to exercise his seniority by reminding some younger boys that what he thought held more weight than what they thought and these exercises seemed to involve me more often than they didn't.

Mash was a different story altogether. He had inherited his nickname from his older brother, was the same age as Jay and he was a vindictive little shit of a thirteen year old. When I was within earshot, Mash would suddenly turn from the hilarious person that all of my friends assured me he was into some sinister prick whose only interest was the absolute destruction of any joy or confidence I possessed. I know that this all seems sensationalised, especially given that Mash and I get on reasonably well now, but that was how he seemed to my eleven-year-old self. We were on a bus to Belfast when the car controversy erupted, heading for the ferry to Scotland. It was 2005 and we were on one of the Goldfield hurling club's sporadic trips to Scotland. My brother had been on one in 2002 and now it was my turn, but things hadn't gone as I had hoped and my inability to criticise a colour that was only mundane to me hung over me for the entirety of the trip. My hopes of enjoying a weekend away in a country I had never seen before with my friends were dashed within the first few hours because of a sentence that I thought was innocuous at worst.

Things simmered, but remained tense for the whole trip. Everything I said aloud in a group setting was shouted down, primarily by Mash. Everything he said, whether it was directed my way or not, seemed to provoke a sense of anger in me that I wasn't aware I had possessed until our sojourn to the Scottish Highlands. I retreated into myself and wished that I had stayed home. I would sit with my head down in the window seat, trying to ignore Mash's barbs, but eventually his words began to cut too much, and so I began answering him back. His abuse grew more fervent, and I could tell that he was taken aback by this challenge to his authority within the group of young Goldfieldian boys. Looking back on it, what happened when our bus pulled up to a waterpark shouldn't have been a surprise, but at the time I didn't think that it would happen. I had wanted it to happen; I thought that I could win if it did happen. I thought I could teach the older boys to stop trying to take the weight away from my opinion by showing them that I was just as strong as they were; that anyone who wanted to try and stop what I was saying would end up in the state in which I was going to leave Mash. I was big for my age; I was about as tall as Mash and the other boys his age. I figured that if something happened, I could at the very least hold my own. When he aimed his apparently hilarious rhetoric my way, I would respond aggressively; sometimes it was just a simple fuck off, but other times I attempted to turn the barrel of the gun back around on him, usually aiming at the mushroom-shaped blond hair that sat on his head.

I'm not sure what it was that I said just after our bus had stopped outside the waterpark, but it sparked my desired reaction in Mash. It was probably something to do with the mushroom haircut; those ones seemed to rankle with him the most. Whatever it was, it was enough to make him spin around in the aisle of the bus. I was still seated and I raised my arms to protect my face as he spun and swung a punch all in one motion. The blows came too quickly and I kept my arms raised over my head and face, waiting for the frequency of his swings to lessen, but they never did.

Eventually, his fists began breaking through my guard and there was nothing I could do about it. It seemed like there was no end, like he had four arms, like others were hitting me too, but all I could see was the anger stretched across his reddened face as he struck down continuously. I lay in the foetal position and whimpered as he pummelled me, never getting the chance to strike back even once. I felt tears breaking through my eyes, but I knew I couldn't cry out; to take a beating this severe was one thing, to take it like a tall-for-his-age baby would end any hope of repairing the reputation that was getting beaten up with me. It came to an end after some time, but still I cowered. My face covered in the tears that streamed from my eyes, the blood that trickled from my lower lip and the spit that shot from my mouth during my spluttered gasps for air as I attempted to process what had just happened. After a while, I rubbed my eyes, cleaned my lip and stood up from my seat into the aisle of the bus. My knees shook as I placed my foot down on the ugly burgundy carpet and I still whimpered and gasped as I made my way to the still-open door. The bus was long deserted, but the door had been left open for me so that I could join the fun in the waterpark once I forgot my beating.

When I finally made it off the bus, arm shaking as I leaned against the door for support, Fiachra, my oldest friend in Goldfields, was standing there, waiting for me. He didn't say anything when I saw him, he just nodded his head in the same sheepish way he does to this day and we walked into the waterpark together. That whole day, only Fiachra spoke to me. It was his usual amount of discussion, which isn't much, but he was there. I saw the others looking at us and looking away when they saw my eyes rise towards them. My eyes dried and my breathing went back to its usual asthmatic rustiness. We never spoke of the fight or my embarrassment; we just went water-skiing.

BIOGRAPHIES

✳

ADAM ANDRUSIER was born in 1974. He studied music at King's College, Cambridge, then turned his childhood hobby of autograph collecting into a business. Adam is working on a novel, *Memoirs of a Child Psychic*, about a child who convinces his family he can bend spoons with his mind.

KATHERINE ALLEN grew up in Bath and then moved to Norwich to do her first degree in Literature and History at UEA. She then stayed on to study for an MA in Biography and Creative Non-Fiction. Some of her writing on photography has been published in *Shooter Literary Magazine*.

MICHAEL ALLEN was born in London in 1986. He studied Fine Art at The Slade, London, and at the École Nationale Supérieure des Beaux-Arts, Paris. He is currently working on a collection of linked short stories set in a fictional caravan park on the English coast.

SAMANTHA ALLEN is from Phoenix, Arizona. She received her BA in English and Creative Writing from Arizona State University and worked as a freelance writer before moving to Norwich with her husband and two cats. She is currently working on a novel that she describes as a Gothic Feminist Western.

JUSTINE ASHFORD is particularly interested in writing about the hidden histories of women who have occupied the margins of others' stories. She has had work published by the Bronte Society and blogs on the subject of loss at afterwards.live. Justine lives with her five-year-old son in Suffolk.

JAMES BARNES was born in 1993 and lives in Norwich. He is working on a short story collection about unconventional religious practices and the ways in which our experiences in the real world and the world on screen can bleed into each other.

ROSS BENAR is a Jew from the American South. He currently lives in Europe.

ANNETTA BERRY has a First and PhD in Art History from Cambridge University. At the National Gallery, her work was nominated for two Interactive BAFTAs. She has worked at Tate and for the Royal Collection. Her novel-in-progress, *The Binding Frame*, was longlisted for the Bath Novel Award 2016.

NICK BRADLEY was born in 1982 and grew up in Bath. He lived and worked in Japan on and off for 10 years, and speaks Japanese fluently. He is currently working on a novel set in Japan after the 2011 disaster, and a linked collection of short stories set in Tokyo.

ROSALIND BROWN received a Malcolm Bradbury Memorial Bursary for the MA. Her story 'General Impression of Size and Shape' appeared in *Lighthouse* in March 2016. Her novel, *Position of Trust*, follows a young woman finally confronting the pain and guilt she experienced after an illegal affair with her female teacher twelve years ago.

DESMOND BYRNE grew up in Dublin but has lived in London since the eighties. Writing in a style that he describes as 'dirty modernism', he cites Joyce, Hubert Selby Junior and Kathy Acker as influences. *Month's Mind* is his first novel.

ROSANNE DAVIES has worked as a teacher in Moscow and London. Her current writing projects explore what happens when different cultures clash. *Beyond, The Fire* is the opening to a historical novel about the impact of the presence of European whalers on the Ngāti Tumatakokiri tribe of Mohua (Golden Bay). She is also working on a novel set in the Lot Valley, France.

NICHOLAS DEPHTEREOS is originally from Northern New York, has worked as a writing instructor and storyteller in Savannah, Georgia, and has lived in New York, New England and the Deep South. He is currently working on a historical novel about the settlement of Upstate New York at the turn of the 18th century.

LISA EVELEIGH's first degree was in English literature at the University of Durham. A BBC researcher before becoming a literary agent, she runs her own boutique agency, Richford Becklow, and a digital imprint, The Paris Press. Lisa lives in London, and before this MA, was a keen cook and gardener.

SALLY FOX is a memoirist and creative non-fiction writer. Current projects include a memoir about the premature birth of her son and his diagnoses with cerebral palsy, epilepsy, and schizophrenia. She is also writing about growing up with a mother who had bipolar disorder. Both affirm positively the complexities of life and love in very difficult circumstances. www.sally-fox.com.

JEHANGIR JILANI is a solicitor and human rights lawyer. He has worked in various organisations for victims of human rights abuses and is writing a related novel.

ADAM BENNETT KEOGH is from County Wicklow, Ireland. He writes short stories, and is currently working on the final draft of his first novel, *Every Other Place*, which was longlisted for the 2015 Bridport First Novel Award under its previous title, *Tilt*.

D M LYNCH is from Cork City in Ireland and holds a BA in English Literature from Trinity College Dublin. His fiction has appeared in *Three Monkeys*, *The Stinging Fly*, *The Irish Times* and the anthology *The Best Small Fictions 2015*, edited by Pulitzer Prize winner Robert Olen Butler.

LUCY MALOUF is an award-winning non-fiction writer. She is the co-author of nine books and contributes to publications in Australia and the UK. The extract is from her first novel; she is also writing a comic crime story set in Margate, near her home in East Kent.

JACINTA MULDERS is from Sydney. She has worked in arts journalism and human rights law. Her writing has appeared in *Meanjin*, *Seizure*, *Oyster* and *Pollen*. She is working on a collection of short stories.

FELICITY NOTLEY is based in Cornwall. Her

published work includes poetry and short stories. She has read at the Port Eliot Festival and on the radio. She came second in the LiteratureWorks First Page Prize, and has been shortlisted for the Bridport Prize for Poetry. She was awarded the Seth Donaldson Memorial Bursary for study at UEA.

WILL NOTT was born in London in 1991. At UEA he is a recipient of the Malcom Bradbury Bursary. He has worked as a journalist, writing for the *Daily Express* and *VICE*. He is finishing a first novel.

KRISTIEN POTGIETER is from Johannesburg, South Africa, and is the recipient of the 2015 UEA Booker Prize Foundation Scholarship. She has worked as a freelance translator and editor, and as an English teacher in France.

RORY POWER graduated from Middlebury College in 2014. She interned in the editorial departments of St Martin's and Knopf before joining the Bent Agency as a reader. She is currently working on a speculative YA novel set at an all-girls boarding school in the Outer Banks of North Carolina.

SAMANTHA PURVIS is from London. She holds an English Literature and Creative Writing BA and a Creative Writing MA from UEA. She has worked at Bloomsbury, Elsevier and *The White Review*. She is currently working on a collection of short stories provisionally titled *Whoever Might Like to Hear It*.

JENNIFER ROE is from Dublin, Ireland. She taught English and Religion before moving to Norwich for the MA. In 2013 she won the *Aesthetica* Short Story Award and was published in their annual magazine.

RASHMEE ROSHAN LALL is a journalist who writes on world affairs. She presented the BBC World Service's *The World Today*, edited *The Sunday Times of India* and has written for *The Guardian*, *The Economist* and *Foreign Policy*. She has lived and worked around the world, including Kabul, Port au Prince and Abu Dhabi. Her website is www.rashmee.com.

VANDANA SARAS grew up in New Delhi, studied engineering in Moscow and then lived as a starving artist and writer in New York City, where she was a featured poet at Nuyorican Poets Café, Bowery Poetry Bar and The louderARTS Project. She was awarded the South Asian Bursary at UEA.

LEIGHTON SEER was raised in Dallas, Texas. She graduated with honours from the University of Texas with a degree in film-making and screenwriting. She now resides in England, where she is working on *The Angler's Edge*, a speculative novel set in the Gulf of Mexico. She's 25.

AVANI SHAH grew up behind the counter in various newsagents' shops around London. As a freelance writer, she has worked on projects ranging from web content to a horror film script. Her short story 'Mira/Meera' appeared in *Words and Women: Two*.

RADHA SMITH grew up in Taiwan, rural Canada, and northern England. She spent her undergraduate years in Vancouver and Paris, earning a degree in international studies. She has worked as a farmhand, bartender, teacher, magazine editor, and non-profit worker. Her writing has appeared in Vancouver's *Ricepaper Magazine*.

TAYMOUR SOOMRO studied at Cambridge and Stanford. He has practised corporate law in London, managed a 2,000-acre rice farm in Pakistan, and been a publicist for a luxury fashion brand. He is currently working on a collection of short stories about love and tyranny entitled *Little Masters*.

LAURA TOPHAM was a journalist for ten years before starting the Creative Writing MA. Most recently she was Commissioning Editor at the *Daily Mail* and she has written freelance for most national newspapers and many magazines. Laura is the recipient of a Malcolm Bradbury Memorial Trust scholarship at UEA. She is currently working on a thriller set in journalism.

LAUREN VAN SCHAIK SMITH was born in Missouri and now lives and works in London. She was one of ten young writers mentored through Writers' Centre Norwich in 2014–5 and at UEA is the recipient of the David Higham Award. More of her work can be found at www.laurenvanschaik.com.

ZAKIA UDDIN is working on a collection of short stories about being lost at night. It includes 'Walking the Dog'. She has written about music, labour and place for *The Wire*, *Dazed & Confused*, *Paris Review* Daily and *LRB* blog, among others.

ODRÁN WALDRON is a non-fiction writer from Kilkenny, Ireland, who is studying for an MA in Biography and Creative Non-Fiction. Odrán graduated from Dublin City University with a BA in Journalism. His main topics are life in post-recession rural Ireland and the Irish sport of hurling, which often go hand in hand.

SAM WEST is an American writer of short stories and essays. He is currently at work on a novel.

J Y YANG lives in Singapore and writes science fiction and fantasy. Her Asian science-fantasy novella *Duology* will be out from Tor.com Publishing in the summer of 2017. She is represented by DongWon Song at Howard Morhaim Literacy Agency, and is working on her first novel.

ACKNOWLEDGEMENTS

Thanks are due to the School of Literature, Drama and Creative Writing at UEA in partnership with Egg Box Publishing for making the UEA MA Creative Writing anthologies possible.

We'd also like to thank the following people:

Trezza Azzopardi, Tiffany Atkinson, Andrew Cowan, Giles Foden, Vesna Goldsworthy, Sarah Gooderson, Rachel Hore, Kathryn Hughes, Sarah Jones, Catrina Laskey, Timothy Lawrence, Jean McNeil, Jeremy Noel-Tod, Beatrice Poubeau, Denise Riley, Sophie Robinson, Kathy Scales, Helen Smith, Henry Sutton, Ian Thomson, Steve Waters, Peter Womack

Nathan Hamilton at Egg Box Publishing, Thom Swann and Ray O'Meara of A New Archive and Daniel Frost.

Editorial team:
Katherine Allen
Justine Ashford
Meghann Boltz
Sally Fox
Patrick Hughes
Rashmee Roshan Lall
Keely Celia Laufer
James McDermott
Lucy Malouf
Richard O'Halloran
Arron Westbrook
J Y Yang

COLOPHON

UEA Creative Writing MA Anthology:
Prose, 2016

International © 2016 retained by individual authors

Designed by A New Archive.

Cover illustration by Daniel Frost.

Proofread by Sarah Gooderson.

Printed and bound in the UK by TJ International.

Distributed by
NBN International,
10 Thornbury Road
Plymouth PL6 7PP
t. +44 (0)1752 2023102
e. cservs@nbninternational.com

ISBN: 978-1911343097